D0999896

SUCCULENTS II

THE NEW ILLUSTRATED DICTIONARY

SUCCULENTS II

THE NEW ILLUSTRATED DICTIONARY

Maurizio Sajeva

and

Mariangela Costanzo

Timber Press
Portland, Oregon

First published in Italy 2000
by Le Lettere, Firenze

© Copyright 2000 by Le Lettere, Firenze
All rights reserved.

First published in North America in 2000
by Timber Press, Inc.
The Haseltine Building
133 S.W. Second Ave., Suite 450
Portland, Oregon 97204, USA.

Reprinted 2001

ISBN 0–88192–449–0
A catalog record for this book is available from the Library of Congress.

Printed and bound in Italy by Tipografia ABC.

CONTENTS

ACKNOWLEDGEMENTS

Several people contributed to the preparation of this book. We would like to thank the following people who supplied illustrations: Roberto Mangani, Alberto Marvelli, Alessandro Mosco, Annarosa Nicola and Gaetano Palisano (Italy); Duke Benadom, Leo Pickoff, Ann Wayman (USA); Ernst van Jaarsveld (South Africa) who, besides supplying illustrations, helped with the identification of several habitat shots. A special thanks to Charles H. Everson (Rainbow Gardens, USA) both for supplying photographs and for his constant help and encouragement; to Ms Jacqueline A. Roberts for her skillful checking of the English text and for precious suggestions; to Ms Elena Fontana for the editing and for her patience and courtesy even when we were very late in supplying due text.

The plants illustrated have been photographed in habitat, in the authors' collections and in the public collections of Kirstenbosch Botanical Garden (RSA), Karoo Botanical Garden (RSA), Orto Botanico di Palermo (Italy). They have also been photographed in the collections of Vivai F.lli Colombo di Casatenovo (Lecco, Italy), Vivai Fiore Verde di Montecchio E. (Reggio Emilia, Italy), Vivaio Botaniké di Baveno (Verbania, Italy).

All the photographs were taken by Pierfranco Costanzo, Daniele Costanzo and Maurizio Sajeva, unless otherwise stated in the text.

We would like to emphasize that we assume all responsibilities for any errors still present in the book despite the help of the above mentioned people.

FOREWORD

When we decided to publish *Succulents: The Illustrated Dictionary* (our first book), we tried to provide a wide choice of illustrations of succulent plants that are normally scattered in several specialized books and journals. We knew it was a difficult task and we received many different reactions from readers. Luckily, most of those reactions were positive and we received nice comments, suggestions and few complaints.

We are aware that there were mistakes and omissions and we naturally take full responsibility for them.

In this second volume, we have tried to supply additional illustrations, either of species not included in the previous *Dictionary* or of different aspects of those plants already illustrated. We imagine that there will be omissions and mistakes here too, for which we would like to apologize in advance.

With regard to the illustrations, the main difference between cacti and the other succulents is that cacti are easier to photograph: the stems and flowers usually fit well into a single shot. With the other succulents, the flowers are sometimes too big compared to the stem and at least two photographs are required to show both parts. In other instances, flowers are too small and a close-up is necessary. Sometimes stems are too thin and long and too far from the main trunk. In some species the young plant is quite different from the adult one. We could go on trying to explain the difficulties that one meets when photographing succulents, but we just ask for your understanding. The ideal book should contain at least three or four illustrations for a single species to show the entire plant: the flower, the juvenile stage, and the differences between cultivated and wild plants. Unfortunately, such a book would need hundreds of pages, thousands of illustrations and a lot of money. In this volume we have tried, with some plants, to present several illustrations of the same species, with others we have tried to show the most important features. In other cases, we have just published what was available from various private or public collections.

We hope that this book will be of interest both to experienced collectors and neophytes. We also hope to receive comments and suggestions, and we would welcome your help in finding any errors.

INTRODUCTION

SUCCULENTS IN HABITAT

The general idea that succulent plants grow in deserts is not strictly correct. By definition a desert is a place where almost nothing can grow, like the Sahara desert or the Gobi desert or the Sand Plains of Australia. It is better to say that succulents can grow in a semi-desert habitat, together with other plants that adopt different strategies to survive water deficit. Succulents have adapted to survive in environments where water is not constantly available, therefore they may grow in habitats where water is only abundant at certain times of the year, or in some restricted areas.

The greatest diversity of habits and families of succulent plants is to be found in the southern part of Africa, where this adaptive strategy has been very successful. Most of the plants illustrated in this book come from that part of the world, and particularly from the Cape Province area. The American continent is the home of several species of succulent plants, but most of them belong to the Cactaceae family which is not included in this book.

A few illustrations can give an idea of the diverse habitats where succulents have their home.

Fig. 1

Fig. 2

Fig. 3

Fig. 4

Fig. 1) shows the Namib Desert. *Welwitschia mirabilis* is the only succulent that has adapted to this extreme environment. This species uses the fog that covers the area almost every day and its seeds germinate only during the very rare rains. Low reproductive rate and slow growth are compensated by the lack of competition with other perennial species and a very difficult environment for predators.

Fig. 2) South of Tenerife, rich in succulents plants. Several endemic plants grow in the Canary Islands, and succulents are present with a broad selection of species.

Fig. 3) shows an alpine environment. Here water is usually available and succulents can occupy areas not suitable for other plants. The crevices of rocks exposed to the sun can supply enough soil and the succulence permits conservation of the short water supply.

Fig. 4) shows the tropical forest in Palenque (Mexico). Here succulent plants grow epiphytically and take up water that may have been caught in the branches for a short time. In this condition succulents occupy relatively dry places in a humid habitat.

These few examples show how diverse the habitat of succulents can be and indicate that growth condition may be extremely varied.

SUCCULENTS IN CULTIVATION

Almost every person that becomes interested in growing succulents asks for advice on how to grow them: what type of soil, how much water, what kind of container and so on. That is an impossible task in our opinion. Besides the variability due to the plant's original habitat, there is the other great variable, the habitat of the grower. The authors of this book live in Italy some 1,400 km distance from each other. One lives in Sicily where almost every species of succulent can grow outside all year long, while the other lives in Lombardy where succulents can grow outside for only part of spring and summer. Spring is also variable between the two locations: in Sicily the typical activities of spring can begin in February, while in the northern part of Italy this may be delayed until the end of March.

Of course, those readers with some experience already know what is necessary to grow their plants to their best. We do not expect to give suggestions to those experienced collectors, but we would like to give some advice to the new enthusiasts.

Cultivation of succulents is relatively easy. The temperature must not drop below 8°C for most species, therefore a greenhouse or relocation of the plants to a heated building may be necessary in winter time. South or southwest facing positions are usually preferred to allow a good amount of sunlight to reach the plants, but in southern regions an east facing position will work well too.

When watered, the soil must be saturated but the water must pass through quickly. To achieve this, it is necessary to mix the soil with coarse sand, pumice or other particles. It will depend on the availability *in situ*. In Sicily pumice is easily available in most builders' warehouses, but in other regions it may be easier to find coarse sand. It is advisable to wash the material before mixing it with the soil to avoid the presence of dust that can become very hard after a few waterings. The soil can be chosen depending on availability, but avoid clay soils and pure peat. Make a mix of garden soil, some peat-moss, and sand (or pumice) until the soil has a good structure and drainage.

When choosing pots remember that clay pots allow more air circulation and dry faster, while plastic pots keep humidity for a longer time and lower air circulation. Simply consider the climate where you grow the plants. If you live in a hot country, plastic pots will permit less watering; if you live in a cold country, the use of clay pots may help to control humidity. Keep in mind that both kind of pots are used almost everywhere in the world, and in the end it is a choice made with experience. Water is necessary for the plants to live. Water the plants until you see the water coming out of the drainage holes at the bottom of the pot. Wait until the soil is dry (this will depend on temperature, humidity, size and type of pots) before watering again. Water must be given only in the growing season, and the succulents should be kept dry during their dormant time. When the first sign of new growth is evident, start watering; at the end of the season growth will slow down until it completely stops. At this point watering must be stopped. This simple rule will keep your plants in good health. From time to time add a very diluted low nitrogen nutrient, only half the suggested dosage. In this way you will give nutrients to your plants without forcing an unnatural growth.

The form of the plant can tell you a lot of information about its requirements. Plants with foliage and vigorous growth usually require more water and nutrients and they will thrive in large containers. Plants with no or very few leaves, with caudex or with a lot of thick spines usually come from areas where water and nutrients are scarce. These plants may be difficult to grow, but to stay on the safe side give them a little water and spend some time getting to know their requirements.

Good luck!

CLASSIFICATION

Succulence has evolved independently in several families of plants. The similar shapes and adaptations found in plants that are distant both from a geographical and phylogenetic point of view are dependent on the same selective pressure: lack of water.

In order to classify a plant, the shape alone is not sufficient, it is also necessary to look at the flowers and fruits. From the time of Linnaeus, taxonomists evolved systems of classification and this evolution is still very active, to the point that sometimes it is difficult to follow all the changes that affect the names of plants. As stated in the first volume, we do not pretend to have found a solution to the chaos affecting the classification of succulent plants. Some help to alleviate the confusion has been provided in the form of CITES (Convention on International Trade in Endangered Species of Wild Fauna and Flora) checklists. The requirement for a standard reference to the names of plants included in the Appendices of CITES prompted the Scientific Authorities to compile checklists for the most commonly traded groups of plants. The following CITES checklists have been published:

CITES Cactaceae Checklist
CITES Cactaceae Checklist (second edition)
The CITES Checklist of Succulent *Euphorbia* Taxa (Euphorbiaceae)
CITES Orchid Checklist Volume 1
CITES Orchid Checklist Volume 2
CITES Bulb Checklist

CONSERVATION AND CITES

The collection of plants in the wild for commercial purposes is still one of the major threats to several species of succulent plants. The CITES convention, signed and ratified by 145 countries as at January 1999, provides rules to prevent the threat to species of fauna and flora due to exploitation for commercial purposes. The aim of the Convention is to allow sustainable use of wildlife so that it is conserved for future generations.

The basic rules of the Convention are simple, but a lack of understanding of them may cause problems to people wishing to export or import CITES-listed species.

CITES monitors and controls the trade across international borders in selected taxa. These taxa are listed in three Appendices:

• Appendix I includes plants threatened with extinction as a result of international trade. Trade in wild-collected plants is prohibited for commercial purposes, but trade in artificially propagated plants is permitted subject to the provision of permits. There are some succulent plants included in this Appendix.

• Appendix II includes plants, which although not currently threatened, may become so if trade is not regulated. Several succulent plants are listed in this Appendix. Trade is permitted for both wild-collected and artificially propagated plants subject to the provision of permits.

• Appendix III includes plants subject to regulation within the territory of a CITES party for which the co-operation of other parties is needed to prevent or restrict their exploitation. No succulent plants are listed in this Appendix. Trade in Appendix III specimens for both wild and propagated plant material is subject to CITES documents.

The implementation of CITES is the responsibility of each country involved in the trade, the exporting country and the importing country. It is very important to become fully acquainted with the CITES regulations before trading any CITES-listed species. Always contact your CITES Management Authority. Information on CITES authorities in all countries can be obtained from:

The CITES Secretariat
15 chemin des Anémones
case postale 456, 1219 Châtelaine
Geneva - Switzerland

The CITES status has been included for each of the illustrated succulent species in the alphabetical section of the *Dictionary*. A further list of all succulent plants included in the CITES appendices is also provided. However, full CITES documentation should be consulted for information on annotations and exemptions.

SUCCULENT PLANTS INCLUDED IN THE CITES APPENDICES

Family	Appendix I	Appendix II
AGAVACEAE	*Agave arizonica* *Agave parviflora* *Nolina interrata*	*Agave victoriae-reginae*
APOCYNACEAE	*Pachypodium baronii* *Pachypodium decaryi*	*Pachypodium* spp.
ASCLEPIADACEAE		*Ceropegia* spp. *Frerea indica*
BROMELIACEAE		*Tillandsia harrisii* *Tillandsia kammii* *Tillandsia kautskyi* *Tillandsia mauryana* *Tillandsia sprengeliana* *Tillandsia sucrei* *Tillandsia xerographica*
CACTACEAE	*Ariocarpus* spp. *Astrophytum asterias* *Aztekium ritteri* *Coryphantha werdermannii* *Discocactus* spp. *Disocactus macdougallii* *Echinocereus ferreirianus* ssp. *lindsayi* *Echinocereus schmollii* *Escobaria minima* *Escobaria sneedii* *Mammillaria pectinifera* *Mammillaria solisioides* *Melocactus conoideus* *Melocactus deinacanthus* *Melocactus glaucescens* *Melocactus paucispinus* *Obregonia denegrii* *Pachycereus militaris* *Pediocactus bradyi* *Pediocactus knowltonii* *Pediocactus paradinei* *Pediocactus peeblesianus* *Pediocactus sileri* *Pelecyphora* spp. *Sclerocactus brevihamatus* ssp. *tobuschii* *Sclerocactus erectocentrus* *Sclerocactus glaucus* *Sclerocactus mariposensis* *Sclerocactus mesae-verdae* *Sclerocactus papyracanthus* *Sclerocactus pubispinus* *Sclerocactus wrightiae* *Strombocactus* spp. *Turbinicarpus* spp. *Uebelmannia* spp.	Cactaceae spp.

Family	Appendix I	Appendix II
CRASSULACEAE	*Dudleya stolonifera* *Dudleya traskiae*	
DIDIEREACEAE		Didiereaceae spp.
DIOSCOREACEAE		*Dioscorea deltoidea*
EUPHORBIACEAE		*Euphorbia* spp. (succulent species)
	Euphorbia ambovombensis *Euphorbia capsaintemariensis* *Euphorbia cremersii* *Euphorbia cylindrifolia* *Euphorbia decaryi* *Euphorbia francoisii* *Euphorbia moratii* *Euphorbia parvicyathophora* *Euphorbia quartziticola* *Euphorbia tulearensis*	
FOUQUIERIACEAE		*Fouquieria columnaris*
	Fouquieria fasciculata *Fouquieria purpusii*	
LILIACEAE		*Aloe* spp.
	Aloe albida *Aloe albiflora* *Aloe alfredii* *Aloe bakeri* *Aloe bellatula* *Aloe calcairophila* *Aloe compressa* *Aloe delphinensis* *Aloe descoingsii* *Aloe fragilis* *Aloe haworthioides* *Aloe helenae* *Aloe laeta* *Aloe parallelifolia* *Aloe parvula* *Aloe pillansii* *Aloe polyphylla* *Aloe rauhii* *Aloe suzannae* *Aloe thorncroftii* *Aloe versicolor* *Aloe vossii*	
PORTULACACEAE		*Anacampseros* spp. *Avonia* spp. *Lewisia cotyledon* *Lewisia maguirei* *Lewisia serrata*
WELWITSCHIACEAE	*Welwitschia mirabilis*	

SUCCULENT FAMILIES
AND GENERA

Brief descriptions of the families illustrated in the *Dictionary* are given in this section. Those readers wishing to study any of the families or genera in detail will find monographic studies and general works in the 'Further Reading' section. New plants are always found in the wild and new taxonomic studies are often published. Journals specializing in succulent plants provide a very good source of up-to-date information.

AGAVACEAE Endl. (Monocotyledons)

The family of the Agavaceae includes about 18 genera. Plants are stemless, short stemmed or trees. Leaves are fleshy or fibrous and are usually arranged in rosettes. Roots are fibrous and stoloniferous. Inflorescences may attain huge sizes and have several flowers.

Most genera within the Agavaceae are easy to cultivate, and several species are hardy. During the growing season they appreciate plenty of water and their growth may be rather fast. For the bigger species it may be a problem to find suitable containers for indoor cultivation, while in the milder climates they can be grown in the field.

DISTRIBUTION: America, tropical Africa, India, Madagascar and Australia.

Genera illustrated

Agave L.
Cordyline Comm. ex R.Br.
Dasylirion Zucc.
Dracaena L.
Furcraea Vente
Nolina Michs.
Sansevieria Thunb.
Yucca L.

AMARYLLIDACEAE J.St.Hill. (Monocotyledons)

Bulbous plants with leaves arranged in rosettes or distichous. Inflorescences bear one to several flowers. Few species can be regarded as succulents and the growers usually appreciate the beautiful flowers. Cultivation is relatively easy; water should be provided during the growing season and the bulbs should be left to dry in the dormant season.

DISTRIBUTION: warm temperate and tropical areas around the world.

Genera illustrated

Boophane Herb.
Brunsvigia Heist.
Gethyllis L.
Haemanthus L.

APOCYNACEAE Juss. (Dicotyledons)

Over 215 genera are included in this family. Plants can be herbs, lianas, shrubs or trees and all contain latex. Leaves are simple and veins are parallel. Flowers can be solitary or in clusters and have five petals. The fruit is divided into two follicles.

In cultivation these plants require minimum temperatures above 8°C and should be kept dry. In milder climates most species can be grown outdoors.

DISTRIBUTION: widespread.

Genera illustrated

Adenium Roem. & Schult.
Pachypodium Lindl.
Plumeria L.

ARALIACEAE Juss. (Dicotyledons)

Family with 57 genera and approximately 800 species ranging from lianas to shrubs, trees and epiphytes. Leaves are compound, large and arranged in spirals.

DISTRIBUTION: tropical regions.

Genus illustrated

Cussonia Thunb.

ASCLEPIADACEAE R.Br. (Dicotyledons)

The family contains over 2,500 species of lianas or low shrubs. Leaves are simple and caducous. Flowers have five sepals and five petals and may be very malodorous. Within the succulents, the Stapeliae group has pollen grains that adhere together to form waxy pollinia. The fruit is divided into two follicles containing several seeds with terminal tufts of hair.

Cultivation of succulent species of this family requires some attention, as the plants are prone to rot when grown in a humid environment. The caudex when present must not be deep in the soil, but should sit just above it. Some topping with gravel may help to prevent rot.

DISTRIBUTION: widespread.

Genera illustrated

Brachystelma R.Br.
Caralluma R.Br.
Ceropegia L.
Dischidia R.Br.
Duvalia Haw.
Echidnopsis Hook.f.
Fockea Endl.
Hoodia Sweet
Hoya R.Br.
Huernia R.Br.
Huerniopsis N.E.Br.
Orbeopsis L.C.Leach
Psedoulithos P.R.O.Bally
Sarcostemma R.Br.
Stapelia L.
Trichocaulon N.E.Br.
Tridentea Haw.

BEGONIACEAE Agardh. (Dicotyledons)

A family with two genera and about 800 species of succulent herbs or shrubs with thick rhizomes or tubers. Stems are usually succulent, with leaves arranged in spirals.

DISTRIBUTION: tropical and warm regions.

Genus illustrated

Begonia L.

BOMBACACEAE Kunth. (Dicotyledons)

This family contains some 30 genera of large soft wooded trees. Leaves are simple or compound and are covered with hairs or hairy scales. Flowers are large and fruit may be woolly and contain numerous seeds.

DISTRIBUTION: tropical Africa and America.

Genera illustrated

Adansonia L.
Chorisia Humb., Bonpl. & Kunth.

BROMELIACEAE Juss. (Monocotyledons)

This family contains approximately 50 genera of plants either terrestrial or epiphytic. Leaves are basal, usually arranged in rosettes, and may have spiny margins. Flowers are borne in spikes and have coloured bracts.
Most of the species grown in succulent collections are epiphytic and can be grown on dry branches or bark. Water should be sprayed on the plants every day during the hot season.

DISTRIBUTION: tropical America.

Genera illustrated

Aechmea Ruiz & Pav.
Dyckia Schult.f.

BURSERACEAE Kunth. (Dicotyledons)

Family with 20 genera; large trees or shrubs with compound leaves and resinous wood. The few species that are suitable for cultivation require water during the growing season, but should be kept dry during the dormant season.

DISTRIBUTION: southern Africa, tropical and subtropical America.

Genera illustrated

Bursera Jacq.
Commiphora Jacq.

CHENOPODIACEAE Vent. (Dicotyledons)

This family contains 120 genera and about 1,300 species of annual and perennial herbs and shrubs, or sometimes small trees. Stems are usually succulent and leaves are alternate, succulent or reduced. Most species are adapted to semi-desert or salty habitats.

DISTRIBUTION: widespread.

Genera illustrated

Beta L.
Suadea Dumort

COMMELINACEAE R.Br. (Monocotyledons)

This family includes annual and perennial herbs with leaves either basal or on jointed stems. Succulent species are perennial and the succulence is usually in the leaves or in tuberous roots. The flowers are usually blue, a rarity among succulents. Cultivation of these plants is quite easy as long as they are watered regularly.

DISTRIBUTION: widespread in tropical regions.

Genus illustrated

Tradescantia L.

COMPOSITAE Giseke (Dicotyledons)

A very large family containing annual and perennial plants ranging from herbs to trees and including epiphytic and aquatic species. The inflorescence may bear one to several heads of stemless flowers. The calyx has bristles and scales which remain attached to the seeds to facilitate wind dispersal.

Within such a large family, there is a great variability of growth conditions. Among the succulents the genus *Othonna* is slow growing and requires extra care with watering.

DISTRIBUTION: widespread.

Genera illustrated

Othonna L.
Senecio L.

CONVOLVULACEAE Juss. (Dicotyledons)

A family with plants of very diverse habit, including some parasitic species. Flowers are campanulate, white or pink.
Few genera are cultivated in succulent collections but they may grow very large. They require plenty of water during the growing season.

DISTRIBUTION: widespread.

Genera illustrated

Ipomoea L.
Jacaratia Rusby

CRASSULACEAE DC. (Dicotyledons)

This family includes over 33 genera and about 1,500 species ranging from annual or perennial herbs to shrubs and small trees with more or less succulent leaves. Plants in this family grow in a wide range of habitats: from deserts to wetlands.
Most species are of easy cultivation and can be propagated by leaf or stem cuttings.

DISTRIBUTION: widespread.

Genera illustrated

Adromischus Lem.
Aeonium Webb & Berthel.
Aichryson Webb & Berthel.
Cotyledon L.
Crassula L.
Dudleya Britton & Rose
Echeveria DC.
Graptopetalum Rose
Greenovia Webb & Berthel.
Kalanchoe Adans.
Lenophyllum Rose
Monanthes Haw.
Orostachys (DC.) Fisch.
Pachyphytum Link, Klotzsch & Otto
Rosularia (DC.) Stapf.
Sedum L.
Sempervivum L.
Tylecodon Toelken
Umbilicus DC.

CUCURBITACEAE Juss. (Dicotyledons)

A family with approximately 120 genera of annual or perennial herbaceous plants, with climbing or trailing habit, usually with tendrils and tuberous root. Leaves are alternate, simply and palmately lobed.

Succulent genera are quite diverse in habit and cultural requirements. It is better to keep them dryish until some confidence has been gained with the particular species.

DISTRIBUTION: tropical and subtropical regions.

Genera illustrated

Ibervillea B.D.Greene
Kedrostis Medik.
Momordica L.
Xerosicyos Humbert

DIDIEREACEAE Drake (Dicotyledons)

A family with xerophytic spiny shrubs and small trees, closely related to the Cactaceae family. This family is endemic to Madagascar.

In cultivation these plants require minimum temperatures above 8°C and water only in the growing season.

DISTRIBUTION: Madagascar.

Genera illustrated

Alluaudia Drake
Decaryia Choux.
Didierea Baill.

DIOSCOREACEAE R.Br. (Monocotyledons)

Herbs with twining shoots arising from tubers rich in starch.

DISTRIBUTION: southern Africa, South and Central America

Genus illustrated

Dioscorea L.

EUPHORBIACEAE Juss. (Dicotyledons)

A very large family with approximately 320 genera and over 8,000 species, ranging from annual herbs to large trees. All the Euphorbiaceae contain a milky sap that may be harmful to the touch. The inflorescence is based on a cyathium constituted by an involucre containing one reduced female flower and several male ones. There are protective bracts that can be very showy, and nectaries to attract insects. The capsule containing the seeds explodes at maturity and disperses the seeds to a distance of over 3 m.

The cultivation of these plants is quite easy, but there are some species that may require extra care in watering.

DISTRIBUTION: widespread.

Genera illustrated

Euphorbia L.
Jatropha L.
Monadenium Pax

FOUQUIERIACEAE DC. (Dicotyledons)

A monotypic family with a few species of spiny shrubs or trees to 10 m tall. The genus *Idria* is considered to be a synonym.

DISTRIBUTION: Mexico, southwestern USA.

Genus illustrated

Fouquieria Humb., Bonpl. & Kunth.

GERANIACEAE Juss. (Dicotyledons)

The plants of this family range from herbs to shrubs. Stems are usually jointed and have leaves arranged in spirals. Several species have aromatic oils in glandular hairs.
The succulent species require little water only during the growing season, which for some species is in winter.

DISTRIBUTION: temperate and tropical regions.

Genera illustrated

Pelargonium L'Hér.
Sarcocaulon (DC.) Sweet.

LABIATAE Juss. (Dicotyledons)

This family includes herbaceous plants and shrubs with simple leaves. Several species contain fragrant oils. Among the several species of interest in horticulture only a few are succulent.

DISTRIBUTION: widespread.

Genera illustrated

Aeolanthus Mart.
Plectranthus L'Hér.

LEGUMINOSAE Juss. (Dicotyledons)

This very large family contains over 16,000 species with very diverse habit. The Leguminosae are very important as cultivated crops, but only a few are cultivated for succulent collections.

DISTRIBUTION: widespread.

Genus illustrated

Erythrina L.

LILIACEAE Juss. (Monocotyledons)

A large family of herbaceous plants with a few tree-like species. The family has actually been split into several other families (Asphodelaceae, Aloaceae etc...) but we prefer to use Liliaceae in the old broad sense.
Cultivation requirements vary depending on the plant habit and geographical origin.

DISTRIBUTION: widespread.

Genera illustrated

Aloe L.
Astroloba Uitewaal
Bowiea Harv. ex Hook.f.
Bulbine L.

Dipcadi Medik.
Gasteria C.J.Duval
Haworthia C.J.Duval
Massonia Thunb. ex L.
Ornitogalum L.
Scilla L.
Trachyandra J.C.Manning
Veltheimia Gled.

MENISPERMACEAE (Dicotyledons)

Family with about 70 genera of woody or herbaceous vines or lianas. Leaves are alternate and simple, flowers are small.

DISTRIBUTION: tropical and subtropical regions.

Genus illustrated

Tinospora Miers

MESEMBRYANTHEMACEAE Baill. (Dicotyledons)

Over 100 genera and 2,000 species are included in this family. The habit ranges from extremely specialized stemless plants to shrubs or creeping plants, all with succulent leaves. Flowers are usually showy, with several petals. The fruit responds to water and opens to release seeds when conditions are suitable for germination. Cultivation is easy for shrubby species, while the stemless ones require some skills.

DISTRIBUTION: southern Africa and Mediterranean regions.

Genera illustrated

Aloinopsis Schwantes
Aptenia N.E.Br.
Argyroderma N.E.Br.
Carpobrotus N.E.Br.
Carruanthus Schwantes
Cephalophyllum N.E.Br.
Chasmatophyllum N.E.Br.
Cheiridopsis N.E.Br.
Conicosia N.E.Br.
Conophyllum Schwantes
Conophytum N.E.Br.
Cylindrophyllum Schwantes
Delosperma N.E.Br.
Dinterantus Schwantes
Drosanthemum Schwantes
Faucaria Schwantes
Fenestraria N.E.Br.
Frithia N.E.Br.
Gibbaeum Haw.
Glottiphyllum Haw.
Jordaaniella H.E.K.Hartmann
Lampranthus N.E.Br.
Lithops N.E.Br.
Malephora N.E.Br.
Mesembryanthemum L.
Mitrophyllum Schwantes
Monilaria Schwantes
Muiria N.E.Br.
Nananthus N.E.Br.
Oophytum N.E.Br.

Orthopterum L.Bolus
Oscularia Schwantes
Pleiospilos Dinter & Schwantes
Psilocaulon N.E.Br.
Rabiea N.E.Br.
Rhinephyllum N.E.Br.
Ruschia Schwantes
Schlechteranthus Schwantes
Sphalmanthus N.E.Br.
Tanquana H.E.K.Hartmann & Liede
Titanopsis Schwantes
Trichodiadema Schwantes

MORACEAE Link (Dicotyledons)

There are more than 50 genera and over 1,200 species of very diverse habit, ranging from herbaceous plants to large trees, usually having a milky latex. Flowers are small and grouped in inflorescences with thickened axes forming an invaginated receptacle. Most species are wind pollinated while others are pollinated by insects.

DISTRIBUTION: tropical and temperate regions.

Genus illustrated

Dorstenia L.

MORINGACEAE Dumort. (Dicotyledons)

A monotypic family of deciduous, succulent trees with large alternate leaves.

DISTRIBUTION: Africa, Arabia, India, Madagascar.

Genus illustrated

Moringa Adans.

OXALIDACEAE R.Br. (Dicotyledons)

This family includes herbs with tubers or small trees. Leaves are trilobed and the fruits are capsules.

DISTRIBUTION: tropical and temperate regions.

Genus illustrated

Oxalis L.

PASSIFLORACEAE Juss. (Dicotyledons)

Plants with very diverse habit ranging from lianas, shrubs or trees with lobed leaves.

DISTRIBUTION: tropical and temperate regions.

Genus illustrated

Adenia Forssk.

PEDALIACEAE R.Br. (Dicotyledons)

Family including herbs and shrubs with opposite hairy leaves and campanulate flowers. The fruits are capsules often armed with spines or prickles.

DISTRIBUTION: temperate and warm regions.

Genera illustrated

Pterodiscus Hook.
Uncarina Stapf.

PIPERACEAE G.Agardh (Dicotyledons)

A family of herbaceous plants and small trees, many of which are aromatic. Leaves are simple and flowers are small.

DISTRIBUTION: tropical regions.

Genus illustrated

Peperomia Ruiz & Pav.

PORTULACACEAE Juss. (Dicotyledons)

A family with over 20 genera and 400 species of herbaceous plants and shrubs. Leaves are succulent, entire and often bear long hairs at their base. Flowers are small and can be very showy.

DISTRIBUTION: tropical and temperate regions.

Genera illustrated

Anacampseros L.
Avonia (Mey. ex Fenzl) G.D.Rowley
Ceraria Pearson & Stephens.
Portulaca L.
Portulacaria Jacq.
Talinum Adans.

RUBIACEAE Juss. (Dicotyledons)

This large family includes lianas, shrubs and trees, but few are of interest to succulent growers. Some species have large tubers with a series of cavities inhabited by ants.

DISTRIBUTION: Africa, Asia and Europe.

Genus illustrated

Myrmecodia Jack

SOLANACEAE Juss.

A large family with 90 genera and over 2,600 species of diverse habit including herbs, lianas, shrubs and trees with prickles and hairs. Leaves are simple or lobed, arranged in spirals. Several species are edible.

DISTRIBUTION: widespread.

Genus illustrated

Lycium L.

VITACEAE Juss. (Dicotyledons)

A family with approximately 12 genera and 700 species ranging from lianas to small trees. The two genera illustrated in this *Dictionary* are the only ones of interest to succulent collectors.

DISTRIBUTION: widespread in tropical regions.

Genera illustrated

Cissus L.
Cyphostemma Alston

WELWITSCHIACEAE Markgr. (Gymnosperms)

A monotypic family belonging to the Gymnosperms. It was considered to be pollinated by wind dispersal, but investigations (Wetschnig & Debisch, 1999) have indicated that at least 6 species of flies and other insects are involved in pollination.

DISTRIBUTION: Angola and Namibia.

Genus illustrated

Welwitschia Hook.f.

ZYGOPHYLLACEAE

A family with some 25 genera of herbs or shrubs. Stems are usually jointed at nodes, leaves are opposite, pinnately compound.

DISTRIBUTION: tropical regions.

Genus illustrated

Zygophyllum L.

USING THE DICTIONARY

Name of the author who described the species, abbreviated according to the accepted international standard (Brummit & Powell, 1992). Where the original name has been changed, the name of the author who originally described the species is in brackets and is followed by the author who published the new name.

Name of variety, subspecies, forma, where present, are in **bold**, and are followed by the name of the author. In the case of cultivar, the name of the creator is given. For some undescribed taxa, there may be a code number that denotes the reference number of the plant.

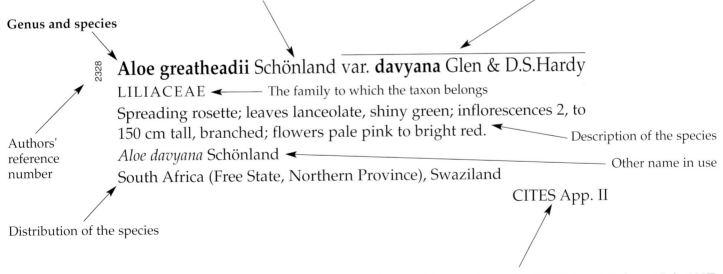

Genus and species

2328

Aloe greatheadii Schönland var. **davyana** Glen & D.S.Hardy

LILIACEAE ◄——— The family to which the taxon belongs

Spreading rosette; leaves lanceolate, shiny green; inflorescences 2, to 150 cm tall, branched; flowers pale pink to bright red. ◄——— Description of the species

Aloe davyana Schönland ◄——— Other name in use

South Africa (Free State, Northern Province), Swaziland

Authors' reference number

Distribution of the species

CITES App. II

Status of the species under CITES (up-dated as at July 1997)
App. I = species listed in Appendix I
App. II = species listed in Appendix II

COLOUR
ILLUSTRATIONS

Adansonia digitata L.
BOMBACACEAE
Deciduous tree, to 20 m and over, massive trunk to 10 m in diameter; branches relatively short; leaves variable, simple to 7-digitate; flowers white, opening at night, fruits woody. Plant photographed in habitat.
Sub-Saharan Africa

Adansonia grandidieri Baill.
BOMBACACEAE
Stem to 30 m tall and 7 m in diameter with reddish bark; leaves bluish-green, hairy, digitate, deciduous; flowers white. Plant photographed in habitat by Paolo Ormas.
Madagascar

Adenia fruticosa Burtt Davy
PASSIFLORACEAE
Large caudex to 1 m tall and 50 cm in diameter; several grey-brown branches in the upper part of stems; leaves roundish-ovate, deciduous; flowers yellowish. Adult specimen.
South Africa (Transvaal)

Adenia fruticosa
Burtt Davy
PASSIFLORACEAE
Young specimen.

Adenia pechuelii
Engl. & Prantl
PASSIFLORACEAE
Caudex fleshy, to 50 cm in diameter and to 1 m tall, with several branches; leaves lanceolate, caducous; inflorescence small, flowers pale green to yellow.
Echinothamnus pechuelii Engl.
Namibia

Adenia venenata Forssk.
PASSIFLORACEAE
Semi succulent plant, tree-like with thin pendent branch. The plant illustrated is a young specimen.
Arabia, East Africa

Adenium obesum
(Forssk.) Roem.
& Schult.
APOCYNACEAE
Shrubs to 2 m tall, caudex thick and many short branches; leaves at ends of branches; flowers pink. Plant photographed in habitat.
Kenya, Tanzania, Zimbabwe

Adenium obesum
(Forssk.) Roem.
& Schult. ssp.
bohemianum
(Schinz) G.D.Rowley
APOCYNACEAE
A mature specimen.

Adenium obesum
(Forssk.) Roem.
& Schult.
APOCYNACEAE
The flowers.

Adromischus alveolatus Hutchison
CRASSULACEAE
Tuberous root, stem 2-3 cm long; leaves 3-4 cm long, 2 cm wide, grey-green to yellowish green, variable in colour; inflorescence to 17 cm tall. Considered a form of *A. marianae* var. *antidorcatum*.
South Africa (Cape Province)

Adenium obesum (Forssk.) Roem. & Schult. ssp.
bohemianum (Schinz) G.D. Rowley
APOCYNACEAE
This subspecies has pink to pink-purple flowers with dark throat.
Angola, Namibia

Adromischus cooperi A.Berger
CRASSULACEAE
Stems erect, much branched, to 10 cm tall; leaves green to grey-green with or without darker or purple spots, 5-8 cm long; inflorescence to 40 cm long; flowers pale pink.
Adromischus cuneatus V.Poelln., *A. halesowensis* Uitew., *A. festivus* C.A.Smith.
South Africa (Cape Province)
Note - According to Pilbeam plants cultivated with the name *A. halesowensis*, like the one illustrated here, do not match well with the species.

27

Adromischus cristatus Lem.
CRASSULACEAE
Stems short, erect, much branched, covered with aerial roots; leaves 2-4 cm long, convex on both sides, green, covered with soft hairs; inflorescence to 2 cm long; flowers whitish-red or grey-green with pink edges.
South Africa (Cape Province)

Adromischus filicaulis (Eckl. & Zeyh.) C.A.Sm.
CRASSULACEAE
Prostrate to ascending stems to 35 cm long, branching; leaves 2-8 cm long, lanceolate to oblong, green to grey-green with dark purple spots; inflorescence to 35 cm tall; flowers yellow-green with mauve tinged lobes.
Namibia, South Africa (Cape Province)

Adromischus cristatus Lem. var. zeyeri (Harv.) Toelken
CRASSULACEAE
Variety with stems lacking aerial roots; inflorescence and flowers with glandular hairs.
South Africa (Cape Province)

Adromischus filicaulis (Eckl. & Zeyh.) C.A.Sm.
CRASSULACEAE
A well grown specimen. Photograph by Annarosa Nicola.

Adromischus fallax Toelken
CRASSULACEAE
Stems decumbent to 20 cm long, little branched; leaves to 5 cm long, concave on the upper surface, convex below; inflorescence to 30 cm long; flowers greenish. Photograph by Annarosa Nicola.
South Africa (Cape Province)

Adromischus filicaulis (Eckl. & Zeyh.) C.A.Sm. ssp. marlothii (Schönl.) Toelken
CRASSULACEAE
Subspecies with thicker root, flaking bark and leaves rarely purple spotted.
South Africa (Little Karoo)

Adromischus kubusensis Uitewal
CRASSULACEAE
Stems 8-10 cm tall, reddish-brown, coated with wax; leaves green, becoming pruinose with age, erect, club-shaped, tapering at the end; flowers purple.
South Africa (Cape Province)

Adromischus marianae (Marloth) Berger var. **immaculatus** Uitewaal
CRASSULACEAE
Another form of this very variable subspecies.

Adromischus marianae (Marloth) A.Berger var. **immaculatus** Uitewaal
CRASSULACEAE
Small plant, much branched; leaves variable in size and shape, usually elliptic, 2-5 cm long, verrucose, without purple spots; flowers pale pink.
South Africa (Cape Province)

Adromischus montium-klinghardtii (Dinter) A.Berger
CRASSULACEAE
Erect stems to 20 cm tall; leaves obovate to orbicular 1.5-3 cm long, 1.2-2 cm wide, grey-green to greyish-brown; flowers white to pale yellow.
Namibia

Adromischus marianae (Marloth) A.Berger var. **immaculatus** Uitewaal
CRASSULACEAE
Flowers.

Adromischus roaneanus Uitewaal
CRASSULACEAE
Erect stems, freely branching; leaves grey-green, 3 cm long with numerous waxy markings; flowers light green with pink tips.
South Africa (Cape Province)

Adromischus rotundifolius (Haw.) C.A.Sm.
CRASSULACEAE

Suberect or decumbent branches to 20 cm long; leaves oblanceolate, 1.5-2.5 cm long, 1-2 cm wide, grey-green with flaking wax ; flowers white tinged with pink. Reputedly a synonym of *A. hemisphaericus* (L.) Lem.

South Africa (Cape Province)

Adromischus subdistichus Mekin ex Bruyns
CRASSULACEAE

Low shrub branched from the base; leaves 1.2-2.7 cm long and 1-2.2 cm wide; flowers pink.

South Africa (Cape Province)

Adromischus schuldtianus (Poelln.) H.E.Moore ssp. juttae (Poelln.) Toelken
CRASSULACEAE

Dwarf shrub with many branches to 7 cm tall; leaves roundish or elongate, 2-4 cm long, green with numerous waxy spots; inflorescence 10 cm long; flowers green to red-brown.
Adromischus juttae V.Poelln.

Namibia

Adromischus triflorus (L.f.) A.Berger
CRASSULACEAE

Stems to 10 cm tall with few branches at the base; leaves convex on both sides, pale green with waxy spots; inflorescence to 35 cm; flowers pale pink. Plant photographed in habitat.

South Africa (Cape Province)

Adromischus sphenophyllus C.A.Sm.
CRASSULACEAE

Dwarf shrub; leaves 5-10 cm long, 3.5-4.5 cm wide, grey-green, with cartilaginous margin and short tip; flowers pale pink.

South Africa (Cape Province)

Aechmea lindeni E.Morren ex K.Koch
BROMELIACEAE

Leaves to 60 cm long, 4-5 cm wide, green, turning brown at tips; inflorescence on scape 40-50 cm long, fast withering; flowers with red bracts and yellow petals, fast withering.

Brazil

Aeolanthus subacaulis Hua & Briq. ex Briq.
LABIATAE
Small plant; underground caudex with short aerial stems; leaves green, hairy; flowers inconspicuous.
Southern Africa

Aeonium canariense (L.) Webb & Berthel.
CRASSULACEAE
Short stems with offsetting rosettes to 50 cm in diameter; leaves green, covered with hairs; flowers pale yellow. Plant photographed in habitat.
Canary Islands (Tenerife)

Aeonium arboreum var. **atropurpureum**
(W.A.Nicholson) A.Berger
CRASSULACEAE
Stems erect, to 1 m tall with dense rosettes 20 cm diameter, leaves dark purple (light green in the type species); inflorescence to 30 cm tall; flowers yellow.
Morocco, Canary Islands, naturalized in several Mediterranean regions

Aeonium canariense × **cuneatum**
CRASSULACEAE
A natural hybrid with intermediate characters between the parental species.
Canary Islands (Tenerife)

Aeonium balsamiferum Webb & Berthel.
CRASSULACEAE
Shrubs with strong balsamiferous odour, to 1.5 m tall; branches brown to greyish-brown; rosettes 7-18 cm in diameter; leaves 5-6 cm long, 2.5-3.5 cm wide, greyish-green with brownish stripes; flowers yellow.
Canary Islands (Lanzarote, Fuerteventura)

Aeonium castello-paivae Bolle
CRASSULACEAE
Stems freely branching with rosettes to 10 cm in diameter; leaves glaucous-green, with red margins in older ones; inflorescence sticky; flowers greenish-white.
Canary Islands (Gomera)

Aeonium cuneatum Webb & Berthel.
CRASSULACEAE
Short stem with large rosette; leaves green-glaucous, erect, with mucronate apex and ciliate margins; inflorescence to 1 m tall, flowers yellow. Plant photographed in habitat.
Canary Islands (Tenerife)

Aeonium holochrysum Webb & Berthel.
CRASSULACEAE
Shrub, stems to 1 m tall; leaves 15-25 cm long, arranged in rosettes, yellowish-green with brown-red stripes when grown in full sun, hairy; inflorescence to 1 m tall; flowers yellow. Plant photographed in habitat.
Canary Islands (Tenerife, Gomera, La Palma, Hierro)

Aeonium goochiae Webb & Berthel.
CRASSULACEAE
Subshrub to 40 cm tall; branches sticky; leaf rosettes 3-12 cm in diameter, leaves pale green to yellow-green, occasionally tinged with red, viscid; flowers pale yellow with central portion pink.
Canary Islands (Palma)

Aeonium lancerottense Praeger
CRASSULACEAE
Shrub to 60 cm tall, freely branching; branches pale brown to silver; leaves in tight rosettes of 10-18 cm in diameter, pale green, red marginated in full sun, to 8 cm long and 4 cm wide; flowers whitish-pink. Photograph by Roberto Mangani.
Canary Islands (Lanzarote)

Aeonium haworthii (Salm-Dyck) Webb & Berthel.
CRASSULACEAE
Bush to 60 cm tall, freely branching; numerous rosettes 6-8 cm in diameter; leaves bluish-green with red-brown cartilaginous teeth; flowers pale yellow flushed with rose. Plant photographed in habitat.
Canary Islands (Tenerife)

Aeonium nobile Praeger
CRASSULACEAE
Short stems, unbranched; leaves 20-30 cm long, yellow-green, arranged in rosettes, ciliate margins, viscid when young; inflorescence 50 cm tall, flowers red. A young plant photographed in habitat.
Canary Islands (La Palma)

Aeonium palmense Webb & Berthel.
CRASSULACEAE
Rosettes cup-shaped; leaves hairy, often with portions of margin strongly undulate; flowers yellow-green. Reputedly a subspecies of *A. canariense* (L.) Webb & Berthel
Canary Islands (Hierro, La Palma)

Aeonium percarneum (Murray) J.Pitard & L.Proust
CRASSULACEAE
Shrub to 1.5 m tall; rosettes 8-20 cm in diameter; leaves 8-10 cm long, 4 cm wide, dark green or glaucous to purple in full sun, red edged; flowers whitish, median portion pink variegated.
Canary Islands (Gran Canaria)

Aeonium sedifolium (Webb ex Bolle) A.Pit. & Proust
CRASSULACEAE
Bushes to 15 cm tall; leaves arranged in rosettes, green to yellowish-green with red stripes; flowers yellow.
Canary Islands (La Palma, Tenerife)

Aeonium simsii
(Sweet) Stearn
CRASSULACEAE
Rosettes forming low clumps; leaves green with reddish lines; inflorescence 15-20 cm tall; flowers yellow. Plant photographed in habitat.
Aeonium caespiitosum (C.Sm.) Webb & Berthel.
Canary Islands (Gran Canaria)

Aeonium smithii
(Sims) Webb
& Berthel.
CRASSULACEAE
Branched stems to 60 cm long, covered with white hairs; leaves green with reddish lines, arranged in rosettes 10 cm in diameter; flowers yellow. Plant photographed in habitat.
Canary Islands (Tenerife)

Aeonium spathulatum (Hornem.) Praeger
CRASSULACEAE
Branches to 60 cm tall with small rosettes; leaves sticky 3-4 cm long, green marked with brown stripes, cartilaginous margins; flowers yellow. Plant photographed in habitat.
Canary Islands (Gran Canaria, Gomera, Hierro, La Palma, Tenerife)

Aeonium tabulaeforme (Haw.) Webb & Berthel.
CRASSULACEAE
Large flat solitary rosettes to 50 cm in diameter; leaves green; inflorescence branching to 60 cm tall; flowers yellow. Rosette dies after flowering.
Aeonium bertoletianum Bolle, *A. macrolepum* Webb
Canary Islands (Tenerife)

Aeonium tabulaeforme (Haw.) Webb & Berthel.
CRASSULACEAE
Plant photographed in habitat.
Canary Islands (Tenerife)

Aeonium undulatum Webb & Berthel.
CRASSULACEAE
Shrubs to 2 m tall; branches arise from near or below ground; leaf rosettes with centre flattened, 10-30 cm in diameter; leaves 6-18 cm long, 3-5 cm wide, green, occasionally variegated with brown lines; flowers yellow.
Canary Islands (Gran Canaria)

Aeonium urbicum
Webb & Berthel.
CRASSULACEAE
Unbranched stems to 1 m tall; leaves oblong, arranged in rosettes to 25 cm in diameter; flowers greenish-white borne in large pyramids. Plant photographed in habitat.
Canary Islands (Tenerife)

Aeonium urbicum Webb & Berthel.
CRASSULACEAE
A very young specimen photographed in habitat.

Aeonium virgineum Webb & Berthel.
CRASSULACEAE
Rosettes to 25 cm in diameter; leaves hairy, green with reddish or yellowish tinge; flowers green-yellow. Reputedly a subspecies of *A. canariense* (L.) Webb & Berthel.
Canary Islands (Gran Canaria)

Agave angustifolia Haw.
AGAVACEAE
Offsetting stems to 40 cm long; leaves variable in size 50-90 cm, light green to grey-green, with pale margins armed with teeth and 1-2 cm long terminal spine; inflorescence 3-5 m tall; flowers green to yellow.
Costa Rica, Mexico

Agave atrovirens
Karw.
AGAVACEAE
The tall inflorescence.

Agave arizonica Gentry & J.H.Weber
AGAVACEAE
Rosette 40 cm in diameter and to 30 cm tall; leaves to 25 cm long, widening in the middle, dark green, reddish-brown or grey margins; inflorescence 3-4 m tall; flowers pale yellow. Photograph by Gaetano Palisano.
USA (Arizona)

CITES App. I

Agave avellanidens Trel.
AGAVACEAE
Rosettes with smooth leaves to 60 cm long, marginal teeth and grey terminal spine; inflorescence 4-6 m tall; flowers pale yellow.
Mexico

Agave atrovirens
Karw.
AGAVACEAE
Rosettes to 4 m in diameter; leaves 1.5-4 m long, to 30 cm and over wide at base, green to light glaucous or glaucous variegated, armed with brown teeth and terminal spine 3-5 cm long; inflorescence to 12 m tall; flowers yellowish.
Mexico

Agave celsii var. albicans (Jacobi) Gentry
AGAVACEAE
Rosettes of pale green, undulate leaves to 70 cm long, armed with 3 mm long teeth and brown terminal spine 2 cm long; inflorescence 2-3 m tall.
Agave mitis Jacobi.
Mexico

Agave cv.
AGAVACEAE
A dwarf variegated culti-
var.
Garden origin

Agave flexispina Trel.
AGAVACEAE
Rosettes to 70 cm in diameter; leaves 15-30 cm long, glaucous to yellowish-
green, undulate margins armed with 5-10 mm teeth; inflorescence 2-3 m
tall; flowers greenish-yellow.
Mexico

Agave ensifera Jacobi
AGAVACEAE
Caespitose rosettes; leaves to 60 cm long, strongly convex, smooth, dark
green, margins with a grey border and curved teeth; inflorescence 2-3 m
tall; light green to yellowish.
Garden origin

Agave fourcroydes Lem.
AGAVACEAE
Stem to 170 cm tall and 25 cm in diameter; leaves to 180 cm long with
dark-brown teeth on the margins and black terminal spine to 3 cm long;
inflorescence 5-6 m tall; flowers greenish-yellow.
Agave rigida var. *elongata* Bak
Mexico

Agave filifera Salm-Dyck
AGAVACEAE
Stemless rosettes to 65 cm in diameter, with lateral shoots; leaves nume-
rous, to 25 cm long and 3 cm wide, shiny green with white lines and filife-
rous margins; inflorescence to 3 m tall; flowers greenish-yellow.
Agave filamentosa Salm-Dyck
Mexico

Agave ghiesbrechtii K.Koch
AGAVACEAE
Offsetting rosettes; leaves grey-green to dark green, to 40 cm long , stron-
gly armed; inflorescence 3 m tall; flowers greenish-brown to purplish.
Guatemala, Mexico

Agave henriquesii Baker
AGAVACEAE
Simple rosettes; leaves to 100 cm long, rigid, green to glossy green, margins with horny edge and irregular teeth, brown terminal spine 3-4 cm long; inflorescence to 3 m tall.
Mexico

Agave horrida Lem. ex Jacobi
AGAVACEAE
Rosettes strongly armed, solitary; leaves numerous, dark green to yellow-green, teeth 1.5 cm long, grey; terminal spine to 4 cm long, grey with darker tip; inflorescence 2.5 m tall.
Mexico

Agave leguayana Baker
AGAVACEAE
A doubtful species, grown at the Botanical Garden of Palermo. Could be a variety of *A. ghiesbregthii*, with darker, shorter leaves. Unknown, probably of garden origin.

Agave longisepala Tod.
AGAVACEAE
Stemless rosette; leaves grey-green, terminal spine black-brown, 2-3 cm long; inflorescence 2-4 m tall; flowers yellow. The validity of this species is doubtful.
Probably Mexico

Agave macroacantha Zucc.
AGAVACEAE
Rosettes stemless or short-stemmed, leaves to 55 cm long, terminal spine 3 cm long; inflorescence to 3 m tall; flowers numerous, reddish, flushed with grey.
Mexico (Tehuacán, Oaxaca)

Agave macroacantha Zucc.
AGAVACEAE
The plant illustrated here is the form «compacta», with shorter leaves and more compact habit.

Agave macroculmis Tod.

AGAVACEAE

Short stems; leaves to 90 cm long and 15-25 cm wide, widest at base, dark green to light green, corneous margins with teeth 1 cm long, brown to greyish; terminal spine 4-7 cm long, dark brown to greyish; inflorescence to 5 m tall; flowers yellow.

Mexico

Agave multifilifera Gentry

AGAVACEAE

Single stems, 70-100 cm tall; leaves arranged in rosettes, green, to 60 cm long, margins finely filiferous (sometimes non-filiferous) and terminal spine greyish, to 7 mm long; inflorescence 4-6 m tall; flowers greenish, flushed with red.

Mexico

Agave maculosa (Rose) Hook.

AGAVACEAE

Offsetting rosette, forming large mats; leaves herbaceous, to 30 cm long, grey-green with brown markings and cartilaginous teeth; inflorescence to 1 m tall; flowers greenish-white, scented.

USA (Texas)

Agave ochauii Gentry

AGAVACEAE

Stems to 50 cm tall with leaves arranged in rosette; leaves green, erect to ascending to 50 cm long, margins lined, border reddish-brown, terminal spine 1-2 cm long, grey; inflorescence to 3 m tall; flowers yellow.

Mexico

Agave mckelveyana Gentry

AGAVACEAE

Rosettes single or offsetting, to 40 cm tall; leaves 20-35 cm long and 3-5 cm wide, light glaucous green or yellowish, margins with greyish-red tipped teeth; inflorescence to 3 m tall; flowers yellow.

USA (Arizona)

Agave pelona Gentry

AGAVACEAE

Rosettes dark green to purplish, shiny, to 80 cm in diameter; leaves toothless, to 50 cm long, terminal spine 4-7 cm long; inflorescence 3 m tall; flowers dark red.

Mexico

Agave polyacantha Haw.
AGAVACEAE
Rosettes 100-150 cm in diameter; leaves to 65 cm long, ascending to recurving, green or yellow-green, armed with closely-spaced brown teeth and 2-3 cm long terminal spine; inflorescence 3 m tall; flowers reddish.
A. engelmannii Trelease.
Mexico

Agave potatorum Zucc.
AGAVACEAE
Rosette with 30-80 leaves glaucous green to white, 30 cm long and 11 cm wide at base, armed with sharp spines and terminal spine to 4 cm long; inflorescence 3-6 m tall; flowers light green to yellowish. The plant illustrated here is a horticultural form with a dwarf habit.
A. saundersii Lem., *A. scolymus* Karw., *Agave verschaffeltii* Lem.
Mexico

Agave pumila De Smet ex Baker.
AGAVACEAE
In the juvenile stage, persisting to 12 years, rosettes are 3-4 cm in diameter with 5-8 short thick leaves. Inflorescence unknown. When cultivated in the ground, the plants lose the dwarf habit. It could be a hybrid of *A. lechuguilla* Torr. Photograph by Gaetano Palisano.
Mexico

Agave ragusae
Terracciano
AGAVACEAE
Offset rosette to 1.5 m tall; leaves to 80 cm long and 30 cm wide at base, bright green, margins armed with dark brown teeth; terminal spine to 8 cm long, dark brown to black; inflorescence 7-8 m tall; flowers greenish-yellow. Probably a horticultural variety of *A. salmiana*.
Possibly garden origin

Agave schottii Engelm.
AGAVACEAE
Offset rosettes; leaves 20-30 cm long, green, margins with horny edges, terminal spine 1 cm long, brown; inflorescence 1.5-2 m tall, flowers light-yellow. Young specimen.
USA (Arizona)

Agave shawii Engelm.
AGAVACEAE
Rosettes single or caespitose with stems to 2 m long; leaves glossy to dark green, to 50 cm long, corneous margins dark reddish-brown to grey, teeth variable in shape and size; inflorescence to 4 m tall; flowers yellow to reddish.
Mexico

Agave sp.
AGAVACEAE

An unidentified species from Mexico (San Luis Potosì); leaves glaucous-green, striped brownish; margins toothed; flowers not seen. Photographed in habitat by Alessandro Mosco.
Mexico

Agave stricta Salm-Dyck
AGAVACEAE

Spherical rosette, forming a branched thick stem with many leaves about 35 cm long, thick at the base, then narrowing with 2 cm long terminal spine; inflorescence 2 m tall. The photograph shows a dwarf hybrid with shorter and wider leaves.
Mexico (Tehuacán)

Agave tequilana Weber.
AGAVACEAE

Rosettes to 1.8 m tall, with short stems to 50 cm, leaves glaucous-bluish to grey-green, to 1.5 m long with 3-6 mm long teeth and 2 cm terminal spine; inflorescence 5-7 m tall; flowers green.
Mexico

Agave titanota Gentry
AGAVACEAE

Rosettes single or offset; leaves glaucous-white, to 55 cm long, corneous margins, variable teeth and 4 cm long terminal spine; inflorescence 3 m tall; flowers yellow.
Mexico

Agave titanota Gentry
AGAVACEAE

A young specimen. Photograph by Roberto Mangani.
Mexico

Agave toumeyana Trel. var. bella (Breitung) Gentry
AGAVACEAE

Small rosette with 100 or more (in adult specimens) leaves, filiferous, 10-20 cm long, light green, denticulate margins on lower half; inflorescence 1-2 m tall, flowers greenish.
USA (Arizona)

Agave victoriae-reginae T.Moore.
AGAVACEAE
Solitary rosettes, spherical; leaves numerous, 10-15 cm long, green with white margins and terminal spine 2 mm long; inflorescence to 4 m tall; flowers varicoloured, often red tinged.
Mexico   CITES App. II

Agave victoriae-reginae T.Moore
AGAVACEAE
The plant illustrated here is the form «compacta». Photograph by Charles H. Everson.
Mexico   CITES App. II

Agave victoriae-reginae T.Moore
AGAVACEAE
A variegated form.
Horticultural origin
                                                   CITES App. II

Aichryson laxum (Haw.) Bramwell
CRASSULACEAE
Stems 30-50 cm long, succulent, green or reddish, covered with short hairs; leaves hairy, arranged in rosettes at the tip of stems; inflorescence branched with small flowers. Plant photographed in habitat.
Canary Islands (Tenerife, Gran Canaria, La Palma, Hierro, Gomera)

Aichryson × **domesticum** f. foliis **variegatis** Praeger
CRASSULACEAE
Subshrub small, hairy, 15-30 cm tall, much branched; leaves alternate, hairy, 2 cm long, 1 cm wide, dark green with yellowish-white margins; flowers golden yellow.
Canary Islands

Alluaudia procera
Drake
DIDIEREACEAE
Tree 3-15 m tall, armed with conical thorns; main stem with few branches; leaves ovate, to 2.5 cm long and 5-10 mm wide; inflorescence crowded at end of stems; flowers very small.
Madagascar
CITES App. II

Aloe aculeata Pole-Evans
LILIACEAE

Single rosette, to 1 m tall and wide; leaves dark green to bluish, 50-60 cm long, with reddish-brown teeth on the margins and thorns on the upper and lower surfaces; inflorescence 1 m tall; flowers yellow.

South Africa (Northern Province), Zimbabwe   CITES App. II

Aloe acutissima H.Perrier
LILIACEAE

Shrub to 1 m across, stems several, erect or procumbent branches, to 1 m long; leaves grey-green with reddish tinge, margins dentate with pale brown teeth; inflorescence 50 cm tall; flowers reddish-scarlet.

Madagascar   CITES App. II

Aloe albiflora Guillaumin
LILIACEAE

Stemless plant with cylindrical roots, offset from the base and forming small clumps of compact rosettes; leaves 15 cm long, upper surface grey-green with numerous white spots, margins cartilaginous; inflorescence to 35 cm; flowers white.
Guillauminia albiflora (Guillaumin) Bertrand
Madagascar
CITES App. I

Aloe amudatensis Reynolds
LILIACEAE

Stemless plant offset from the base and forming dense groups; leaves erect, to 25 cm long and 5 cm wide at base, dull green, sometimes reddish-brown tinged, with whitish spots, the lower surface milky green with pale greenish spots; margins dentate with cartilaginous edge armed with small teeth; inflorescence to 65 cm long; flowers rose-pink to coral-red.

Kenya, Uganda   CITES App. II

Aloe angelica Pole-Evans
LILIACEAE

Usually single stemmed, to 4 m tall; upper leaves horizontal, lower leaves recurved, green to reddish-green, with sharp teeth along the margins. Inflorescence branched; flower buds reddish, turning greenish-yellow when open. Young specimen.

South Africa (Northern Province)   CITES App. II

Aloe arborescens Mill.
LILIACEAE

Rosettes on erect stems to 4 m tall, branched from base (or taller) and covered by persistent dry leaves; leaves to 60 cm long and 5 cm wide, grey-green to dark green, spiny margins; inflorescence to 80 cm tall; flowers scarlet.

Malawi, Mozambique, South Africa (Cape Province, Natal), Zimbabwe
CITES App. II

Aloe arborescens Mill.
LILIACEAE
Plant photographed in habitat (Natal).

CITES App. II

Aloe arborescens Mill.
LILIACEAE
The flowers.
CITES App. II

Aloe arenicola Reynolds
LILIACEAE
Shrubs with several creeping stems; leaves to 20 cm long, erect, bluish-green with whitish spots on both surfaces, margins whitish with small teeth; inflorescence simple or branched, flowers pale red.
South Africa (Cape Province)
CITES App. II

Aloe barberae Dyer
LILIACEAE
Trees, branched, to 18 m tall; trunks to 3 m in diameter; bark greyish-brown; leaves recurved, deeply channelled, with small whitish teeth; inflorescence branched, to 50 cm long; flowers salmon-pink to orange. Plant photographed in habitat (KwaZulu-Natal).
Aloe bainesii Dyer
Mozambique, South Africa (KwaZulu-Natal, Cape Province), Swaziland
CITES App. II

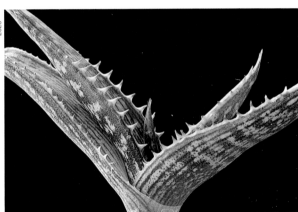

Aloe branddraaiensis Groenew
LILIACEAE
Stemless rosettes forming small clumps; leaves green to reddish with white spots in longitudinal lines, margins armed with brown teeth; inflorescence to 150 cm tall, much branched, flowers coral-red.
South Africa (Mpumalanga)
CITES App. II

Aloe brevifolia Mill.
LILIACEAE
Rosettes densely leaved to 30 cm in diameter forming large clumps; leaves to 15 cm long and 6 cm wide, greyish-green, soft spines on lower surface, margins with white triangular spines; inflorescence unbranched to 60 cm tall; flowers red to yellow. Plant photographed in habitat.
South Africa (Cape Province)
CITES App. II

Aloe buettneri A.Berger
LILIACEAE

Solitary plant, stemless, with leaf base forming a bulb-like swelling 8-10 cm in diameter below the soil; leaves to 55 cm long, green; margins with white to pink cartilaginous edge armed with teeth; inflorescence to 90 cm tall; flowers variable from greenish-yellow to pinkish-brown or bright red.

Angola, Congo, Ghana, Malawi, Mali, Nigeria, Zambia   CITES App. II

Aloe burgersfortensis Reynolds
LILIACEAE

Rosettes single or occasionally 2-3 headed; leaves brownish-green to bright green, densely or scarcely spotted; inflorescence 1-2 branched with pinkish-red flowers.

South Africa (Transvaal)   CITES App. II

Aloe caesia
Salm-Dyck
LILIACEAE

Stems to 1.5 m tall, branching from the base; leaves to 50 cm long, erectly spreading, with marginal teeth; inflorescence 80-100 cm tall; flowers pale red to whitish. A natural hybrid: *A. arborescens × A. ferox.*

South Africa (Cape Province)
CITES App. II

Aloe castanea
Schönland
LILIACEAE

Trees, small with several branches covered with the remains of old leaves; leaves to 1 m long, margins armed with brown teeth; inflorescence to 150 cm long, curled, flowers orange-brown.

South Africa (Mpumalanga, Northern Province)
CITES App. II

Aloe chabaudii Schönland
LILIACEAE

Rosettes stemless, erect, forming clumps; leaves green, white spots on both surfaces of young leaves, faint lines on both surfaces of mature leaves, margins with white teeth; inflorescence much branched, flowers red to pinkish.

Malawi, Mozambique, South Africa (Northern Province), Swaziland, Tanzania, Zambia, Zimbabwe   CITES App. II

Aloe chabaudii
Schönland
LILIACEAE

Plant photographed in habitat.
CITES App. II

Aloe chabaudii
Schönland
LILIACEAE
A flowering plant photo-
graphed in habitat.
CITES App. II

Aloe compressa H.Perrier var. **rugosquarrosa** H.Perrier
LILIACEAE
Solitary plant with very short stems or stemless; leaves to 15 cm long,
glaucous with green marginal teeth sometimes with red apices; inflorescence to 70 cm tall; flowers white. The variety illustrated differs from the
type in having longer leaves (to 25 cm) and being more robust with bigger
flowers.
Madagascar   CITES App. I

Aloe chabaudii Schönland
LILIACEAE
Another specimen in different habitat.
CITES App. II

Aloe dichotoma Masson
LILIACEAE
Tree, dichotomously branching, to 10 m tall, 1 m diameter, leaves 20-30 cm
long, arranged in rosettes at the end of branches; flowers yellow.
Namibia, South Africa (Bushmanland)   CITES App. II

Aloe ciliaris Haw.
LILIACEAE
Stems to 6 m long, shiny, usually supported by surrounding plants; leaves
dark green; white marginal hair-like thorns present only on the apical part
of the stems; inflorescence unbranched, to 50 cm long; flowers orange-red
with yellow tips.
South Africa (Eastern Cape Province)   CITES App. II

Aloe dichotoma
Masson
LILIACEAE
Plant photographed in
habitat with the author's
family.
CITES App. II

Aloe dichotoma
Masson
LILIACEAE
Young specimen photographed in habitat.
CITES App. II

Aloe dolomitica Groenew.
LILIACEAE
Single stems, to 2 m tall, covered with dry leaves; leaves to 50 cm long, dark green to greyish-green, turning to red in winter; up to 6 inflorescences simultaneously, to 60 cm tall; flowers greenish-yellow to yellowish. The plant illustrated is a young one.
South Africa (Transvaal)   CITES App. II

Aloe dichotoma
Masson
LILIACEAE
The bark.
CITES App. II

Aloe elgonica Bullock
LILIACEAE
Plant forming clusters to 1 m in diameter; leaves dull green often with reddish tinge, recurved, margins armed with white teeth; inflorescence branched, pendulous, 30-50 cm long; flowers yellowish with a red vertical line. In habitat most of the plants hang down vertical cliffs.
South Africa (Bushmanland)
CITES App. II

Aloe distans Haw.
LILIACEAE
Stems to 3 m long, creeping, sprawling, forming dense groups; leaves bluish-green with whitish spots on both surfaces, margins armed with yellowish teeth; inflorescence to 1 m tall, branched, flowers orange-red to bright red.
South Africa (Cape Province)   CITES App. II

Aloe erinacea
D.S.Hardy
LILIACEAE
Rosettes forming large clumps; leaves greyish-green, well armed with spines; inflorescence 1 m tall; flowers yellow.
Namibia
CITES App. II

Aloe excelsa A.Berger
LILIACEAE
Stem unbranched, erect, to 4 m tall, with persistent dry leaves; leaves to 70 cm long and 7 cm wide at base, dull green, teeth on the lower surface and margins; inflorescence 80-100 cm tall, flowers reddish or orange. Plant photographed in habitat.
Malawi, Mozambique, South Africa, Zimbabwe
CITES App. II

Aloe excelsa A.Berger
LILIACEAE
Plant photographed in habitat.

CITES App. II

Aloe excelsa A.Berger
LILIACEAE
Cultivated specimen.

CITES App. II

Aloe ferox × **speciosa**
LILIACEAE
A natural hybrid with large stem and persistent old dry leaves; inflorescence branched and racemes bicoloured.
South Africa (Southern & Eastern Cape)
CITES App. II

Aloe fosteri Pillans
LILIACEAE
Stemless rosettes to 1 m in diameter; leaves bluish-green, striped, spots on the lower surface forming an 'H'; inflorescence to 120 cm; flowers yellow to orange or scarlet. Young specimen.
South Africa (Mpumalanga)   CITES App. II

Aloe gariepensis Pillans
LILIACEAE
Stems to 1 m tall, branching and forming small groups, leaves dark green with horny edges, stems covered with old dry leaves; inflorescence to 1.2 m tall; flowers yellow. Photograph by Charles H. Everson.
Aloe gariusana Dinter
Namibia, South Africa (Cape Province)   CITES App. II

Aloe greatheadii Schönland
LILIACEAE

Rosette stemless, solitary or forming clumps; leaves triangular, shiny green with white spots arranged in irregular bands, margins armed with sharp brown teeth; inflorescence to 150 cm; flowers pale pink to bright red.

Botswana, Malawi, Mozambique, South Africa (Northern Province), Swaziland, Zambia, Zimbabwe   CITES App. II

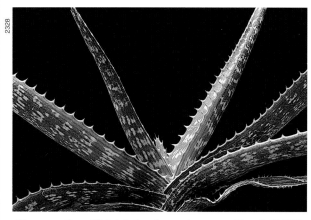

Aloe greatheadii Schönland var. davyana Glen & D.S.Hardy
LILIACEAE

Spreading rosette; leaves lanceolate, shiny green; inflorescences 2, to 150 cm tall, branched; flowers pale pink to bright red.
Aloe davyana Schönland
South Africa (Free State, Northern Province), Swaziland
          CITES App. II

Aloe hambury Borzì
LILIACEAE

Stem 1-1.5 m tall; leaves green to bluish, to 50 cm long arranged in a dense rosette; inflorescence 60 cm tall, branched; flowers red. Probably a hybrid of *A. ferox*.
Garden origin   CITES App. II

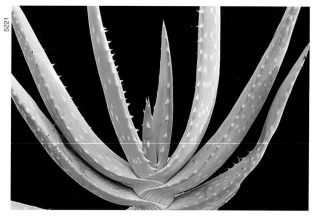

Aloe hereroensis Engl.
LILIACEAE

Rosettes on horizontal stems, single or sometimes divided into more heads; leaves greyish-green with whitish spots, margins cartilaginous armed with reddish-brown teeth; inflorescence to 1 m tall, branched; flowers orange-red, or yellow.

Angola, Namibia, South Africa (Northern Cape and Free State)
          CITES App. II

Aloe jucunda Reynolds
LILIACEAE

Rosette short stemmed; leaves to 4 cm long, 2-5 cm wide at base, recurved, dark green with numerous transparent spots, margins with 2 mm long teeth; inflorescence 35 cm tall; flowers pale pink.
Somalia   CITES App. II

Aloe juvenna
Brandham & S.Carter
LILIACEAE

Stems erect to 25 cm tall, branching from the base, with procumbent longer stems to 45 cm long; leaves bright green to brownish in dry conditions, paler green spots on both surfaces, margins armed with small teeth; inflorescence to 25 cm tall; flowers bright coral-pink with yellow mouth.
Kenya
CITES App. II

Aloe krapohliana Marloth
LILIACEAE
Stemless rosettes, single or caespitose; leaves to 20 cm long, grey-green with greyish-brown transverse bands, margins with white teeth; up to 4 inflorescences from each rosette, simple or 1-2 branched; flowers dull red with greenish-yellow tips. Photograph by Charles H. Everson.
South Africa (Northern Cape)   CITES App. II

Aloe linearifolia A.Berger
LILIACEAE
Solitary plant; leaves narrow, to 25 cm long and 10 cm wide; margins may have minute teeth near the base; inflorescence to 40 cm high; flowers yellow. Plant photographed in habitat.
South Africa (Natal)   CITES App. II

Aloe longistyla Baker
LILIACEAE
Stemless plant, to 20 cm in diameter, solitary or sometimes forming clusters of 3 to 10; leaves to 15 cm long, greyish-green with a waxy layer, both surfaces and margins with white spines; inflorescence to 20 cm tall, unbranched, flowers salmon-pink to coral-red. Plant photographed in habitat.
South Africa (Little Karoo, Great Karoo)   CITES App. II

Aloe lutescens
Groenew.
LILIACEAE
Horizontal stems from which several groups of rosettes arise; leaves narrow, yellowish-green to red when grown in full sun with incurved tips, margins with sharp teeth; inflorescence to 150 cm tall with 3 branches, buds dark red, open flowers bright yellow.
South Africa
(Northern Province)
CITES App. II

Aloe marlothii A.Berger
LILIACEAE
Single stemmed plant, 4 m tall and over; leaves wide, 40-60 cm long, dull green to greyish-green, brown spines on the margins and on both surfaces, dry leaves are persistent on the stem; inflorescence 50 cm long with several horizontal racemes (erect in the KwaZulu-Natal); flowers bright orange-red, or red or yellow. Plant photographed in habitat (Natal).
Botswana, Mozambique, southern Africa (KwaZulu-Natal), Swaziland, Zimbabwe
CITES App. II

Aloe marlothii
A.Berger
LILIACEAE
Plants in their natural habitat (Natal).
CITES App. II

Aloe marlothii A.Berger
LILIACEAE
Cultivated specimen. Photograph by Charles H. Everson.

CITES App. II

Aloe marlothii A.Berger
LILIACEAE
Young cultivated specimen.

CITES App. II

Aloe melanacantha A.Berger
LILIACEAE
Rosettes forming groups up to 10; stems short; leaves 20 cm long, brownish-green, curved upwards and inwards giving a ball-shape to the rosette, black thorns along the margins and the keel; inflorescence 1 m tall, flowers bright red turning yellow when open.
Namibia, South Africa (Bushmanland, Northern Cape Province)   CITES App. II

Aloe meyeri
vanJaarsv.
LILIACEAE
Stems to 1 m tall, branching from the base; leaves to 30 cm long, bluish-green, margins armed with white teeth; inflorescence simple with reddish-orange tips. In habitat the plants usually grow hanging from vertical cliffs.
Namibia, South Africa (northern Cape Province)
CITES App. II

Aloe microstigma
Salm-Dyck
LILIACEAE
Rosettes, single or forming small groups; stems short or to 50 cm in older specimens, leaves to 30 cm long, reddish-green with white spots on both surfaces, margins armed with reddish-brown teeth; inflorescence simple, to 1 m tall, with dull red buds turning yellow when open. Plant photographed in habitat.
South Africa (eastern and western Cape Province)
CITES App. II

Aloe mudenensis Reynolds
LILIACEAE
Solitary or clump-forming plant with stems to 80 cm tall; leaves 25-30 cm long, bluish-green with scattered spots, margins with teeth 7 mm long; inflorescence to 1 m tall; flowers yellowish-orange to red.
South Africa (KwaZulu-Natal)   CITES App. II

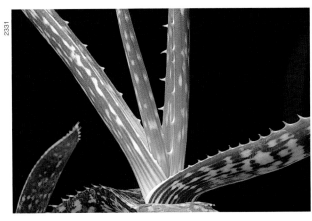

Aloe nyeriensis Christian
LILIACEAE
Stems to 2 m tall, offset; leaves green, white spotted when young, 55 cm long, margins with teeth to 1.5 long; inflorescence 60 cm tall, branched; flowers coral-red. Young specimen.
Kenya   CITES App. II

Aloe ortholopha Christian & Milne-Redhead
LILIACEAE
Stemless rosettes; leaves 40-50 cm long, green to bluish-green, horny margins armed with teeth; inflorescence to 1 m tall, flowers pale yellowish to red.
Zimbabwe   CITES App. II

Aloe ortholopha
Christian
& Milne-Redhead
LILIACEAE
A flowering specimen.
Zimbabwe
CITES App. II

Aloe pachygaster
Dinter
LILIACEAE
Stemless, 20 cm in diameter; leaves grey-green, arranged in spiral, yellow marginal teeth; inflorescence 90 cm tall, flowers red.
Namibia
CITES App. II

Aloe parvibracteata Schönland
LILIACEAE
Stemless or sometimes short stemmed creeping plant; leaves variable in shape and colour, from bright green to purplish-green, upper surface with white margins armed with prickles; inflorescence branched at top; flowers orange or red.
Mozambique, South Africa (KwaZulu-Natal), Swaziland   CITES App. II

Aloe pearsonii Schönland
LILIACEAE
Large shrubs, much branched, to 2 m in diameter; leaves dull bluish-green, red during drought periods; inflorescence 40 cm tall; flowers red to orange-red or yellow. Photograph by Charles H. Everson.
Namibia, South Africa (Cape Province)   CITES App. II

Aloe pearsonii
Schönland
LILIACEAE
Flowers. Photograph by
Duke Benadom.
CITES App. II

Aloe pictifolia D.S.Hardy
LILIACEAE
Short stems, creeping or hanging, with rosettes forming small groups; leaves 15 cm long, reddish-green or pinkish with white spots on both surfaces and reddish-brown teeth along the margins; inflorescence to 35 cm tall; flowers dull red.
South Africa (eastern Cape Province)   CITES App. II

Aloe peglerae Schönland
LILIACEAE
Rosettes solitary or in small groups; leaves 25 cm long, greyish-green or reddish-green, curved inwards, margins with brown teeth and short rows of spines along the middle upper and lower surfaces; inflorescence 40 cm tall; flowers dull red.
South Africa (Transvaal)   CITES App. II

Aloe pirottae A.Berger
LILIACEAE
Stemless plant usually in small groups; leaves recurved, to 50 cm long, green during the rainy season, becoming brownish during drought, marked with dull whitish spots, margins armed with brown teeth; inflorescence to 1 m tall; flowers pinkish-scarlet.
Ethiopia, Kenya, Somalia   CITES App. II

Aloe pendens Forssk.
LILIACEAE
Shrubs with pendent stems 30-40 cm long; leaves 30 cm long, recurved, pale green with a narrow red edge on the margins; inflorescence 90 cm tall; flowers red-yellow.
Yemen   CITES App. II

Aloe pluridens Haw.
LILIACEAE
Plant single stemmed; leaves bright green, 70 cm long, armed with soft teeth; inflorescence to 1 m tall, flowers pinkish-red or yellow.
South Africa (Eastern Province, KwaZulu-Natal)   CITES App. II

Aloe pluridens Haw.
LILIACEAE
Young cultivated specimen.

CITES App. II

Aloe polyphylla
Schönland ex Pillans
LILIACEAE
Single rosette with a peculiar spiral arrangement of leaves; leaves 30 cm long, grey-green with the tips turning purplish-black; inflorescence to 60 cm tall; flowers red to salmon. Photograph by Ernst van Jaarsveld.
Lesotho
CITES App. I

Aloe purpurascens (Aiton) Haw.
LILIACEAE
Stems to 80 cm tall, leaves 40-50 cm long, dull green to grey-green with white spots; inflorescence 90 cm tall; flowers light red.
South Africa (Cape Province)   CITES App. II

Aloe ramosissima Pillans
LILIACEAE
Shrubs to 2 m, with several branches; leaves 20 cm long, glaucous-green with pale yellow margins and pale brownish teeth; inflorescence 20 cm long; flowers yellow to greenish-yellow. Plant photographed in habitat by Charles H. Everson.
Namibia, South Africa (Cape Province)   CITES App. II

Aloe ramosissima Pillans
LILIACEAE
Several plants in their natural environment. Photograph by Charles H. Everson.
CITES App. II

Aloe ramosissima
Pillans
LILIACEAE
A cultivated specimen.
CITES App. II

Aloe rauhii Reynolds
LILIACEAE

Rosettes stemless or short stemmed to 10 cm in diameter forming dense groups; leaves 10 cm long, 2 cm wide at the base and narrowing to acute at apex, grey-green with white spots, margins dentate; inflorescence 30 cm tall; flowers rose-scarlet.

Madagascar
CITES App. I

Aloe rivae Baker
LILIACEAE

Plant short stemmed; leaves to 20 cm long, green to bluish-green with marginal horny teeth; inflorescence 15-20 cm tall; flowers yellow.

Somalia
CITES App. II

Aloe reynoldsii Letty
LILIACEAE

Plant stemless or short stemmed; leaves to 35 cm long, pale bluish-green to yellow with H-shaped whitish spots, margins with pinkish-red teeth; inflorescence 40-60 cm tall; flowers yellow tinged with orange.

South Africa (eastern Cape Province)   CITES App. II

Aloe rubroviolacea Schweinf.
LILIACEAE

Stem thick, unbranched, to 1 m tall; leaves to 60 cm long and 10 cm wide at base, blue-reddish or purplish-violet, armed with red teeth; inflorescence 1 m tall, flowers bright red.

Yemen   CITES App. II

Aloe riccobonii Borzì
LILIACEAE

Rosette unbranched to 30 cm tall; leaves to 50 cm long and 6 cm wide at base, tapering, margins with reddish teeth 2-3 mm long, dull green; inflorescence to 60 cm tall, flowers yellow.

Garden origin   CITES App. II

Aloe rupestris Baker
LILIACEAE

Simple stems to 8 m tall; leaves 70 cm long, green with reddish-brown marginal teeth; inflorescence to 130 cm tall; flowers yellow to bright orange.

Mozambique, South Africa (KwaZulu-Natal), Swaziland
CITES App. II

Aloe rupestris Baker

LILIACEAE

Plant photographed in habitat (Natal).
CITES App. II

Aloe saponaria Haw.

LILIACEAE

Rosettes stemless; leaves 15-20 cm long, light green with horny, dark brown marginal teeth; flowers orange.
South Africa (Cape Province, Natal, Lesotho, Zimbabwe)
CITES App. II

Aloe saponaria Haw. var. **latifolia** (Aiton) Haw.

LILIACEAE

This variety is more robust than the species, with larger, greener leaves and spots elongate and less numerous.
South Africa (Cape Province)
CITES App. II

Aloe secundiflora Engl.

LILIACEAE

Plant stemless or short stemmed; leaves to 45 cm long, dull green, unspotted, margins armed with brown teeth; inflorescence to 1.5 m tall, branched; flowers rose-pink.
Ethiopia, Kenya, Sudan
CITES App. II

Aloe sp.

LILIACEAE

An unidentified species from Somalia with greenish, unspotted leaves and white teeth.
Somalia
CITES App. II

Aloe sp.

LILIACEAE

An unidentified species from Somalia with brownish-green, unspotted leaves and white teeth.
Somalia
CITES App. II

Aloe speciosa Baker
LILIACEAE
Plant single stemmed to 6 m tall; leaves to 90 cm long, blue-green with pinkish edges armed with teeth; inflorescence 50 cm tall; flowers red to greenish-white.
South Africa (eastern Cape Province)
CITES App. II

Aloe striata Haw.
LILIACEAE
Stemless rosettes; leaves 40-50 cm long and 10-15 cm wide with white marginal teeth; inflorescence 1 m tall, branched; flowers coral-red to bright orange and yellow. Plant photographed in habitat by Charles H. Everson.
Aloe paniculata Jacq., *A. albo-cincta* Haw., *A. hanburyana* Naud., *A. rhodocincta* Hort.
Namibia, South Africa (eastern Cape Province)   CITES App. II

Aloe squarrosa Baker
LILIACEAE
Stems to 15 cm long, branching from the base; leaves 8 cm long and 2 cm wide at base, green with whitish spots, margins with uncinate teeth; inflorescence to 15 cm long; flowers red.
South Yemen (Socotra)
CITES App. II

Aloe striata Haw.
LILIACEAE
A flowering plant photographed in habitat by Charles H. Everson.
CITES App. II

Aloe steudneri Schweinf.
LILIACEAE
Plant branching at base; leaves to 60 cm long, green with rose-coloured edges armed with teeth; inflorescence to 50 cm tall; flowers yellow-orange.
Eritrea, Ethiopia   CITES App. II

Aloe striata Haw.
LILIACEAE
The flowers.
CITES App. II

Aloe striata Haw.
LILIACEAE
A cultivated specimen.

CITES App. II

Aloe thompsoniae
Groenew.
LILIACEAE
Flowers.
CITES App. II

Aloe tenuior Haw.
LILIACEAE
Bushes with stems to 3 m tall; leaves 10-15 cm long, bluish-green, crowded in terminal rosettes, margins with horny white edge; inflorescence 10-20 cm tall; flowers from yellow to red.
South Africa (eastern Cape Province)   CITES App. II

Aloe thraskii Baker
LILIACEAE
Stem unbranched at least 2 m tall, covered with dry leaves; leaves to 1.5 m long and 20 cm wide at base, dull green to glaucous, tapering towards the apex and recurved, margins concave, armed with triangular teeth; inflorescence 30 cm tall, flowers yellow to pale orange.
South Africa (Cape Province, Natal)   CITES App. II

Aloe thompsoniae
Groenew.
LILIACEAE
Rosettes more or less stemless, offset and forming dense groups; leaves 15 cm long, light green, with small spots on the lower or sometimes the upper surface, margins with minute white teeth; inflorescence 20 cm tall; flowers red.
South Africa (Northern Province)
CITES App. II

Aloe vacillans Forssk.
LILIACEAE
Stem to 50 cm tall, prostrating; leaves dull glaucous-green, to 60 cm long; lower surface with a few small teeth in the median line; inflorescence to 2 m tall; flowers red.
Saudi Arabia, Yemen   CITES App. II

Aloe vaombe Decorse & J.Poiss.
LILIACEAE
Plant single stemmed, to 3 m tall; leaves to 1 m long, tapering towards the apex, dull green, unspotted, margins dentate; inflorescence branched, to 90 cm tall; flowers crimson-red.
Madagascar   CITES App. II

Aloe × laetococcinea A.Berger
LILIACEAE
Rosettes stemless; leaves 20 cm long, 5 cm wide at base, green to bluish-green with elongate white irregular spots and margins with pink horny teeth; inflorescence 20 cm tall; flowers red.
Garden origin   CITES App. II

Aloe variegata L.
LILIACEAE
Rosettes stemless, elongated, to 25 cm tall, offsetting and forming dense groups; leaves to 15 cm long, 4 cm wide at base, green to brownish-green with white spots arranged in bands; inflorescence 30 cm tall; flowers pink. Plant photographed in habitat.
Aloe punctata Haw.
South Africa (Cape Province, Karoo, Namaqualand)   CITES App. II

Aloe zebrina Baker
LILIACEAE
Plant stemless or short stemmed; leaves dull green, striated and marked with whitish spots, margins dentate armed with horny teeth; inflorescence to 1.5 m tall; flowers reddish.
Angola, Botswana, Mozambique, Namibia, Zambia, Zimbabwe
                                              CITES App. II

Aloe vogtsii Reynolds
LILIACEAE
Solitary or offsetting rosettes to 20 cm tall; leaves 20-25 cm long, grey-green to pale green, spotted with minute spots, margins with triangular teeth; inflorescence 60 cm tall; flowers bright red to scarlet.
South Africa (Northern Province)
CITES App. II

Aloinopsis malherbei (L.Bolus) L.Bolus
MESEMBRYANTHEMACEAE
Leaves erect, lanceolate, glaucous-green, 1.8-2.5 cm long with small white tubercles more evident at apex; flowers 2.5 cm in diameter, pale brown to flesh coloured.
Nananthus malherbei L.Bolus
South Africa (Calvinia)

Aloinopsis orpenii (N.E.Br.) L.Bolus
MESEMBRYANTHEMACEAE
Leaves bluish-green, 1.5-2 cm long with dark spots, forming dense clumps; flowers 3.5 cm in diameter, yellow.
Nananthus orpenii L.Bolus
South Africa (Cape Province)

Anacampseros arachnoides (Haw.) Sims
PORTULACACEAE
Plant photographed in habitat.
CITES App. II

Anacampseros arachnoides (Haw.) Sims
PORTULACACEAE
Branches to 5 cm long with fibrous root; leaves 1-2 cm long, acuminate, green, flushed purple with a few white bristle-hairs; inflorescence 8 cm tall; flowers white, tinged with pale purple or pink. Plant photographed in habitat.
South Africa (Great and Little Karoo)
CITES App. II

Anacampseros baeseckei Dinter
PORTULACACEAE
Short rootstock about 1 cm in diameter; stems 2-8 cm tall, with numerous branches; leaves minute, 3-7 mm long, hairy; flowers white to rose.
Namibia
CITES App. II

Anacampseros arachnoides (Haw.) Sims
PORTULACACEAE
Specimen in flower.
CITES App. II

Anacampseros baeseckei Dinter
PORTULACACEAE
A cultivated specimen.

CITES App. II

59

Anacampseros crinita (Dieter) A.Poelln
PORTULACACEAE

Stems with small branches 8 cm tall, 1 cm thick; leaves 4 mm long, light green with brownish hairs to 1.5 cm long; flowers carmine-red with white margins. Considered synonym of *A. baesekei*.

Namibia, South Africa (Cape Province)　　　CITES App. II

Anacampseros retusa Poelln.
PORTULACACEAE

Caudex 1-2 cm long, with small branches to 8 cm tall; leaves to 1 cm long, green to reddish-brown axils with long brownish hairs to 1.5 cm; flowers carmine-red to pink with white margins.

Namibia, South Africa (Cape Province)　　　CITES App. II

Anacampseros lanceolata (Haw.) Sweet
PORTULACACEAE

Plant clump-forming to 8 cm tall with fibrous roots; leaves brown, 4 cm long with a minute spiny tip; flowers carmine or white. Plant photographed in habitat.

South Africa (Cape Province)　　　CITES App. II

Anacampseros sp. DT 2482
PORTULACACEAE

An unidentified plant, probably a new species recently collected and distributed.

South Africa (Cape Province)　　　CITES App. II

Anacampseros namaquensis H.Pears. & Stephens
PORTULACACEAE

Small shrub, branched, to 12 cm tall; leaves 5-10 mm long and 5 mm wide, green covered with hairs; flowers pink. Considered a subspecies of *A. filamentosa*.

Namibia　　　CITES App. II

Anacampseros sp. SB 684
PORTULACACEAE

An unidentified plant, possibly a new species recently collected and distributed.

South Africa (Cape Province)　　　CITES App. II

Anacampseros telephiastrum DC.
PORTULACACEAE
Several stems to 5 cm tall arising from a thickened root, leaves 1 cm long and 8 mm wide, brownish-green, with bristly hairs; flowers rose-carmine. Plant photographed in habitat.

South Africa (Cape Province)   CITES App. II

Aptenia cordifolia (L.f.) Schwantes
MESEMBRYANTHEMACEAE
Flowering specimen.

Anacampseros telephiastrum DC.
PORTULACACEAE
A specimen among rocks. Plant photographed in habitat.
Namibia, South Africa (Cape Province)   CITES App. II

Argyroderma carinatum L.Bolus
MESEMBRYANTHEMACEAE
Solitary plant; leaves rounded, to 2 cm long, pale bluish; flowers pink-purple.
South Africa (Cape Province)

Aptenia cordifolia (L.f.) Schwantes
MESEMBRYANTHEMACEAE
Small shrub, with several green succulent stems to 60 cm long growing flat on the ground; leaves fresh green, papillose, to 2.5 cm long; flowers purple-red.
South Africa (Eastern Cape)

Astroloba foliolosa (Willd.) Uitewaal
LILIACEAE
Stems erect, to 30 cm tall, leaves spirally arranged, 1-1.5 cm long and wide at base, dark green to black; flowers yellow.
South Africa (Cape Province)

Avonia dinteri (Schinz) G.D.Rowley
PORTULACACEAE
Dwarf, creeping plant branching from the base with prostrate shoots to
10 cm long; leaves 3 mm long and wide covered by silvery scales; flowers
red.
Anacampseros dinteri Schinz
Namibia   CITES App. II

Avonia papyracea (Poelln.) G.D.Rowley
PORTULACACEAE
Plant photographed in habitat.   CITES App. II

Avonia mallei G.Will.
PORTULACACEAE
Small shrub, much branched, to 10 cm tall; leaves covered with white sca-
les, dark spot at the tip of each; flowers white.
South Africa (Cape Province)   CITES App. II

Avonia papyracea ssp. **namaensis** G.D.Rowley
PORTULACACEAE
Very similar to the species but with dentate scales.
Anacampseros meyeri Poelln.
Namibia   CITES App. II

Avonia papyracea (Poelln.) G.D.Rowley
PORTULACACEAE
Tuberous root with several 5-10 cm long shoots; leaves 2 mm long and
3 mm wide, pure white with ovate scales; flowers white.
Anacampseros papyracea Poelln.
Namibia, South Africa (Cape Province)   CITES App. II

Avonia papyracea ssp. **namaensis** G.D.Rowley
PORTULACACEAE
Large clump.   CITES App. II

Avonia quinaria ssp. **alstonii** (Schönland) G.D.Rowley
PORTULACACEAE
Caudex to 6 cm in diameter with numerous 2 cm long branches; leaves in rows covered with silvery stipules; flowers white or rarely pink.
Anacampseros alstonii Schönland
Namibia   CITES App. II

Begonia dregei Otto & A.Dietrich
BEGONIACEAE
Caudex brown, 10 cm in diameter; leaves green with reddish petiole, 5-10 cm long, very variable; margins denticulate; inflorescence with few flowers.
South Africa (Cape Province, Zululand)

Avonia recurvata (Schönland) G.D.Rowley
PORTULACACEAE
Tuberous root with many decumbent to erect shoots to 8 cm long; leaves 1-2 mm long and 2-3 mm wide, pale or purplish-green, with a few short hairs arising from the axils; flowers white.
Anacampseros recurvata Schönland
Namibia, South Africa (Cape Province)   CITES App. II

Beta procumbens (Ch.Sm.) Williams, Scott & Ford-Lloyd
CHENOPODIACEAE
Stems herbaceous, procumbent, and very variable; leaves ovate to triangular.
Canary Islands (Fuerteventura, Gomera, Gran Canaria, Lanzarote, La Palma)

Avonia rhodesica (N.E.Br.) G.D.Rowley
PORTULACACEAE
Caudex 2-3 cm in diameter with several erect or prostrate tiny shoots to 3 cm tall; leaves covered by silvery scales; flowers white to pink.
Anacampseros rhodesica N.E.Br.
Somalia, South Africa (Transvaal), Zimbabwe
CITES App. II

Boophane haemanthoides Snijman
AMARYLLIDACEAE
Leaves to 50 cm long, arising from a large bulb; inflorescence to 30 cm tall; flowers cream with reddish tips.
South Africa (Namaqualand, Western Cape)

Bowiea gariepensis vanJaarsv.
LILIACEAE
Bulbs spherical, to 30 cm in diameter, green; shoots 50-100 cm long, twining; leaves small, caducous; flowers white.
Namibia, South Africa (Cape Province)

Brachystelma coddii R.A.Dyer
ASCLEPIADACEAE
Tuber 2-5 cm in diameter and to 3 cm tall; stems simple or branched from the base, to 20 cm long, hairy; leaves ovoid, 2.5 cm long; flowers solitary, wine-coloured with red spots.
Swaziland

Brachystelma barberae Harv. ex Hook.
ASCLEPIADACEAE
Flat caudex 10 cm in diameter and over; stems to 10 cm long; leaves 10-20 cm long; stems and leaves deciduous; flowers dirty purple with yellow centre, malodorous.
South Africa (Cape Province, Natal, Transvaal), Zimbabwe

Brachystelma longifolium (Schltr.) N.E.Br.
ASCLEPIADACEAE
Rootstock producing clusters of fleshy roots; stems 10-30 cm tall; leaves narrow, 3-7 cm long; flowers greenish tinged with brown.
South Africa (Transvaal)

Brachystelma circinatum E.Mey.
ASCLEPIADACEAE
Caudex to 13 cm in diameter; stems 25 cm long, branching from the base; leaves 1-2 cm long; flowers in clusters, colour variable.
Namibia, South Africa (Cape Province)

Brachystelma meyerianum Schltr.
ASCLEPIADACEAE
Tuber 4-6 cm in diameter; stems annual, to 1.5 m long, spreading or ascending; leaves to 3 cm long, hairy or hairless; flowers pinkish to greyish-green.
South Africa (Eastern Cape), Transkei

Brachystelma ngomense R.A.Dyer
ASCLEPIADACEAE
Tuber 2-3 cm in diameter; stems annual, prostrate, branching, 1 m long or to 2 m in cultivation; leaves to 1.5 cm long; flowers dark red or maroon, with white tip.
South Africa (Natal)

Bulbine haworthioides B.Nord
LILIACEAE
Caudex 1-2 cm in diameter; leaves to 10 cm long, arranged in a flat rosette, inflorescence 15 cm tall; flowers yellow.
South Africa (Cape Province)

Brachystelma sp.
ASCLEPIADACEAE
Unidentified species with tuber 10-15 cm in diameter. Plant photogaphed in habitat.
Zimbabwe

Bulbine latifolia (L.f.) Roem. & Schult.
LILIACEAE
Stemless, aloe-like rosette; leaves 20-30 cm long, recurved, pale green; inflorescence 15-25 cm tall; flowers yellow.
South Africa (Cape Province)

Brunsvigia sp.
AMARYLLIDACEAE
Unidentified species with stout bulb above ground and variegated leaves. Photograph by Charles H. Everson.
South Africa

Bulbine sp.
LILIACEAE
A recently discovered species with leaves arranged in rosettes, pale green; inflorescence to 30 cm tall, flowers yellow. Plant photogaphed in habitat.
South Africa (Cape Province)

Bulbine sp.
LILIACEAE
The inflorescence.
Plant photographed
in habitat.

Bulbine sp.
LILIACEAE
A view of the habitat.

Bulbine sp.
LILIACEAE
A flowering specimen in
habitat.

Bursera fagaroides Engl.
BURSERACEAE
Shrub or small tree to 5 m tall, bark of the trunk pale reddish-orange, lea-
flets with leaves heart-shaped; flowers reddish.
Mexico

Caralluma burchardii
N.E.Br.
ASCLEPIADACEAE
Clump-forming plant;
stems to 45 cm long, qua-
drangular, grey-green with
red spots; flowers in clusters at apices of stems,
olive green to red-brown
with outer corona yellow.
Photograph by Roberto
Mangani.
Canary Islands, Morocco

Caralluma dodsoniana Lavranos
ASCLEPIADACEAE
Clump-forming plant; stems to 60 cm long, 4-angled; flowers deep red-
brown. Photograph by Gaetano Palisano.
Somalia

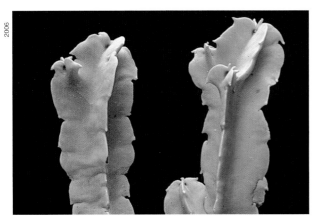

Caralluma retrospiciens (Ehrenb.) N.E.Br.
ASCLEPIADACEAE
Erect 4-angled stems freely branching and forming dense bushes; edges with teeth; black-brown flowers with dark violet-red cilia.
Eritrea, Somalia, Sudan

Carruanthus ringens (L.) Boom
MESEMBRYANTHEMACEAE
Plant to 10 cm tall; leaves crowded, yellowish-green, to 5 cm long, with margins finely toothed; flowers yellow.
South Africa (eastern Cape Province)

Carpobrotus edulis (L.) L.Bolus
MESEMBRYANTHEMACEAE
Stems prostrate, to 1 m long, branching; leaves dull green, turning reddish in dry, sunny location, triangled; flowers 8-10 cm in diameter, yellowish-pink to purple; fruits edible.
South Africa, naturalized in Mediterranean regions

Cephalophyllum spongiosum (L.Bolus) L.Bolus
MESEMBRYANTHEMACEAE
Shrub to 30 cm tall; branches more or less ascending, yellow-brown, spongy; leaves light to dark green, erect 3-angled, in pairs of unequal length, to 11 cm long; flowers scarlet.
South Africa (Cape Province)

Carpobrotus muirii (L.Bolus) L.Bolus
MESEMBRYANTHEMACEAE
Stems 20-30 cm long; leaves green, to 6 cm long, erect, spreading; flowers 6 cm in diameter, pink-purple.
South Africa (Cape Province)

Cephalophyllum spongiosum (L.Bolus) L.Bolus
MESEMBRYANTHEMACEAE
The flower. Photograph by Charles H. Everson.

Ceraria fruticulosa G.Pearson & Stephen
PORTULACACEAE
Shrub to 60 cm tall, freely branching; leaves small, to 6 mm long, green to grey-green; flowers small, pink. Young specimen.
Namibia, South Africa (Cape Province)

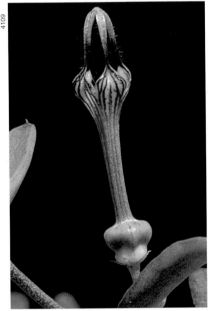

Ceropegia africana R.Br.
ASCLEPIADACEAE
Tuber 5 cm in diameter, with auxillary tubers; stems annual, branching sparsely from base; leaves to 2.5 cm long and 1 cm wide; flowers greenish striped with violet-brown. Photograph by Leo Pickoff.
South Africa (Cape Province)
CITES App. II

Ceropegia ampliata E.Mey
ASCLEPIADACEAE
Stems thick, grey-green; leaves absent or scale-like; flowers cylindrical, 2-5 cm long with swollen base, pale green outside, with a purple band inside. Photograph by Leo Pickoff.
South Africa (Natal)
CITES App. II

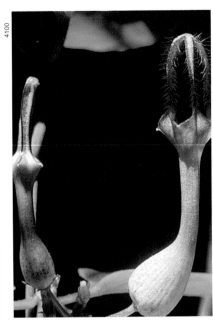

Ceropegia bulbosa Roxb.
ASCLEPIADACEAE
Stems twining, to 50 cm long and over; leaves thin, 3 cm long, pale green turning to reddish in full sun; flowers 3-5 together, to 2 cm long, greenish below, purple above. Photograph by Leo Pickoff.
Ethiopia, India, Oman, N. Yemen, Pakistan
CITES App. II

Ceropegia cimiciodora Oberm.
ASCLEPIADACEAE
Stems succulent, prostrate to erect, to 150 cm long; flowering stems thinner and leafless; flowers with red-brown lobes. Photograph by Leo Pickoff.
South Africa (Cape Province)
CITES App. II

Ceropegia dimorpha Humb.
ASCLEPIADACEAE
Stems erect, grey-violet, to 15 cm tall; leaves lanceolate, to 3.5 cm long; flowers pale violet to pale red with dark violet stripes.
Madagascar   CITES App. II

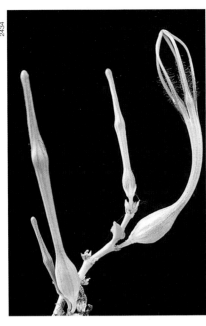

Ceropegia fortuita
R.A.Dyer
ASCLEPIADACEAE
Tuber to 5 cm in diameter and 3 cm tall; stem annual, branching sparsely, climbing and twining to 1 m tall; leaves to 2.5 cm long and 1.2 cm wide with few hairs on margins; flowers purple, hairy.
South Africa (Natal)
CITES App. II

Ceropegia fortuita R.A.Dyer
ASCLEPIADACEAE
Stems and flower.

CITES App. II

Ceropegia fusca Bolle
ASCLEPIADACEAE
Stems erect, to 1 m tall with several spreading cylindrical branches, greyish or purplish; leaves 4 cm long and 3 mm wide borne only during growing season; flowers brown. Plant photographed in habitat.
Canary Islands (Tenerife)
CITES App. II

Ceropegia fusca Bolle
ASCLEPIADACEAE
The flowers. Plant photographed in habitat.
Canary Islands
CITES App. II

Ceropegia krainzii Svent.
ASCLEPIADACEAE
Stems erect, numerous, to 60 cm tall, simple or dichotomously branched, olive green to whitish; leaves only on the younger parts, 1-3 cm long, grey; flowers whitish-yellow.
Canary Islands

CITES App. II

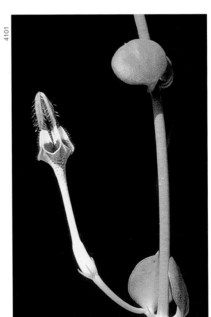

Ceropegia radicans
Schltr.
ASCLEPIADACEAE
Low shrub with creeping stems rooting at nodes; leaves 2-5 cm long; flowers green-white with purple blotches. Photograph by Leo Pickoff.
South Africa (Cape Province)
CITES App. II

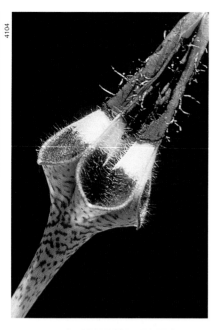

Ceropegia radicans
Schltr.
ASCLEPIADACEAE
Close-up of the flower.
Photograph by Leo Pickoff.
CITES App. II

Ceropegia somaliensis Chiov.
ASCLEPIADACEAE
Stems twining, glabrous; leaves small, ovate; flowers hairy, whitish with darker spots. Photograph by Leo Pickoff.
Kenya, Somalia   CITES App. II

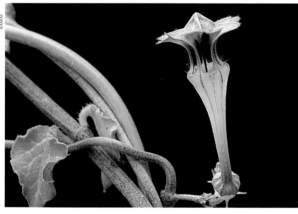

Ceropegia rendallii N.E.Br.
ASCLEPIADACEAE
Stems 8-15 cm long arising from a tuber and twining; leaves 1.5-3 cm long; flowers purple at base, white towards the apex.
South Africa (Transvaal)
CITES App. II

Ceropegia sp.
ASCLEPIADACEAE
The flower of an unidentified species with succulent leafless stems.
Photograph by Gaetano Palisano.
CITES App. II

Ceropegia rendallii
N.E.Br.
ASCLEPIADACEAE
Close-up of the flower.
Photograph by Leo Pickoff.
CITES App. II

Ceropegia sp.
Transvaal
ASCLEPIADACEAE
An unidentified species in trade as originating from Transvaal. Tuber large, stems twining, leaves long, green, flowers small.
South Africa (Transvaal)
CITES App. II

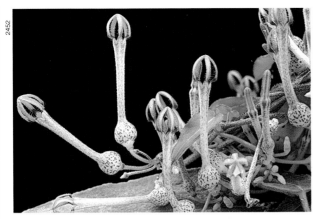

Ceropegia sp. Transvaal
ASCLEPIADACEAE
The flowers of the Transvaal species.

CITES App. II

Ceropegia woodii Schltr.
ASCLEPIADACEAE
Stems creeping, branches filamentous with tubers at the nodes; leaves heart-shaped, dark green with white marks; flowers brown. Some authors consider this species a variety of *C. linearis* E.Meyer.
South Africa (Natal), Zimbabwe

CITES App. II

Ceropegia stapeliiformis Haw.
ASCLEPIADACEAE
Stems to 1.5 m tall, grey-brown, trailing; leaves tiny, inconspicuous; flowers brownish with whitish spots. Photograph by Leo Pickoff.
South Africa (Cape Province)
CITES App. II

Chasmatophyllum muscolinum (Haw.) Dinter & Schwantes
MESEMBRYANTHEMACEAE
Plant forming dense groups; branches prostrate; leaves 1.5-2 cm long, 3-angled to semi-cylindrical, grey-green with minute transparent spots; flowers yellow.
Namibia

Ceropegia variegata (Forssk.) Decne
ASCLEPIADACEAE
Stems creeping, very fleshy and leafless, flowers pale green or pink, with dark red spots. Photograph by Leo Pickoff.
Arabia
CITES App. II

Cheiridopsis cigarettifera (A.Berger) N.E.Br.
MESEMBRYANTHEMACEAE
Stems with 2-4 pairs of leaves of unequal size, the longest pair 3-6 cm; leaves grey-green with translucent spots; flowers yellow. Plant photographed in habitat.
South Africa (Cape Province)

71

Cheiridopsis peculiaris N.E.Br.

MESEMBRYANTHEMACEAE

Small plant; leaves in 2 pairs, grey-green with darker spots; flowers yellow. Photograph by Charles H. Everson.

Namibia, South Africa (Little Namaqualand)

Chorisia speciosa A.St.-Hil.

BOMBACACEAE

Tree over 20 m tall with very spiny stems and branches; leaves digitate; flowers 10 cm in diameter, yellowish or reddish; fruits very woody.

Brazil

Chorisia speciosa A.St.-Hil.

BOMBACACEAE

The flower.

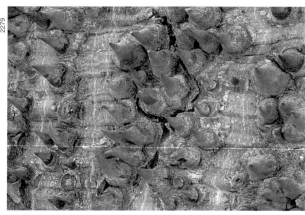

Chorisia speciosa A.St.-Hil.

BOMBACACEAE

The spiny trunk.

Cissus lanigera Harv.

VITACEAE

Trailing stems to 2 m long; leaves ovate to lanceolate, hairy, 7-10 cm long and 3-5 cm wide; flowers yellowish-white; fruit red, hairy.

South Africa (Natal)

Cissus quadrangularis L.

VITACEAE

Stems green, climbing, much branched, 4-angled, constricted at nodes and rooting; leaves only on growing portions of the stems; inflorescence 5 cm long; flowers yellow to green. Plant photographed in habitat.

Tropical Africa, southern Asia, Malaysia

Cissus quadrangularis L.
VITACEAE
Flowering specimen in habitat.

Cissus trifoliata (L.) L.
VITACEAE
Stems slender, striated, to 10 m long, with long tendrils; leaves tripartite, succulent; flowers greenish-yellow.
USA (New Mexico)

Cissus quadrangularis L.
VITACEAE
Plant photographed in habitat.

Cissus tuberosa Moç. & Sessé
VITACEAE
Caudex swollen; stems with thick internodes, long tendrils and aerial roots; leaves 5-10 cm long, palmate; flowers greenish-yellow.
Mexico

Cissus sp.
VITACEAE
An unidentified species with thick caudex and long, trailing stems.
Kenya

Commiphora capensis (Sond.) Engl.
BURSERACEAE
Bush to 2 m tall; branches thick, covered with brown to green bark, peeling in small papery flakes; leaves almost circular, smooth, green; flowers inconspicuous, greenish to yellow. Photograph by Charles H. Everson.
Namibia, South Africa (Cape Province)

Commiphora saxicola
Engl.
BURSERACEAE
Base swollen with several stems, 50-100 cm tall and to 2 m in diameter; bark yellowish-green or grey, rarely reddish-brown, not peeling; leaves small, shiny green; flowers very small, yellowish. Photograph by Charles H. Everson.
Namibia

Conophyllum framesii
(L.Bolus.) L.Bolus
MESEMBRYANTHEMACEAE
Branches to 15 cm long, brown, those bearing flowers thinner and with shorter internodes; leaves rounded, to 7 cm long; flowers pale pink.
Namibia, South Africa (Little Namaqualand)

Conicosia pugioniformis (L.) N.E.Br.
MESEMBRYANTHEMACEAE
Stems erect, to 30 cm tall; leaves to 20 cm long, 3-angled, grey-green with reddish base; flowers yellow. Plant photographed in habitat.
South Africa (Cape Province)

Conophytum blandum L.Bolus
MESEMBRYANTHEMACEAE
Plant caespitose; leaves whitish to bluish-green, sometimes flushed with red; flowers white to very pale pink.
South Africa (Cape Province)

Conophyllum angustifolium L.Bolus
MESEMBRYANTHEMACEAE
Shrub, freely branching; branches to 30 cm long with red-brown internodes; leaves to 10 cm long, rounded on the lower surface; flowers whitish to lemon yellow.
Namibia, South Africa (Little Namaqualand)

Conophytum cupreatum Tischer
MESEMBRYANTHEMACEAE
Bodies to 1.5 cm tall, conical, coppery-brown with dark windows and grey spots; flowers white. Hammer considers this species a variety of *C. pellucidum* Schwant.
South Africa (Cape Province)

Conophytum fraternum (N.E.Br.) N.E.Br.
MESEMBRYANTHEMACEAE
Branches to 5 cm long, thick; bodies numerous, to 1 cm long, forming clumps, reddish-green with dark green spots; flowers white-pink.
South Africa (Cape Province)

Conophytum jacobsenianum Tischer
MESEMBRYANTHEMACEAE
Plant forming large clumps; bodies pear-shaped to 1.5 cm long, whitish to grey-green with several dark green spots; flowers whitish-pink. Hammer considers this species a synonym of *C. gratum* N.E.Br.
South Africa (Cape Province)

Conophytum giftebergense Tischer
MESEMBRYANTHEMACEAE
Bodies to 1 cm long and 1 cm diameter, olive green with darker spots; flowers white. Considered by Hammer a form of *C. obcordellum* N.E.Br.
South Africa (Cape Province)

Conophytum lambertense Schick & Tischer
MESEMBRYANTHEMACEAE
Bodies to 1 cm tall, grey-green with a darker line around the fissure and prominent green to reddish lines on the apical part; flowers white. Hammer considers this species synonym of *C. obcordellum* N.E. Br.
South Africa (Cape Province)

Conophytum gratum (N.E.Br.) N.E.Br.
MESEMBRYANTHEMACEAE
Bodies to 2.5 cm tall and wide, forming mats, glaucous-green with grey or dark spots; flowers red-magenta. Photograph by Charles H. Everson.
South Africa (Cape Province)

Conophytum maximum Tischer
MESEMBRYANTHEMACEAE
Bodies to 3 cm tall and 2.5 cm wide, grey-glaucous with dark green spots; flowers pink. Hammer considers this species a synonym of *C. gratum* (N.E.Br.), but flattish and larger.
South Africa (Cape Province)

Conophytum minutum (Haw.) N.E.Br.
MESEMBRYANTHEMACEAE

Bodies to 1.2 cm tall, 1 cm wide, bluish-grey-green with darker spots; flowers pink to pink lilac or rarely white.
South Africa (Cape Province)

Conophytum ornatum Lavis
MESEMBRYANTHEMACEAE

Plant caespitose; bodies to 2 cm tall, bluish-green with isolated dark spots; flowers yellow. Hammer considers this species a population of *C. flavum* N.E.Br.
South Africa (Cape Province)

Conophytum pearsonii N.E.Br.
MESEMBRYANTHEMACEAE

Plant forming clumps; bodies conical to 1.6 cm long, glaucous to yellowish-green, occasionally with darker spots; flowers violet-pink. Hammer considers this species a variety of *C. minutum* (Haw.) N.E.Br. Photograph by Charles H. Everson.
South Africa (Cape Province)

Conophytum praecox N.E.Br.
MESEMBRYANTHEMACEAE

Bodies over 1 cm long, forming clumps, pale grey to pale bluish-green, several dark green spots; flowers white.
South Africa (Cape Province)

Conophytum quaesitum (N.E.Br.) N.E.Br.
MESEMBRYANTHEMACEAE

Bodies elliptical, to 1.2 cm tall and 1.5 cm wide, light grey to bluish-green with dark green spots; flowers white.
South Africa (Cape Province)

Conophytum ricardianum Loesch & Tischer
MESEMBRYANTHEMACEAE

Plant forming clumps; bodies conical to 1.8 cm tall, grey-green with dark green spots; flowers whitish.
Namibia

Conophytum saxetanum (N.E.Br.) N.E.Br.
MESEMBRYANTHEMACEAE
Plant forming large clumps; bodies to 1 cm long, variable in colour, green to greyish-green, pale blue, purple-red or orange, spotted or immaculate; flowers white. Photograph by Charles H. Everson.
Namibia

Conophytum spectabile Lavis
MESEMBRYANTHEMACEAE
Bodies to 1.2 cm tall and 0.8 cm wide, green marked with red-brown lines; flowers white. Hammer considers this species synonym of *C. obcordellum* N.E.Br.
South Africa (Cape Province)

Conophytum subfenestratum Schwantes
MESEMBRYANTHEMACEAE
Plant forming clumps; bodies to 2.5 cm long, cylindrical, light green with dark green spots; flowers white to violet-pink.
South Africa (Cape Province)

Conophytum tantillum N.E.Br. ssp. **helenae** (Rawe) S.Hammer
MESEMBRYANTHEMACEAE
Plant forming mats; bodies pale greyish-green, lined with red; flowers pink to magenta.
Conophytum helenae Rawe
South Africa (Cape Province)

Conophytum tischeri Schick
MESEMBRYANTHEMACEAE
Plant with short stems forming small mats; bodies to 1.3 cm tall, grey-green with dark red spots; flowers lilac. Hammer considers this species as synonym of *C. ectypum* N.E.Br.
South Africa (Cape Province)

Conophytum truncatum (Thunb.) N.E.Br. var. **wiggettiae** (N.E.Br.) Rawe
MESEMBRYANTHEMACEAE
Plant forming small cushions to 5 cm in diameter; bodies to 1.5 cm long, whitish-green to reddish-grey-green with spots green to reddish; flowers white to pale pink.
Conophytum calitzdorpense Tischer, *C. wiggettiae* N.E.Br.
Namibia, South Africa (Cape Province)

Conophytum truncatum (Thunb.) N.E.Br. var. **wiggettiae** (N.E.Br.) Rawe
MESEMBRYANTHEMACEAE
Plant photographed in habitat.

Cotyledon campanulata Harv.
CRASSULACEAE
Shrub to 20 cm tall; stem rigid and bare at the base with age; leaves opposite, yellowish-green, 3-12 cm long, 0.6-1.2 cm wide, covered with soft hairs; flowers yellow.
Cotyledon teretifolia Thunb.
South Africa (Cape Province)

Conophytum violaciflorum Schick & Tischer
MESEMBRYANTHEMACEAE
Plant forming small mats; bodies dark green with darker green spots; flowers violet-pink.
South Africa (Cape Province)

Cotyledon campanulata Marloth
CRASSULACEAE
A young plant.

Cordyline indivisa (J.R.Forst.) Steud.
AGAVACEAE
Plant to 8 m tall, stems sparsely branched; leaves lanceolate, to 1.5 m long, green above, glaucous beneath; inflorescence to 1.5 m tall; flowers white.
New Zealand

Cotyledon elisae vanJaarsv.
CRASSULACEAE
Erect, much-branched shrublet, to 20 cm tall; leaves 1.5-3 cm long, green with purple margins in the upper third; inflorescence to 20 cm tall; flowers orange-red. Plant photographed in habitat.
South Africa (Cape Province)

Cotyledon elisae
vanJaarsv.
CRASSULACEAE
Plant photographed in habitat.
South Africa (Cape Province)

Cotyledon elisae
vanJaarsv.
CRASSULACEAE
Specimen growing on a rock. Plant photographed in habitat.
South Africa (Cape Province)

Cotyledon orbiculata L.
CRASSULACEAE
Shrub to 1 m tall, branched; leaves green to grey-green, often with red margins, covered with pruinose wax; inflorescence to 70 cm tall; flowers red or orange-red. Photograph by Charles H. Everson.
Cotyledon ausana Dintr; *C. elata* Haw.; *C. ramosa* Haw.
Angola, Namibia, South Africa (Cape Province)

Cotyledon orbiculata
L. var. **spuria**
(L.) Toelken
CRASSULACEAE
Taller variety, with flowers yellow-orange, occasionally red. Plant photogaphed in habitat.
Cotyledon spuria L.
Angola, Namibia, South Africa (Cape Province)

Cotyledon orbiculata
L. var. **spuria** Toelken
CRASSULACEAE
Plant photographed in habitat.

Cotyledon orbiculata
L. var. **spuria** Toelken
CRASSULACEAE
Plant photographed in habitat.

Cotyledon undulata Harv.
CRASSULACEAE
Shrub 50 cm tall; leaves rhomboidal-ovate, 8-12 cm long, 6 cm wide, white pruinose; flowers orange-yellow. Close-up of flowers.
South Africa (Cape Province)

Cotyledon velutina Hook.f.
CRASSULACEAE
The flowers.

Cotyledon velutina Hook.f.
CRASSULACEAE
Plant to 2 m tall; leaves green to grey-brown often with red margins, velvety, 5-10 cm long; flowers orange to copper with yellow margins.
South Africa (Cape Province)

Crassula albiflora Sims
CRASSULACEAE
Shrublets to 40 cm tall; leaves papillose, ciliate, green to yellowish-green; flowers white. A reputed synonym of *C. dejecta* Jacq.
Rochea albiflora DC; *Crassula obvallata* Thunb.
South Africa (Cape Province)

Cotyledon velutina Hook.f.
CRASSULACEAE
Plant photographed in habitat.

Crassula alstonii Marloth
CRASSULACEAE
Low plant 8-10 cm tall, densely leaved; leaves grey-green, obtuse or rounded, forming a spherical rosette 2 cm wide; flowers white-cream to pale yellow.
South Africa (Cape Province)

Crassula atropurpurea (Haw.) A.Dietr.

CRASSULACEAE

Shrublets to 60 cm tall with carnous or woody branches; leaves glabrous or papillose, 1.5-3 cm long, 0.6-2.5 cm wide, green to deep red with horny margins; flowers cream. Plant photographed in habitat.
South Africa (Cape Province)

Crassula capitella Thunb. ssp. thyrsifolia (Thunb.) Toelken

CRASSULACEAE

Stems woody, leaves to 12 cm long, arranged in rosettes, green often spotted red, glabrous with marginal cilia; inflorescence 10-30 cm tall; flowers white tinged with pink. Plant photographed in habitat.
South Africa (Cape Province)

Crassula barbata Thunb.

CRASSULACEAE

Plant to 30 cm high when flowering; leaves arranged in rosettes, 1-3.5 cm long, 1.5-3.5 cm wide, grey-green with marginal white hairs; flowers white tinged with pink. Photograph by Charles H. Everson.
South Africa (Cape Province)

Crassula cephalophora Thunb.

CRASSULACEAE

Plant with several basal rosettes; leaves oblong-elliptic, 2.5 to 7 cm long, grey-green to yellowish-green; flowers yellowish. Reputed synonym of *C. nudicaulis* L.
South Africa (Cape Province)

Crassula biplanata Haw.

CRASSULACEAE

Much branched, 15-20 cm tall; leaves lanceolate 0.8-1.5 cm. long, 0.1-0.2 cm wide, dark green; flowers white to cream. Plant photographed in habitat.
Crassula punctulata Schönland & Bak.
South Africa (Cape Province)

Crassula coccinea L.

CRASSULACEAE

Shrub to 60 cm tall with reddish stem; leaves 1.5-2.5 cm long, 1-1.5 cm wide, with margins curved upwards, green to brownish; flowers scarlet red.
Rochea coccinea (L.) DC.
South Africa (Cape Province)

Crassula coccinea L.
CRASSULACEAE
Cultivated specimen.

Crassula columnaris Thunb.
CRASSULACEAE
Plant photographed in habitat.

Crassula columella Marloth & Schönland
CRASSULACEAE
Shrub to 15 cm tall; stems 8-10 cm tall; leaves green to yellowish-green, tinged with red when grown in full sun, compressed; flowers greenish-white. Photograph by Anna Rosa Nicola.
South Africa (Cape Province)

Crassula cooperi Regel
CRASSULACEAE
Forming dense low cushions; leaves oblanceolate or obovate 0.6-3.5 cm long, 0.3-1 cm wide, light green with marginal cilia; flowers white. A reputed subspecies of *C. exilis* Harv.
Crassula bolusii Hook.

Crassula columnaris Thunb.
CRASSULACEAE
Erect stems 0.3-1 cm tall; leaves 0.3-1.2 cm long, 1-2.5 cm wide, grey-green to brown, completely enveloping the short stem; flowers white to pale yellow often tinged with red. Photograph by Gaetano Palisano.
South Africa (Cape Province)

Crassula cotyledonis Thunb.
CRASSULACEAE
Basal rosettes with woody stems to 20 cm tall; leaves 3-6 cm long, 1-2.5 cm wide, grey-green to yellowish-green, covered with hairs; flowers cream to pale yellow. Plant photographed in habitat.
Namibia

Crassula cv.
CRASSULACEAE
Cultivar with stems covered with compressed leaves, green to yellowish-green.

Crassula cv. «Coralita» ISI 1387
CRASSULACEAE
Cultivar with adpressed leaves in rows. (*C. suzannae* × *C. perfoliata* var. *falcata*). Photograph by Anna Rosa Nicola.
Garden origin

Crassula cv. «Blue Hale»
CRASSULACEAE
Cultivar with branched stems and large bluish-green ovate leaves.

Crassula cv. «Emerald»
CRASSULACEAE
Cultivar with leaves in dense rosettes, dull green, covered with white papillae; flowers cream-yellowish.
Garden origin

Crassula cv. «Hobbit»
CRASSULACEAE
Cultivar related to *C. portulacea* and *C. lactea*. Leaves green, cup-shaped; flowers white.
Garden origin

Crassula cv. «Budda's Temple»
CRASSULACEAE
A beautiful small cultivar with erect stem and adpressed green hairy leaves. Photograph by Gaetano Palisano.

Crassula cv. «Moonglow»
CRASSULACEAE
Nice cultivar, with small leaves covering stems. Hybrid between *C. decep-tor* var. *arta* × *perfoliata* var. *falcata*. Photograph by Anna Rosa Nicola.
Garden origin

Crassula dejecta Jacq.
CRASSULACEAE
Shrublets to 40 cm tall; leaves 0.8-1.5 cm long, 0.4-1.3 cm wide, green to yellowish-green; flowers white.
South Africa (Cape Province)

Crassula cv. «Morgan Beauty»
CRASSULACEAE
Compact cultivar (*C. falcata* × *C. mesembryanthemopsis*), leaves grey-green; flowers salmon-pink.
Garden origin

Crassula dejecta Jacq.
CRASSULACEAE
Flowering specimen.

Crassula cv. «Silver Springtime»
CRASSULACEAE
Small, beautiful cultivar; stems covered with compressed leaves, green to yellowish-green. Photograph by Anna Rosa Nicola.
Garden origin

Crassula dejecta Jacq.
CRASSULACEAE
Young plant. Photograph by Anna Rosa Nicola.

Crassula deltoidea Thunb.
CRASSULACEAE
Small shrub, rarely more than 8 cm tall; leaves rhombic to oblanceolate, 1-1.5 cm long, 0.4-0.8 cm wide, grey-green; flowers white.
Crassula rhomboidea N.E.Br.
South Africa (Cape Province, Little Namaqualand)

Crassula elegans Schönland
CRASSULACEAE
Cultivated specimen. Photograph by Anna Rosa Nicola.

Crassula deltoidea Thunb.
CRASSULACEAE
Specimen photographed in habitat by Charles H. Everson.

Crassula exilis Harv. ssp. **sedifolia** (N.E.Br.) Toelken
CRASSULACEAE
Plant much branching; leaves 0.4-1.5 cm long, 0.2-0.3 cm wide, with a row of dark spots along the ciliate margins; flowers white.
South Africa (Cape Province)

Crassula elegans Schönland
CRASSULACEAE
Plant much branched to 8 cm tall; leaves 0.5-1.5 cm long, 0.4-0.8 cm wide, closely packed, glabrous or covered with fine hairs, green to deep red; flowers cream or white. Plant photographed in habitat by Charles H. Everson.
Namibia, South Africa (Cape Province)

Crassula expansa Dryand.
CRASSULACEAE
Decumbent branches to 40 cm long; leaves 0.6-2 cm long, 0.2-0.4 cm wide, green or yellowish-green; flowers white tinged with red. Plant photographed in habitat.
South Africa (Namaqualand)

Crassula falcata Wendl.
CRASSULACEAE

Plant to 1 m tall, rarely branched; leaves 7-10 cm long, 3-4 cm wide, grey-green; flowers red. Reputedly a subspecies of *C. perfoliata* L. Close-up of flowers.
Rochea falcata DC.
South Africa (Cape Province)

Crassula glomerata
Berg.
CRASSULACEAE

Annual plant, branches to 15 cm tall; leaves 0.6-1 cm long, 1-3 cm wide, green to brown; flowers white.
South Africa (Cape Province)

Crassula garibina
Marloth & Schönland
CRASSULACEAE

Small shrublets to 25 cm tall with swollen base and spreading branches; leaves 2-4 cm long, 1 cm wide, grey-green to dull brown covered with fine hairs; flowers cream-white.
Namibia, South Africa (Cape Province)

Crassula grisea
Schönland
CRASSULACEAE

Small plant, rarely more than 15 cm tall; leaves linear-lanceolate 2-8 cm long, 0.8 cm wide, green to brown, hairy; flowers white.
Crassula bakeri Schönl.
South Africa (Cape Province, L. Namaqualand)

Crassula garibina Marloth & Schönland
CRASSULACEAE

Close-up of flowers.

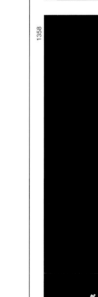

Crassula hemisphaerica
Thunb.
CRASSULACEAE

Plant to 15 cm tall; leaves flat, adpressed, 1.5-2 cm long, 1.5-2.5 cm wide, arranged in rosettes; leaf margins with white hairs; flowers white. A flowering stem.
Crassula alooides Dryand
South Africa (Cape Province)

Crassula heterotricha Schinz
CRASSULACEAE
Plant to 40 cm tall, branched; leaves lanceolate to oblong, 7-15 cm long, 1-1.5 cm wide, light green; flowers white. Reputedly a subspecies of *C. perfoliata* L.
South Africa (Natal)

Crassula hirtipes Harv.
CRASSULACEAE
Stems spreading to 15 cm long; leaves 0.8-1.5 cm long, 0.4-0.7 cm wide, grey-green with short hairs; flowers cream to yellow.
Crassula hystrix Schönland
South Africa (Cape Province)

Crassula hystrix Schönland
CRASSULACEAE
Low subshrub 2-3 cm tall; leaves 0.6-0.8 cm long, 0.4-0.6 cm wide, grey-green with hairs; flowers cream. A reputed synonym of *C. hirtipes* Haw.
Photograph by Anna Rosa Nicola.

Crassula lanuginosa Harv.
CRASSULACEAE
Little subshrub to 15 cm tall; leaves semi-cylindrical, soft, hairy, green or grey-green; flowers white.
South Africa (Cape Province)

Crassula littlewoodii Friedr.
CRASSULACEAE
Low tufted plant; leaves lanceolate or elliptic, 2-4 cm long, 0.1 cm wide, covered with hairs; flowers white.
Namibia, South Africa

Crassula mesembryanthemopsis Dinter
CRASSULACEAE
Short stem with leaves arranged in rosettes of 4-8 pairs of leaves; leaves 1-2 cm long, 0.3-0.6 cm wide with truncate tips; flowers white.
Namibia

Crassula mesembryanthemopsis Dinter
CRASSULACEAE
A flowering specimen.

Crassula muscosa Thunb.
CRASSULACEAE
Cristated specimen.

Crassula muscosa Thunb.
CRASSULACEAE
Slender branched stems to 30 cm tall; leaves small, closely arranged in rows, grey-green to yellowish-green; flowers small, yellowish-white. Photograph by Charles H. Everson.
Crassula lycopodioides Lam.
Namibia, South Africa (Cape Province)

Crassula nudicaulis L.
CRASSULACEAE
Densely leafy branched stem; leaves semi-cylindrical 0.2-0.8 cm long, 0.6-1.5 cm wide, green to reddish-brown; flowers cream. Plant photographed in habitat.
South Africa (Cape Province)

Crassula muscosa Thunb.
CRASSULACEAE
Specimen growing among rock crevices. Plant photographed in habitat.

Crassula pellucida L.
CRASSULACEAE
Decumbent or prostrate stems to 60 cm long; leaves 1-2.5 cm long, 0.5-1.2 cm wide, green with brown stripes and papillose red margins; flowers white tinged with pink.
South Africa (Cape Province)

Crassula perforata Thunb.
CRASSULACEAE
Small shrub with branches to 60 cm long; leaves 0.8-2 cm long, 0.3-1.5 cm wide, greyish-green constricted towards base and fused to the opposite one; flowers cream to pale yellow. Plant photographed in habitat.
Crassula anthurus E.Mey, *C. conjuncta* N.E.Br., *C. perfossa* Lam., *C. perfilata* Scop.
South Africa (Cape Province)

Crassula portulacea Lam.
CRASSULACEAE
Branched shrub to 1.5 m tall; old leaves caducous, new leaves glossy green with red margins; flowers white. A reputed synonym of *C. ovata* (Mill.) Druce.
Crassula lucens Gram., *C. nitida* Schönland
South Africa (Cape Province to Transvaal)

Crassula phyturus Mildbr.
CRASSULACEAE
Small branched plant; leaves semi-cylindrical or linear, 0.6-0.7 cm long, 0.2 cm wide, green; flowers white.
Tropical Africa

Crassula remota Schönland
CRASSULACEAE
Small branched shrub; leaves 2 cm long, 1.2 cm wide, grey-green with fine hairs; flowers cream-white. A reputed synonym of *C. subaphylla* Harv.
South Africa (Cape Province)

Crassula picturata Boom
CRASSULACEAE
Plant much branched forming dense cushions; leaves 0.6-3.5 cm long, 0.3-1 cm wide, green with dark spots and marginal cilia; flowers white to pale pink. A reputed synonym of *C. exilis* Harv. subspecies *cooperi* (Regel) Toelken. Photograph by Anna Rosa Nicola.
South Africa (Cape Province)

Crassula rupestris Thunb.
CRASSULACEAE
Shrublets to 50 cm tall, much branched; leaves 0.5-1.5 cm long, 0.3-1 cm wide, glaucous-green to reddish-brown with red or yellow horny margins; flowers white tinged with pink or red. Plant photographed in habitat.
Crassula monticola N.E.Br., *C. perfossa* Harv.
South Africa (Cape Province)

Crassula rupestris Thunb.
CRASSULACEAE
A large bush in habitat.

Crassula sarcocaulis Eckl. & Zeyh.
CRASSULACEAE
Plant photographed in habitat.

Crassula rupestris Thunb.
CRASSULACEAE
Another specimen in habitat.

Crassula sarcocaulis Eckl. & Zeyh. ssp. **rupicola** Toelken
CRASSULACEAE
Subspecies forming dense shrubs; stems very fleshy; leaves linear.
Plant photographed in habitat.

Crassula sarcocaulis Eckl. & Zeyh.
CRASSULACEAE
Shrub to 60 cm tall; leaves linear lanceolate, 1-4 cm long, 0.1-0.8 cm wide, dark green; flowers white to cream. Cultivated specimen.
South Africa (Cape Province)

Crassula subulata L.
CRASSULACEAE
Plant to 15 cm tall; leaves lanceolate, usually deciduous at the end of season. A reputed synonym of *C. rhodesica* ssp. *transvaalensis* (Kuntze) Toelken. Plant photographed in habitat.
Namibia

Crassula tecta Thunb.
CRASSULACEAE
Plant with basal rosettes, much branched, forming clumps; leaves
2-3.5 cm long, 0.5-1.5 cm wide, grey-green, rounded, covered with papil-
lae; flowers white or cream. Photograph by Anna Rosa Nicola.
Crassula decipiens N.E.Br.
South Africa (Cape Province)

Crassula tecta Thunb.
CRASSULACEAE
Plant photographed in habitat.

Crassula volkensii Engl.
CRASSULACEAE
Plant 10-12 cm tall, symmetrically branching; leaves lanceolate, fleshy,
2-2.5 cm long, 0.5-0.6 cm wide; flowers white.
Tanganyika

Cremmosedum cv. «Crocodile» ISI 1641
CRASSULACEAE
Nice cultivar (*Cremnophila* × *Sedum*) with scaly stems and green leaves.
Garden origin

Cremmosedum cv. «Little Gem» ISI 1256
CRASSULACEAE
Another beautiful cultivar, mat forming; leaves green in small rosettes.
Photograph by Anna Rosa Nicola.
Garden origin

Cussonia paniculata
Eckl. & Zeyh.
ARALIACEAE
Tree to 4 m tall with rough
bark; leaves digitate,
oblong in juvenile plants,
ovate in adult plants;
flowers white.
Southern Africa

Cussonia paniculata
Eckl. & Zeyh.
ARALIACEAE
Young specimen.

Cyphostemma bainesii
(Hook.f.) Desc.
VITACEAE
A very well grown specimen.

Cylindrophyllum dyeri L.Bolus
MESEMBRYANTHEMACEAE
Branches to 8 cm long, forming dense cushions; leaves erect, to 7 cm long, green to grey-green; flowers pale pink.
South Africa (Cape Province)

Cyphostemma currori (Hook.f.) Desc.
VITACEAE
Stem over 4 m tall, branching at the top; bark yellow, peeling, leaves tripartite; flowers yellowish.
Angola, Namibia

Cyphostemma bainesii
(Hook.f.) Desc.
VITACEAE
Stems swollen, bottle-shaped; to 1 m tall; leaves tripartite, green, lanate; flowers greenish-yellow.
Namibia

Cyphostemma elephantopus Desc.
VITACEAE
Large subterranean caudex, ovoid to disk-shaped, to 70 cm tall and 50 cm in diameter; main stem to 1 m tall with climbing branches to 2 m long; leaves 3-4 cm long; flowers yellowish.
Madagascar

Cyphostemma juttae (Hook.f.) Desc.
VITACEAE
Stem to 2 m tall, forming a massive caudex with thick branches; stem covered with yellow bark and papery skin falling off with age; leaves to 20 cm long, 6 cm wide; flowers greenish-yellow; red berries.
Namibia

Cyphostemma laza Desc.
VITACEAE
Stem to 1 m tall, swollen; stems 3-5 m long, prostrate or climbing; leaves to 15 cm long; flowers yellowish. Young specimen.
Madagascar

Dasylirion wheeleri S.Watson
AGAVACEAE
Trunk to 1.5 m tall; leaves yellowish-green to rust-brown, in rosette, to 90 cm long, glaucous, margins spiny; inflorescence to 5 m tall; flowers cream-white tinged with green.
USA (Arizona, Texas)

Decaryia madagascarensis Choux
DIDIEREACEAE
Arborescent plant to 6 m tall; stem with spreading thorny branches; leaves small, fleshy, 5 mm long and 3 mm wide, arising below the thorns; inflorescence 5 cm long; flowers small, pale yellow.
Madagascar

Delosperma ashtonii L.Bolus
MESEMBRYANTHEMACEAE
Low shrub with tuberous roots; branches 3-5 cm long, green with soft hairs; leaves lanceolate to linear, green to greyish-green, 4-5 cm long; flowers purplish.
South Africa (Transvaal)

Delosperma bosseranum Marais
MESEMBRYANTHEMACEAE
Erect or decumbent stems 5-20 cm long; tuberous root; leaves to 2 cm long, green, papillae and red tip; flowers white.

Delosperma davii N.E.Br.
MESEMBRYANTHEMACEAE
Stems 7-15 cm long, weak; leaves ascending, to 6 cm long, green to grey-ish-green, upper surface grooved; flowers white.
South Africa (Cape Province)

Delosperma minimum Lavis
MESEMBRYANTHEMACEAE
Plant to 15 cm tall; branches spreading, thick, green to reddish, leaves triangular; flowers purple-red.
South Africa (Cape Province)

Delosperma harazianum (Deflleurs) H.H.Poppend. & H.D. Hilenf.
MESEMBRYANTHEMACEAE
Plant forming clumps to 12 cm in diameter; leaves to 1.8 cm long and 4 mm wide, green with small papillae and reddish tips; flowers white to pink-purplish.

Delosperma sp. (van Jaarsveld & Sajeva 14653)
MESEMBRYANTHEMACEAE
An unidentified species photographed in habitat (Karoo).

Delosperma litorale (Kensit) L.Bolus
MESEMBRYANTHEMACEAE
Stems elongate, creeping, to 40 cm long; leaves triangular, 3 cm long, blui-sh-green, edges whitish; flowers white.
South Africa (Cape Province)

Delosperma tradescantioides (Berger) L.Bolus
MESEMBRYANTHEMACEAE
Low shrub, freely branching; branches rooting at the nodes, grey-brown; leaves 2-3 cm long, 1 cm wide, 1-2 mm thick; flowers white.
South Africa (Cape Province)

Didierea trollii Capuron & Rauh.
DIDIEREACEAE
Young stems horizontal, forming a bush 50 cm tall from which adult stems develop into trunks; leaves 1-2 cm long, grouped at the centre of the thorns; flowers greenish-yellow.
Madagascar

Dinterantus microspermus Schwantes
MESEMBRYANTHEMACEAE
One to many headed plant; branches to 5 cm long, covered with remains of old dry leaves; leaves in pair, united for half of their length to 3 cm long, reddish-grey-green to grey-violet; flowers yellow with reddish tips.
Namibia

Dioscorea elephantipes (L'Hér.) Engl.
DIOSCOREACEAE
Caudex semi-globose to 1 m in diameter; bark separated into knobs; stems twining, 1-2 m long; leaves green, triangular; flowers yellow.
Testudinaria elephantipes (L'Hér.) Lindl.
Southern Africa

Dioscorea hemicrypta
Burkill
DIOSCOREACEAE
Caudex mostly subterranean, with polygonal knobs; stems erect with thinner branches; leaves heart-shaped; flowers inconspicuous, yellowish.
South Africa (Cape Province)

Dioscorea sylvatica
DIOSCOREACEAE
Caudex flattened; stems spreading; leaves 6 cm long and 6 cm wide, heart-shaped; flowers greenish.
Southern Africa

Dipcadi brevifolium
(Thumb.) Fourc.
LILIACEAE
Bulb 5-10 cm in diameter; leaves 15-30 cm long, triangular to linear; inflorescence to 60 cm tall; flowers pale green tinged with red. Photograph by Charles H. Everson.
Southern Africa

Diplocyatha ciliata (Thunb.) N.E.Br.
ASCLEPIADACEAE
Plant forming clumps; branches 3-5 cm long, 4-angled; flowers 7-8 cm in diameter, yellowish-brown, papillose, hairy.
Stapelia ciliata Thunb.; *Tromotriche ciliata* (Thunb.)
South Africa (Cape Province)

Dischidia astephana Scort. ex King & Gamble
ASCLEPIADACEAE
Stem hairy; leaves green, purple below, 2.5 cm long and 2.5 cm wide; flowers yellow-orange to red with blue marks. Photograph by Charles H. Everson.
Borneo, Malaysia

Dischidia rafflesiana Wall.
ASCLEPIADACEAE
Stems 50-90 cm long, thin, cylindrical, climbing; leaves opposite, fleshy-green; flowers yellowish. Considered a synonym of *D. major* (Vahl) Merr. Photograph by Charles H. Everson.
Malaysia, Australia.

Dorstenia sp.
MORACEAE
Flower of an unidentified species with small caudex, erect branches and green hairy leaves.

Dorstenia zanzibarica Oliv.
MORACEAE
Stems erect; root tuberous; leaves to 20 cm long, variable in shape; flowers dish-like, greenish.
Kenya, Tanzania, Zanzibar

Dracaena draco (L.) L.
AGAVACEAE
Tree to 10 m tall; stem thick, unbranched until first inflorescence is produced, then with several spreading branches; leaves 30-60 cm long, arranged in rosettes at ends of branches; flowers white, tinged with red outside. Plant photographed in habitat.
Canary Islands (Tenerife, Palma, Gran Canaria)

Drosanthemum crassum L.Bolus
MESEMBRYANTHEMACEAE
Shrub; stem erect to prostrate; leaves 1-2 cm long; flowers white.
South Africa (Cape Province)

Dudleya affinis densiflora
CRASSULACEAE
Unrecognized species probably close to *D. densiflora* (Rose) Moran, with short stems, few branches; leaves linear, farinose, arranged in rosettes; flowers pink.
USA (California)

Drosanthemum speciosum (Haw.) Schwantes
MESEMBRYANTHEMACEAE
Shrub to 60 cm tall, branches grey-green, spotted; leaves 1-1.5 cm long, green with crystalline papillae; flowers orange-red. Plant photographed in habitat.
South Africa (Cape Province)

Dudleya affinis saxosa
CRASSULACEAE
Unrecognized species close to *D. saxosa* (M.E.Jones) Br. & R. with short stem, caespitose; leaves in rosettes; flowers yellow marked orange-red.
USA (California)

Drosanthemum speciosum (Haw.) Schwantes
MESEMBRYANTHEMACEAE
Plant in habitat.

Dudleya antonyi Rose
CRASSULACEAE
Stem to 80 cm long; 30-90 leaves in rosettes, 8-25 cm long, 3-7 cm wide, whitish farinose; floral stem 40-100 cm tall; flowers red.
Mexico (Baja California)

5239

Dudleya attenuata (S.Watson) Moran
CRASSULACEAE
Stem branching and forming clumps; rosette 2-5 cm in diameter with 5-20 leaves, linear to lanceolate; flowers yellow-red.
Mexico

5274

Duvalia polita N.E.Br. var. **parviflora** White & Sloane
ASCLEPIADACEAE
Stems erect or decumbent, hexagonal, toothed; flowers purplish-brown mottled with yellowish-green.
Botswana, South Africa (Transvaal), Zimbabwe

5148

Duvalia reclinata (Masson) Haw.
ASCLEPIADACEAE
Stems to 10 cm long, 4-6-angled, green, with tuberculate teeth; flowers green-brown.
Stapelia reclinata Masson
South Africa (Cape Province)

3016

Dyckia rariflora Schult.
BROMELIACEAE
Leaves arranged in a rosette, 20-25 cm long, 1-2 cm wide at base, narrowing towards the pungent tip, green with whitish vertical lines on the lower surface, small marginal teeth; inflorescence 40-60 cm, flowers orange-yellow.
Central Brazil

2557

Echeveria affinis E.Walther
CRASSULACEAE
Leaves in dense rosettes, oblanceolate, acuminate, olive-brownish, to 5 cm long and 2 cm wide; flowers scarlet red.
Mexico

2043

Echeveria albicans E.Walther
CRASSULACEAE
Rosettes stemless; leaves 3-5 cm long, 1.2-2.5 cm wide, glaucous-pruinose; flowers pink-red at base, yellow-green at apex.
Mexico

Echeveria amoena De Smet
CRASSULACEAE
Stemless or short stemmed rosettes, leaves arranged in rosettes, oblong, bluish-green, somewhat pruinose, 2-2.5 cm long and 6-10 mm wide; flowers yellow-red to red.
Echeveria pusilla A.Berger.
Mexico

Echeveria cv. «Blackprince»
CRASSULACEAE
Cultivar with brownish leaves arranged in dense rosettes.
Garden origin

Echeveria atropurpurea (Baker) E.Morren
CRASSULACEAE
Stems to 20 cm long; leaves in rosettes, obovate to spatulate, 10-14 cm long and 3-5 cm wide, dark red; flowers red. A cristate form.
Echeveria sanguinea Hort.
Mexico

Echeveria cv. «Ebony»
CRASSULACEAE
Cultivar with leaves in compact rosettes; leaves grey-green with acute brown tips.
Garden origin

Echeveria chihuahuaensis Poelln.
CRASSULACEAE
Rosette stemless; leaves to 4 cm long and 2 cm wide, pruinose-grey with red edges; flowers red.
Mexico

Echeveria cv. «Lola»
CRASSULACEAE
Cultivar with small rosettes; leaves pale green.
Garden origin

Echeveria cv. «Perle von Nurberg»
CRASSULACEAE
Rosette to 15 cm in diameter; leaves bluish tinged with pink. A hybrid of *E. gibbiflora* var. *metallica* × *E. potosina*.
Garden origin

Echeveria gigantea Rose & Purpus
CRASSULACEAE
Stems to 30 cm high; leaves in rosettes 25 cm long and 15 cm wide, rounded at the tips, light green to grey, pruinose, margins red; flowers red.
Mexico

Echeveria desmetiana De Smet
CRASSULACEAE
Rosette stemless or short stemmed; leaves sub-ovate to oblong, 3-7 cm long and 2-4 cm wide, white-pruinose often with reddish margins; flowers red. A reputed synonym of *E. paecockii* Croucher.
Mexico

Echeveria harmsii (Rose) MacBryde
CRASSULACEAE
Small subshrub; leaves in rosettes, lanceolate-spatulate, green, 2-3 cm long and 1 cm wide; flowers red.
Echeveria elegans A.Berger
Mexico

Echeveria difractens Kimnach
CRASSULACEAE
Rosettes 8-10 cm in diameter; leaves oblong-lanceolate, flesh-coloured; flowers orange-red.
Mexico

Echeveria lilacina Kimnach & Moran
CRASSULACEAE
Short stemmed plant 6-8 cm high and 10-20 cm in diameter; leaves obtuse, 5-6 cm long and 2-4 cm wide, brownish-olive green with violet-white to pinkish-white waxy powder; flowers coral-pink.
Mexico

Echeveria lindsayana E.Walther
CRASSULACEAE
Dense rosettes; leaves obovate to oblong with acuminate apex, 5-9 cm long, 3-4 cm wide, green tinged purplish; flowers orange-yellow.
Mexico

Echeveria minima Meyran
CRASSULACEAE
Rosette short stemmed; leaves 1-2 cm long, glaucous-green with margins and tip red; inflorescence to 50 cm high; flowers pink below, red above.
Mexico

Echeveria moranii
E.Walther
CRASSULACEAE
Rosette short stemmed, 2-3 cm high; leaves to 6 cm long and 3 cm wide, green with brown spots; flowers red.
Mexico

Echeveria mucronata (Baker) Schltr.
CRASSULACEAE
Rosette short stemmed; leaves 7-10 cm long and 2.5 cm wide, green; flowers reddish-yellow.
Central Mexico

Echeveria obtusifolia Rose
CRASSULACEAE
Rosette on short stem; leaves obovate-lanceolate, 7.5-10 cm long and 3.5 cm wide, light green; flowers red.
Echeveria scopulorum Rose
Mexico

Echeveria paniculata A.Gray
CRASSULACEAE
Rosette stemless; leaves 6-10 cm long and 1.5-2 cm wide, dark green to blue-green, often spotted; flowers reddish to pale yellow.
Echeveria schaffneri Rose
Mexico

Echeveria prolifica Moran & E.Mey.
CRASSULACEAE
Stemless plant forming small clumps; leaves bluish, to 8 cm long, with dark margins.
Mexico

Echeveria runyonii Rose
CRASSULACEAE
Rosette stemless or short stemmed; leaves 6-8 cm long and 3-4 cm wide, deep green to bluish, upcurved; flowers pink. The photograph shows a cultivated form: cv. «Topsy-turvy» ISI 1647.
Mexico

Echeveria pulvinata Rose
CRASSULACEAE
Subshrub with silvery to brownish felted stems and leaves; leaves 4-5 cm long; flowers red or yellow.
Mexico

Echeveria schaffneri (S.Watson) Rose
CRASSULACEAE
Rosette short stemmed; leaves light green to reddish, 5-7 cm long and 1.5-2 cm wide; flowers red. A reputed synonym of *E. teretifolia* DC.
Mexico

Echeveria rubromarginata Rose
CRASSULACEAE
Stems short, more evident in age; leaves 6-12 cm long to 9 cm wide, green to grey, pruinose with red margins; flowers light pink.
Mexico

Echeveria setosa Rose & Purpus
CRASSULACEAE
Rosette stemless with numerous offsets in older plants; leaves 7-8 cm long, dark green covered with dense white hairs; flowers red-yellow.
Mexico

Echeveria setosa Rose & Purpus
CRASSULACEAE
A cristate form of garden origin.

Echeveria sp.
CRASSULACEAE
Unrecognized species found near Saltillo (Nuevo Leon). Leaves arranged in rosettes, glaucous-pruinose with red margins. Plant photographed in habitat by Alessandro Mosco.
Mexico

Echeveria shaviana E.Walther
CRASSULACEAE
Rosette short stemmed, to 10 cm in diameter; leaves 4-8 cm long, glaucous-green with undulate margins, toothed near the apex; flowers pink.
Mexico

Echeveria sp.
CRASSULACEAE
Unrecognized species found at Maravillas (San Luis Potosì). Stemless; leaves in loose rosettes, green; flowers orange-red. Plant photographed in habitat by Alessandro Mosco.
Mexico

Echeveria sp.
CRASSULACEAE
Unidentified species from Mexico (Dolores Hidalgo) with long narrow leaves.
Mexico

Echeveria sp.
CRASSULACEAE
Another unrecognized species photographed at San Roberto (Nuevo Leon). Stems short; leaves glaucous-green spotted with red; flowers orange-red. Plant photographed in habitat by Alessandro Mosco.
Mexico

Echeveria sp.
CRASSULACEAE
Close-up of leaves of San Roberto's species. Plant photographed in habitat by Alessandro Mosco.
Mexico

Echeveria subalpina
CRASSULACEAE
Flowers.

Echeveria strictiflora A.Gray
CRASSULACEAE
Rosette stemless or with very short stem; leaves glaucous when young, then dark olive green, 7-9 cm long and 1.5-2 cm wide; flowers orange-yellow.
Mexico, USA (Texas)

Echeveria subrigida
(Rob. & Seaton) Rose
CRASSULACEAE
Rosette short stemmed, solitary; leaves grey-white pruinose with red margins, to 25 cm long and 10 cm wide; flowers red.
Echeveria sangusta V. Poelln.; *E. palmeri* Rose
Mexico

Echeveria subalpina Rose & Purpus
CRASSULACEAE
Rosette stemless; leaves greenish-glaucous, 7-14 cm long and 2 cm wide; flowers orange-yellow.
Echeveria akontiophylla Werdermann
Mexico

Echeveria subsessilis Rose
CRASSULACEAE
Rosette short stemmed; leaves green-pruinose, 3 cm long and 3.5 cm wide; flowers pink.
Echeveria peacockii Poelln.
Mexico

Echeveria tenuifolia E.Walther
CRASSULACEAE
Rosette with short stem; leaves linear-lanceolate, to 11 cm long and 1-1.2 cm wide, green to brownish; flowers red-yellow.
Mexico

Echeveria tolimanensis Matuda
CRASSULACEAE
Rosette stemless; leaves oblong-acuminate, pruinose, 4-8.5 cm long, 2-5.5 cm wide; flowers golden yellow.
Mexico

Echidnopsis sp.
ASCLEPIADACEAE
Dwarf plant much branched; stems tuberculate, 8-10-angled; flowers yellow.
Somalia

Erythrina flabelliformis Kearney
LEGUMINOSAE
Shrub or small tree to 5 m high; leaflets papery, triangular, to 8 cm long, rounded; flowers bright red. Young plant.
North America

Euphorbia abyssinica Raeusch.
EUPHORBIACEAE
Plant to 5 m tall and over; stems 8-angled, winged; margins grey-brown, with thorns in pairs; leaves 4-5 cm long at the tips of the branches; inflorescence with yellowish cyathia.
Eritrea, Ethiopia.
CITES App. II

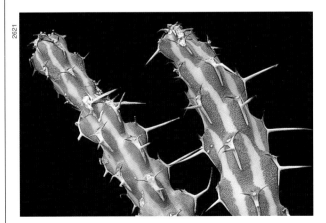

Euphorbia actinoclada S.Carter
EUPHORBIACEAE
Thick fleshy root and main stem to 5 cm high and 2 cm thick; branches erect, then spreading, to 15 cm long, dark green with lighter longitudinal stripes; spines greyish-brown; inflorescence reddish.
Ethiopia, Kenya   CITES App. II

105

Euphorbia aeruginosa
Schweick
EUPHORBIACEAE
Small caudex with numerous branches from base; branches bronze-green, 15 cm long, 4-5-angled; thorns to 7 mm long; inflorescence with yellow cyathia at ends of stems.
South Africa (Transvaal)
CITES App. II

Euphorbia arida N.E.Br.
EUPHORBIACEAE
Stems to 5 cm high; branches numerous, spineless, tuberculate; leaves caducous, persistent peduncles; inflorescence at the tips of branches, green cyathia.
South Africa (Cape Province)
CITES App. II

Euphorbia aggregata A.Berger
EUPHORBIACEAE
Stems to 70 cm tall, branching from the base; branches 9-angled, with thorns 1-2 cm long; inflorescence with reddish cyathia.
Euphorbia enneagona A.Berger
South Africa (Cape Province)
CITES App. II

Euphorbia atrispina N.E.Br.
EUPHORBIACEAE
Plant branching from the base and forming dense cushions to 20 cm high; branches 6-9-angled, dark dull green with a whitish coating; leaves rudimentary, deciduous; peduncles persistent, to 2 cm long; inflorescence with dark purple or purple-brown cyathia. Plant photographed in habitat.
South Africa (Cape Province)
CITES App. II

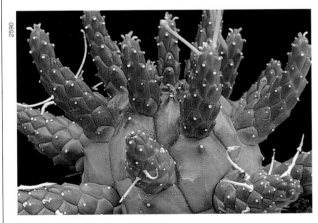

Euphorbia albertensis N.E.Br.
EUPHORBIACEAE
Caudex cylindrical, to 10 cm long; branches numerous from the apex of the caudex, erect, later spreading, with persistent remains of peduncles 1-2 cm long; inflorescence with green cyathia.
South Africa (Cape Province)
CITES App. II

Euphorbia atrispina
N.E.Br.
EUPHORBIACEAE
Young specimen. Plant photographed in habitat.
CITES App. II

Euphorbia atropurpurea Brouss.
EUPHORBIACEAE
Shrub; stems brown, succulent; leaves 5-9 cm long crowned at apex of stems, grey-green; inflorescence with reddish-brown cyathia, capsule dark red or brown. Plant photographed in habitat.
Canary Islands (Tenerife)   CITES App. II

Euphorbia atropurpurea Brouss.
EUPHORBIACEAE
Inflorescence. Plant photographed in habitat.
                                                                CITES App. II

Euphorbia balsamifera Aiton
EUPHORBIACEAE
Shrub up to 2 m high; branches grey, spineless; leaves 2.5 cm long arranged in rosettes at branch apices; inflorescence with yellow cyathia. Plant photographed in habitat.
Canary Islands (Tenerife, Gomera, La Palma, Gran Canaria)   CITES App. II

Euphorbia balsamifera Aiton
EUPHORBIACEAE
Inflorescence with flowers and unripened fruit. Photographed in habitat.
                                                                CITES App. II

Euphorbia avasmontana Dinter
EUPHORBIACEAE
Plant to 2 m high; stems branching from the base, yellowish-green; spines in pairs; leaves rudimentary, caducous; inflorescence with yellow cyathia. Plant photographed in habitat.
Namibia, South Africa (Cape Province)
CITES App. II

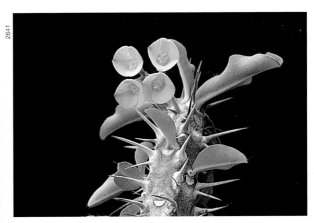

Euphorbia beharensis Leandri
EUPHORBIACEAE
Tuberous root; branches 30-50 cm long, thin, spiny; leaves green, 2-5 cm long; inflorescence on short peduncles from branch apices.
Madagascar   CITES App. II

Euphorbia bongolavaensis Rauh
EUPHORBIACEAE

Shrub to 1 m high; stem 30-40 cm long, covered with grey bark; branches erect; leaves variable in size and shape, to 6.5 cm long, with red petiole; inflorescence with yellow cyathia.

Madagascar

CITES App. II

Euphorbia bourgaeana Gay ex Boiss.
EUPHORBIACEAE

Shrub up to 1.5 m tall, stems light brown; leaves lanceolate, glaucous-green, arranged in rosettes; inflorescence with yellowish-green cyathia, capsule light brown or dark red.

Canary Islands (Tenerife)

CITES App. II

Euphorbia bourgaeana Gay ex Boiss.
EUPHORBIACEAE

Inflorescence.

CITES App. II

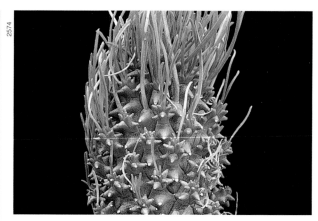

Euphorbia brakdamensis N.E.Br.
EUPHORBIACEAE

Short caudex; branches to 15 cm long, tuberculate, spineless, persistent peduncles to 5 cm long; tubercles arranged in spiral rows; leaves to 1.5 cm long, bluish; inflorescence with green cyathia.

Namibia, South Africa (Cape Province)

CITES App. II

Euphorbia brevirama N.E.Br.
EUPHORBIACEAE

Caudex conical, to 8 cm in diameter, tuberculate; branches short, dull green; leaves inconspicuous, deciduous; peduncles green, persistent, woody and black when ageing; inflorescence with green cyathia.

South Africa (Cape Province)

CITES App. II

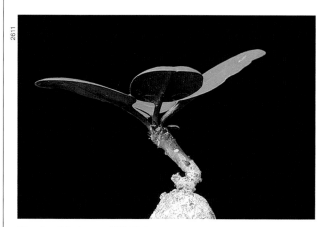

Euphorbia brunellii Chiov.
EUPHORBIACEAE

Tuberous root 5 cm long and 3 cm wide continuing into a long tap-root; leaves to 8 cm long and 3.5 cm wide; inflorescence on peduncles 2 cm long, cyathia pinkish.

Euphorbia rubella Agnew.; *E. rubella Pax* var. *brunellii* (Chiov.) Bally

Kenya, Uganda

CITES App. II

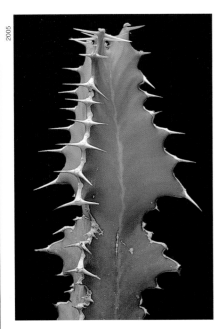

Euphorbia cactus
Ehrenb. ex Boiss.
EUPHORBIACEAE
Shrub up to 3 m high; green with light green bands, 3-4-angled, stems 7-10 cm in diameter with compressed, undulate edges; leaves rudimentary, caducous; spines in pairs 1-4 cm long; cyathia green, later dark red.
Arabia, Eritrea
CITES App. II

Euphorbia canariensis L.
EUPHORBIACEAE
Shrub with numerous 4-6-angled branches to 3 m high (12 m in habitat) arising from base, pairs of small spines; rudimentary caducous leaves; inflorescence on short peduncle with greenish-red cyathia. Plant photographed in habitat.
Canary Islands (La Palma, Hierro, Gomera, Tenerife, Gran Canaria, Fuerteventura, Lanzarote)
CITES App. II

Euphorbia candelabrum
Tremaut
EUPHORBIACEAE
Branched tree up to 10 m high; 4-angled branches with constricted parts, 2-3 cm long; rudimentary caducous leaves; 2-4 mm long spines; inflorescence up to 2 cm long; inflorescence with golden-green cyathia.
Sudan
CITES App. II

Euphorbia «cap-manambabensis»
EUPHORBIACEAE
Probably a new species related to *E. aureo-viridifora* Rauh. Shrub to 70 cm tall, much branched; stems 8-angled; leaves succulent, deciduous; inflorescence yellow to light green.
Madagascar   CITES App. II

Euphorbia capsaintemariensis Rauh
EUPHORBIACEAE
Subterranean caudex 5-10 cm in diameter; branches tipped with a rosette of green to reddish-green leaves, to 2.5 cm long with undulate edges; inflorescence with pale yellow to olive green cyathia.
Madagascar   CITES App. I

Euphorbia capsaintemariensis Rauh
EUPHORBIACEAE
Flowers.

                                              CITES App. I

Euphorbia capuroni Ursch & Leandri
EUPHORBIACEAE
Shrub to 1 m high; stems with thorns to 2 cm long; leaves 3-5 cm long at the end of the stems; inflorescence with several cyathia, green.
Madagascar

CITES App. II

Euphorbia clavaroides Boiss.
EUPHORBIACEAE
Caudex short, thick; branches numerous, tuberculate, 2-7 cm long forming dense cushions to 30 cm in diameter; leaves rudimentary, caducous; inflorescence with greenish-yellow cyathia.
South Africa (Cape Province, Natal, Transvaal)

CITES App. II

Euphorbia clandestina Jacq.
EUPHORBIACEAE
Stems erect, to 60 cm high; prominent tubercles; leaves at tips of stems, 2-4 cm long, 0.2.-0.4 cm wide; inflorescence with green cyathia.
South Africa (Cape Province)
CITES App. II

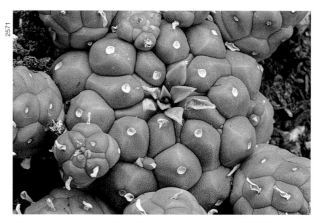

Euphorbia clavaroides Boiss. var. **truncata** (N.E.Br.) A.C.White, R.A.Dyer & B.Sloane
EUPHORBIACEAE
Variety with truncate, shorter branches.
South Africa (Transvaal)

CITES App. II

Euphorbia clandestina Jacq.
EUPHORBIACEAE
Plant photographed in habitat.
CITES App. II

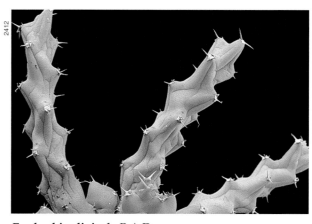

Euphorbia clivicola R.A.Dyer
EUPHORBIACEAE
Main stem and root merging and forming an underground caudex to 15 cm long and 3 cm wide; branches above ground to 6 cm long, yellowish-green; spines in pairs, grey; leaves rudimentary, deciduous.
South Africa (Transvaal)

CITES App. II

Euphorbia coerulescens Haw.
EUPHORBIACEAE
Shrub to 1.5 m high; branches bluish-grey, spines in pairs to 1.5 cm long, white to dark brown; inflorescence with yellow cyathia.
South Africa (Cape Province)
CITES App. II

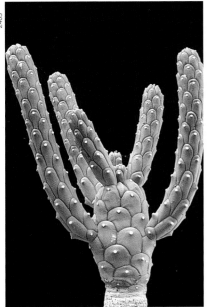

Euphorbia colliculina
A.C.White, R.A.Dyer & B.Sloane
EUPHORBIACEAE
Caudex short, buried in the soil with branches forming rosettes to 25 cm in diameter; root tuberous; branches 5-15 cm long, tuberculate, spineless, remains of peduncles persistent, leaves rudimentary, caducous; inflorescence in clusters at the tip of branches. The photograph shows a cultivated young specimen.
South Africa (Cape Province)
CITES App. II

Euphorbia confinalis
R.A.Dyer
EUPHORBIACEAE
Arborescent plant to 5 m high and over; main trunk with crown of branches curved, ascending and falling with age; spines in pairs, to 1 cm long, longer in young specimens; inflorescences above the spine pairs. The specimen illustrated is a young one, lacking the crown of apical branches.
South Africa (Transvaal)
CITES App. II

Euphorbia cooperi
N.E.Br.
EUPHORBIACEAE
Tree over 5 m high, very much branched above; branches curved, ascending, multi-angled, green with darker transverse bands; spines in pairs, grey with black tips; inflorescence with yellow cyathia.
South Africa (Natal, Transvaal), Zimbabwe
CITES App. II

Euphorbia cooperi
N.E.Br.
EUPHORBIACEAE
Plant photographed in habitat.
CITES App. II

Euphorbia crassipes Marloth
EUPHORBIACEAE
Thick caudex and main root, to 15 cm long, fused together; branches tuberculate, erect, to 6 cm long, arranged in rosette to 30 cm in diameter; inflorescence at tips of branches.
South Africa (Cape Province)
CITES App. II

111

Euphorbia crassipes Marloth
EUPHORBIACEAE
Flowering specimen.

CITES App. II

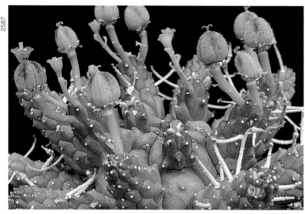

Euphorbia crassipes Marloth
EUPHORBIACEAE
Ripening capsules.

CITES App. II

Euphorbia croizatii Leandri
EUPHORBIACEAE
Shrub to 70 cm high; branches spreading, spiny; leaves to 10 cm long, hairy; spines to 1 cm long, usually 3 together arranged in longitudinal rows; inflorescence at branch apices with yellow cyathia.
Madagascar

CITES App. II

Euphorbia cylindrifolia Marn.-Lap. & Rauh
EUPHORBIACEAE
Branches whitish, subterranean; stems 10-15 cm long; covered with leaf scars; leaves cylindrical, 2-3 cm long, brownish-pink; inflorescence with brownish-pink cyathia.
Madagascar

CITES App. I

Euphorbia davyi N.E.Br.
EUPHORBIACEAE
Caudex semiglobose, buried in the soil, to 8 cm in diameter; branches 5-15 cm long, light green to brownish, tuberculate; leaves at the tips of branches, to 2.5 cm long, caducous; inflorescence borne among leaves at the apex of branches.
South Africa (Transvaal)

CITES App. II

Euphorbia decaryi A.Guill. var. **spirosticha** Rauh & Buchloh
EUPHORBIACEAE
Long stolons, subterranean, pale with reduced leaves; aerial stems erect to curved, with reddish-brown bark, covered scars of deciduous leaves; leaves at end of stems, 3-4 cm long, silvery-green, margins undulate; inflorescence on short peduncles, yellow cyahtia. The illustrated variety differs from the typical species in having leaves arranged in spiral rows.
Madagascar

CITES App. I

Euphorbia decidua P.R.O.Bally & L.C.Leach
EUPHORBIACEAE

Subterranean stem, thick; leaves to 1.2 cm long in the juvenile stage. At maturity the plant produces caducous branches to 12 cm long, 6 mm thick with small caducous leaves; inflorescences with yellow cyathia. The photograph shows a plant with juvenile leaves and a young stem.
Angola, Malawi, Zambia, Zimbabwe

CITES App. II

Euphorbia decidua P.R.O.Bally & L.C.Leach
EUPHORBIACEAE

Seedling showing the characteristic leaves of juvenile stage.

CITES App. II

Euphorbia decussata
E.Mey.
EUPHORBIACEAE

Shrub to 1 m high, much branched from the base; branches ascending or prostrate; leaves rudimentary, caducous. Plant photographed in habitat.
South Africa (Cape Province)

CITES App. II

Euphorbia dichroa S.Carter
EUPHORBIACEAE

Rootstock fleshy, branching from base; branches 15 cm long, yellow-green, darker to purplish-green longitudinal stripes; spines to 1 cm long, brown; inflorescence with yellow cyathia.
Uganda

CITES App. II

Euphorbia dichroa S.Carter
EUPHORBIACEAE

Flowering stem.

CITES App. II

Euphorbia didiereoides Denis
EUPHORBIACEAE

Stems thorny, to 2 m high; leaves at apex of stems, 5-10 cm long, green, often red-margined, arranged in rosettes; inflorescence with yellowish-green or orange cyathia.
Madagascar

CITES App. II

Euphorbia duranii Ursh & Leandri var. **ankaratrae**
Ursch & Leandri
EUPHORBIACEAE
Shrub to 40 cm high; branches 6-8-angled; thorns 1-2 cm long; leaves ovate, to 5 cm long; inflorescence with greenish-yellow to pink cyathia. The variety illustrated is smaller, to 20 cm high, leaves to 3.5 cm long. Photograph by Alberto Marvelli.
Madagascar   CITES App. II

Euphorbia duranii Ursh & Leandri var. **ankaratrae**
Ursch & Leandri
EUPHORBIACEAE
Close-up of flowers. Photograph by Alberto Marvelli.
                                    CITES App. II

Euphorbia duseimata R.A.Dyer
EUPHORBIACEAE
Tuberous caudex 2-3 cm thick; 1-2 subterranean stems to 8 cm long, each with 6-10 branchlets above the ground level, tuberculate; leaves about 1 cm long, deciduous.
South Africa (Cape Province)
                                    CITES App. II

Euphorbia ecklonii (Klotzsch & Garcke) Baill.
EUPHORBIACEAE
Tuberous root 3-4 cm long, fused to the main stem; leaves 2-5 cm long, 2.5 cm wide, elliptic, deciduous; inflorescence to 3 cm long, branched.
South Africa (Cape Province)
                                    CITES App. II

Euphorbia enopla Boiss.
EUPHORBIACEAE
Shrub up to 1 m high, branching from the base and forming large clumps over 1 m in diameter; branches blue or grey-green; persistent peduncles 2-6 cm long, red; inflorescence with dark red cyathia.
South Africa (Cape Province)
                                    CITES App. II

Euphorbia enopla Boiss.
EUPHORBIACEAE
Cristate specimen.
                                    CITES App. II

Euphorbia esculenta Marloth
EUPHORBIACEAE
Tuberous root continuing into the main stem and forming an obconical caudex to 20 cm in diameter; branches arranged in rosette, numerous, tuberculate, 5-20 cm long; inflorescence clustered at the ends of branches. Plant photographed in habitat.
South Africa (Cape Province)   CITES App. II

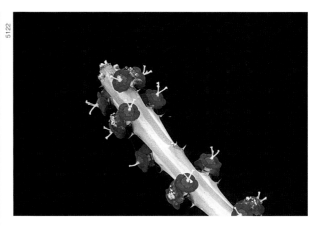

Euphorbia fluminis S.Carter
EUPHORBIACEAE
Stem green-variegated, 4-angled, to 2 m high, spines solitary, 1.5 cm long; leaves rudimentary, caducous; inflorescence with reddish cyathia. Photograph by Alberto Marvelli.
Kenya   CITES App. II

Euphorbia flanaganii N.E.Br.
EUPHORBIACEAE
Conical caudex to 5 cm long; branches in crown of 3-8 rows, tuberculate, erect, older ones spreading; leaves to 1 cm long, deciduous; inflorescence produced at the apex of caudex, yellow cyathia.
South Africa (Cape Province)   CITES App. II

Euphorbia francoisii Leandri
EUPHORBIACEAE
Stoloniferous plant; leaves 5-7 cm long arranged in rosettes, green-variegated with red mid-rib, margins undulate; inflorescence on peduncle 1 cm long with yellowish-green cyathia.
Madagascar   CITES App. I

Euphorbia flanaganii N.E.Br.
EUPHORBIACEAE
Cristate specimen.
                                                CITES App. II

Euphorbia fusca N.E.Br.
EUPHORBIACEAE
Caudex to 30 cm high and 20 cm in diameter with tuberculate head covered with ascending branches; branches tuberculate, 2-15 cm long, green with whitish leaf scars; leaves rudimentary, caducous; inflorescence clustered at tips of branches, yellow cyathia.
Namibia, South Africa (Cape Province)   CITES App. II

115

Euphorbia geroldii Rauh
EUPHORBIACEAE
Shrub to 2 m tall, much branched, spineless; stem green to purplish-green; leaves 3-8 cm long, dark green above, paler below, with red margins; inflorescence with red to purplish cyathia.
Madagascar
CITES App. II

Euphorbia geroldii Rauh
EUPHORBIACEAE
Flowers.
CITES App. II

Euphorbia globosa (Haw.) J.Sims.
EUPHORBIACEAE
Tuberous root; branches numerous, globose, 13 cm long, dark green to reddish, later grey; persistent leaf peduncles to 10 cm long; inflorescence with yellow cyathia.
Euphorbia glomerata Marl.
South Africa (Cape Province)
CITES App. II

Euphorbia globosa (Haw.) J.Sims.
EUPHORBIACEAE
Flowers.
CITES App. II

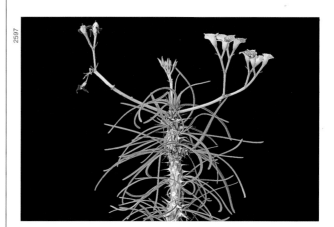

Euphorbia gottlebei Rauh
EUPHORBIACEAE
Shrub to 1.5 m high; main stem to 2 cm thick; leaves of two types; light green, 4-6 cm long and 2 mm wide, and more numerous shorter ones, recurved; spines to 1.5 cm long; inflorescence on long peduncles, cyathia red.
Madagascar
CITES App. II

Euphorbia gottlebei Rauh
EUPHORBIACEAE
Inflorescence.
CITES App. II

116

Euphorbia grandialata R.A.Dyer
EUPHORBIACEAE
Shrub to 2 m high; branches usually 4-angled, constricted into segments, green, marked with yellowish-green bands; margins horny; spines in pair; flowers yellow.
South Africa (Transvaal)   CITES App. II

Euphorbia grandicornis Goebel
EUPHORBIACEAE
Shrub up to 2 m high with main trunk and numerous green, later grey-green, branching 3-angled stems, constricted, angles wavy with horny edges; light brown or grey, 2-5 cm long spines in pairs; fruits yellow and coral-red. The photograph shows apex with fruits.
Euphorbia breviarticulata Pax
South Africa   CITES App. II

Euphorbia grandiendis Haw.
EUPHORBIACEAE
Main trunk 6-10 m high, branching freely to form several stem-like branches ending in slender terminal branchlets; leaves rudimentary, caducous; inflorescence on short peduncles at ends of branches.
South Africa (Transvaal)
CITES App. II

Euphorbia griseola
Pax ssp. **mashonica**
L.C.Leach
EUPHORBIACEAE
Shrub with shortened main trunk branching from base, forming clumps to 80 cm high; branches dark green with yellow-green marks, 4-6-angled, tuberculate, with spines in pairs; inflorescence above spine pairs. The illustrated subspecies has branches multi-angled (9-12-angled) and can reach 3.5 m in height. Plant photographed in habitat.
Zimbabwe
CITES App. II

Euphorbia groenewaldii R.A.Dyer
EUPHORBIACEAE
Root tuberous, to 20 cm tall, 8-10 cm thick, continuing into main stem from which green to purple small spirally twisted branches arise; inflorescences with yellow cyathophylls.
South Africa (Transvaal)   CITES App. II

Euphorbia gymnocalicioides M.G.Gilbert & S.Carter
EUPHORBIACEAE
Stem short, cylindrical, tuberculate, to 10 cm high and 8 cm in diameter; leaves rudimentary, caducous; inflorescence borne on previous year's growth, cyathia white outside, reddish-brown inside. Photograph by Gaetano Palisano.
Ethiopia   CITES App. II

117

Euphorbia
hadramautica Baker
EUPHORBIACEAE
Stem erect or prostrate,
3-12 cm long, 1-3 cm thick,
covered with leaf scars;
leaves 3-9 cm long, green,
glabrous. Young plant.
Arabian peninsula
CITES App. II

Euphorbia hofstaetteri Rauh
EUPHORBIACEAE
Spiny shrub to 1 m high; root tuberous; branches erect to curved, grey-brown, waxy; leaves 3-4 cm long and 1.5 cm wide; margins undulate, red, hairy; inflorescence on short peduncles, yellow-green striped with red-brown.
Madagascar
CITES App. II

Euphorbia handiensis Burch.
EUPHORBIACEAE
Cactus-like plant, freely branched, 80-100 cm high; branches 6-8 cm thick, 8-12-angled; white spine 2-3 cm long. The photograph shows a clump of young plants.
Canary Islands (Fuerteventura)
CITES App. II

Euphorbia hofstaetteri Rauh
EUPHORBIACEAE
Close-up of flowers.

CITES App. II

Euphorbia
hedyotoides N.E.Br.
EUPHORBIACEAE
Tuberous root up to 20 cm
long and 10 cm thick;
aerial spineless stems up to
1 m high, green, later covered with a red-brown bark
and branching in their
upper parts; leaves 3-10 cm
long, deciduous, arranged
in rosettes at the stem
apex; flowers inconspi-
cuous. The photograph
shows a young specimen.
Euphorbia decariana Croizat
Madagascar
CITES App. II

Euphorbia holmsiae
Lavranos
EUPHORBIACEAE
Fleshy root up to 20 cm
long and 5 cm in diameter
with spreading spiny branches up to 30 cm long, purplish to grey-green and
streaked; caducous leaves;
inflorescence with pinkish-
yellow cyathia.
Somalia
CITES App. II

Euphorbia hopetowensis Nel
EUPHORBIACEAE
Caudex 5-8 cm thick; branches erect, 2-4 cm long; peduncles persitent, 1 cm long at ends of branches; inflorescence with green to reddish-brown cyathia.
South Africa (Cape Province)   CITES App. II

Euphorbia horombensis Ursch. & Leandri
EUPHORBIACEAE
Shrub to 1 m tall; stem with thorns 1-2 cm long, in vertical rows; leaves green with red margins, 5-8 cm long, crowded at ends of stems; inflorescence at branch apices with pink cyathia.
Madagascar   CITES App. II

Euphorbia horrida Boiss.
EUPHORBIACEAE
Stems to 15 cm thick, 10-20 prominent angles, very spiny; leaves rudimentary, caducous; inflorescence on peduncles 1 cm long. This is a very variable species, growing in clumps to 1 m high. Several varieties have been described.
South Africa (Cape Province)   CITES App. II

Euphorbia horrida Boiss.
EUPHORBIACEAE
Inflorescence.   CITES App. II

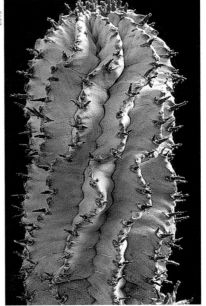

Euphorbia horrida
Boiss.
EUPHORBIACEAE
Dwarf form with whitish stem and short spines. Known only in cultivation.
CITES App. II

Euphorbia horrida
Boiss.
EUPHORBIACEAE
Atypical specimen with dichotomous growth. Photograph by Gaetano Palisano.
CITES App. II

Euphorbia horrida Boiss.var. ES 2971
EUPHORBIACEAE

A new variety collected at Seweekspoort (Cape Province). This new form has purplish-pruinose stem and small green involucre glands.
South Africa (Cape Province)

CITES App. II

Euphorbia jansevillensis Nel
EUPHORBIACEAE

Stems glaucous-green, erect, 5-angled, to 15 cm high, branched and suckering from the base; leaves rudimentary, caducous; inflorescence on short peduncles at stem ends.
South Africa (Cape Province)

CITES App. II

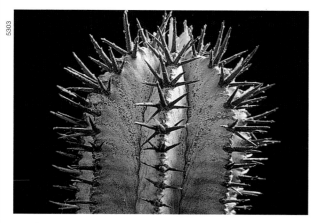

Euphorbia horrida Boiss. var. **noorsveldensis** A.C.White, R.A.Dyer & B.Sloane
EUPHORBIACEAE

Stems dull green or bluish-green, narrow; purple involucre glands.
South Africa (Cape Province)

CITES App. II

Euphorbia jansevillensis Nel
EUPHORBIACEAE

Inflorescence with ripening capsule.

CITES App. II

Euphorbia hottentota Nel
EUPHORBIACEAE

Shrub to 2 m high; main stem not projecting above soil, branching; branches erect, glaucous-green, with spines in pairs to 8 mm long; inflorescence from apices of branches. Photograph by Charles H. Everson.
Namibia, South Africa (Cape Province)

CITES App. II

Euphorbia juttae Dinter
EUPHORBIACEAE

Shrub 10-15 cm high, branching from base; branches spineless, bluish-green; leaves 2-3 cm long; inflorescence at apex of new branches.
Photograph by Charles H. Everson.
Namibia

CITES App. II

Euphorbia keithii
R.A.Dyer
EUPHORBIACEAE
Shrub 2-4 m tall; branches dark green, 1-2 m long, 5-angled; leaves rudimentary, caducous; spine pairs 1 cm long; inflorescence with yellow flowers.
Swaziland
CITES App. II

Euphorbia ledienii
A.Berger
EUPHORBIACEAE
Shrub to 2 m high; branches 5-angled; spines in pairs to 2 cm long; leaves rudimentary, caducous; inflorescence at branch apices, with yellow cyathia.
South Africa (Cape Province)
CITES App. II

Euphorbia lactea Haw.
EUPHORBIACEAE
Shrub to 2 m tall; branches 3-4-angled, dark green with paler band; leaves rudimentary, caducous; inflorescence from new growth, with yellow cyathia.
India   CITES App. II

Euphorbia louwii L.C.Leach
EUPHORBIACEAE
Shrub to 50 cm high; branches bluish, 5-7-angled, spiny; spines purplish; inflorescence yellow.
South Africa (Transvaal)   CITES App. II

Euphorbia lactea Haw.
EUPHORBIACEAE
A cristate specimen.   CITES App. II

Euphorbia maleolens E.Phillips
EUPHORBIACEAE
Short caudex to 10 cm thick continuing into the thick root; branches tuberculate, to 20 cm long; leaves at apices of branches; inflorescence on peduncles 1 cm long among leaves in the upper third of branches.
South Africa (Transvaal)   CITES App. II

121

Euphorbia maleolens E.Phillips
EUPHORBIACEAE
Specimen with several erect branches.

CITES App. II

Euphorbia mammillaris L.
EUPHORBIACEAE
A cristate specimen photographed in habitat.

CITES App. II

Euphorbia mammillaris L.
EUPHORBIACEAE
Stems to 20 cm high and 6 cm in diameter forming dense clumps to 1 m in diameter; branches erect, with hexagonal tubercles; spines solitary, 1 cm long, grey; inflorescence in clusters at apices of branches. Plant photographed in habitat.
South Africa (Cape Province)

CITES App. II

Euphorbia mauritanica L.
EUPHORBIACEAE
Shrub to 1 m high; branches spineless, erect, cylindrical; leaves 1-1.5 cm long, caducous; inflorescence with yellow flowers. Plant photographed in habitat.
Namibia, South Africa (Cape Province)
CITES App. II

Euphorbia mammillaris L.
EUPHORBIACEAE
A large clump photographed in habitat.

CITES App. II

Euphorbia memoralis R.A.Dyer
EUPHORBIACEAE
Shrub to 2 m high; stems cylindrical or 5-7-angled; margins horned, armed with spines in pairs. Small specimen photographed in habitat.

CITES App. II

Euphorbia memoralis
R.A.Dyer
EUPHORBIACEAE
Plant photographed in habitat.
CITES App. II

Euphorbia milii
Des Moul.
EUPHORBIACEAE
Cultivar with dwarf shrub habit and pale pink cyatophylls.
CITES App. II

Euphorbia milii
Des Moul.
EUPHORBIACEAE
Shrub to 1.5 m high in cultivation; branches thorny with leaves at the ends, green, often with red margins, to 15 cm long; inflorescence on long peduncles with red bracts. Several varieties have been described.
Euphorbia boyeri Hook.
Madagascar
CITES App. II

Euphorbia milii Des Moul.
EUPHORBIACEAE
Flowers.

CITES App. II

Euphorbia milii Des Moul.
EUPHORBIACEAE
Inflorescence of a cultivar with curious cristate flowers.

CITES App. II

Euphorbia milii Des Moul.
EUPHORBIACEAE
Cultivar «Short and Sweet», compact and profusely flowering.

CITES App. II

Euphorbia milii Des Moul. var. **tenuispina** Rauh & Razaf.
EUPHORBIACEAE
Variety with tuberous base to 3.5 cm in diameter, several stems to 20 cm tall, thin spines, cyathophylls pale carmine-red.
Madagascar   CITES App. II

Euphorbia milii
Des Moul. var. **vulcani Leandri**
EUPHORBIACEAE
Variety with branches 1 cm thick, spines arranged in horizontal series, leaves to 20 cm long, 4-5 cm wide, cyathophylls bright red.
Euphorbia splendens var. *vulcanii Leandri*
Madagascar
CITES App. II

Euphorbia millotii
Ursch & Leandri
EUPHORBIACEAE
Shrub to 20 cm high, branched from base; leaves green-red, to 4 cm long at growing apices; inflorescence with pendent cyathia, red.
Madagascar
CITES App. II

Euphorbia monteiroi
Hook.f.
EUPHORBIACEAE
Shrub to 1 m tall; branches cylindrical, with tubercles arranged in spirals; leaves at apex of branches, to 15 cm long and 3 cm wide; inflorescence on peduncles 30 cm long; flowers dark brown to red-brown.
Angola, Botswana, Namibia
CITES App. II

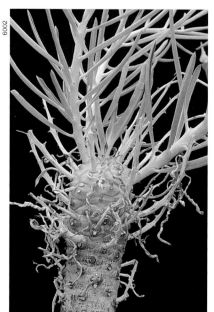

Euphorbia monteiroi
Hook.f.
EUPHORBIACEAE
Another well grown specimen.
CITES App. II

Euphorbia multiceps
A.Berger
EUPHORBIACEAE
Shrub to 30 cm high; many tuberculate branches spreading horizontally; leaves 1.2 cm long, shedding soon. Photograph by Charles H. Everson.
South Africa (Cape Province)
CITES App. II

Euphorbia
multiramosa Nel
EUPHORBIACEAE
Caudex 20 cm long and 15
cm in diameter; branches
tuberculate, 4-11 cm long,
simple or branched, with
persistent peduncles; inflorescence with yellowish-
green cyathia.
Namibia, South Africa
(Cape Province)
CITES App. II

Euphorbia namibiensis Marloth
EUPHORBIACEAE
Young specimen.

CITES App. II

Euphorbia myrsinites L.
EUPHORBIACEAE
Decumbent to erect stems up to 30 cm long; leaves up to 4 cm long, glau-
cous-green, fleshy mucronate tip, arranged in spirals; inflorescence yellow.
Plant photographed in habitat.
Southern Europe   CITES App. II

Euphorbia neobosseri Rauh
EUPHORBIACEAE
Small shrub to 30 cm high, much branched; tuberous root; branches sprea-
ding, green and hairy when young, silver grey with thick bark when
ageing; leaves to 3.5 cm long, deciduous; inflorescence near stem apices,
cyathia yellow-green.
Euphorbia milii var. *bosseri* Rauh
Madagascar   CITES App. II

Euphorbia namibiensis Marloth
EUPHORBIACEAE
Main stem ovoid, 7-20 cm high and 7-15 cm in diameter; branches to 9 cm
long, erect or spreading, persistent peduncles; leaves on young branches,
to 3.5 cm long, caducous; inflorescence in cluster at apex of branches.
Photograph by Charles H. Everson.
Namibia   CITES App. II

Euphorbia
nesemannii R.A.Dyer
EUPHORBIACEAE
Stem and root fused to
form a subterranean cau-
dex; branches in clusters
near the apex of the stem,
to 40 cm long, tuberculate;
persistent peduncles; inflorescence at apex of bran-
ches.
South Africa (Cape
Province)
CITES App. II

125

**Euphorbia
nesemannii** R.A.Dyer
EUPHORBIACEAE
Apex.
CITES App. II

Euphorbia obtusifolia Poir.
EUPHORBIACEAE
Shrub up to 2 m tall; stems light brown; leaves 5-8 cm long, light green, arranged in rosettes at the branch apices; inflorescence with yellow-green cyathia, capsule light brown or red. Plant photographed in habitat.
Euphorbia regis-jubae Webb & Berthel.
Canary Islands (Gran Canaria, Lanzarote, Fuerteventura)   CITES App. II

Euphorbia obesa Hook.f.
EUPHORBIACEAE
Spineless, dwarf, spherical, unbranched plant, grey-green with transverse red-brown or purplish bands; inflorescence on short peduncles at stem apices. This specimen has atypical growth, producing several offsets at the flowering eyes.
South Africa (Cape Province)
CITES App. II

Euphorbia obtusifolia Poir.
EUPHORBIACEAE
Stem with caterpillar of *Hyles tithymali*, a natural enemy of the species. Plant photographed in habitat.
CITES App. II

Euphorbia obesa Hook.f.
EUPHORBIACEAE
Another atypical specimen with dichotomous growth.
CITES App. II

Euphorbia obtusifolia Poir.
EUPHORBIACEAE
Inflorescence. Plant photographed in habitat.
CITES App. II

Euphorbia oncoclada
Drake
EUPHORBIACEAE
Shrub to 50 cm high; branches grey-green, spineless, segmented, covered with leaf scars; leaves rudimentary, deciduous; inflorescence with yellowish cyathia.
Madagascar
CITES App. II

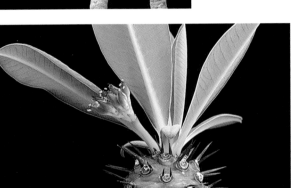

Euphorbia pachypodioides Boiteau
EUPHORBIACEAE
Stems 30-50 cm high, covered with old leaf scars arranged in spiral; leaves bluish-green, 10-15 cm long, at the end of the stems; inflorescence with red purple cyathia.
Euphorbia antankara Leandri
Madagascar
CITES App. II

Euphorbia pedemontana
L.C.Leach
EUPHORBIACEAE
Shrub spineless; branches roundish, green; leaves 2-4 cm long, green.
South Africa (Cape Province)
CITES App. II

Euphorbia peltigera E.Mey.
EUPHORBIACEAE
Shrub to 40 cm high with tuberous root; short trunk branching from base and above; branches green, velvety when young.
South Africa (Cape Province)
CITES App. II

Euphorbia peltigera E.Mey.
EUPHORBIACEAE
Flowering stem.
CITES App. II

Euphorbia perangusta R.A.Dyer
EUPHORBIACEAE
Shrub to 1 m high; main stem mostly underground; branches constricted into segments, 5-to 7-angled, green with lighter bands, margins horny; spines in pairs, to 1.5 cm long; inflorescence at the apices of branches.
South Africa (Transvaal)
CITES App. II

Euphorbia persistens R.A.Dyer
EUPHORBIACEAE
Stem subterranean; branches 3-to 5-angled, 15-20 cm long, glaucous-green with darker stripes; spines brown; inflorescence on short peduncles.
South Africa
CITES App. II

Euphorbia persistentifolia
L.C.Leach
EUPHORBIACEAE
Shrub to 3 m high; branches erect, 4-5-angled, segmented; margins horny, white; spines in pairs to 7 mm long; leaves persistent; inflorescence on short peduncles. Plant photographed in habitat.
Zimbabwe
CITES App. II

Euphorbia persistentifolia
L.C.Leach
EUPHORBIACEAE
A very tall specimen photographed in habitat.
CITES App. II

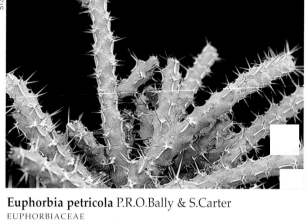

Euphorbia petricola P.R.O.Bally & S.Carter
EUPHORBIACEAE
Sub-cylindrical stem to 75 cm long, green; branches toothed; spines grey, black when young, to 1.5 cm long; inflorescence with yellow cyathia.
Kenya
CITES App. II

Euphorbia pillansii N.E.Br.
EUPHORBIACEAE
Dwarf species to 30 cm tall, much branched; branches 7-9-angled, 3-5 cm thick; spines robust, stellate.
South Africa (Cape Province)
CITES App. II

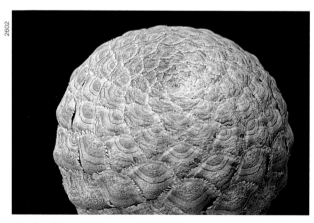

Euphorbia piscidermis M.G.Gilbert
EUPHORBIACEAE
Globular to cylindrical stems, grey to white; tubercles pine-cone shaped, arranged in spirals, covered with scale-like growths; inflorescence on short peduncle, cyathia green outside, yellow inside.
Ethiopia, Somalia
CITES App. II

Euphorbia piscidermis M.G.Gilbert
EUPHORBIACEAE
Grafted flowering specimen. Photograph by Gaetano Palisano.
CITES App. II

Euphorbia polygona
Haw.
EUPHORBIACEAE
Shrub offsetting from base and forming clumps with branches of unequal size; branches to 1.5 m high, 7-10 cm thick, spineless or spiny, 7-20-angled; margins wavy, with persistent peduncles to 1 cm long; leaves rudimentary, caducous; inflorescence from apex of older branches with purple to greyish-purple cyathia.
South Africa (Cape Province)
CITES App. II

Euphorbia piscidermis M.G.Gilbert
EUPHORBIACEAE
Crestate form. Photograph by Gaetano Palisano.
CITES App. II

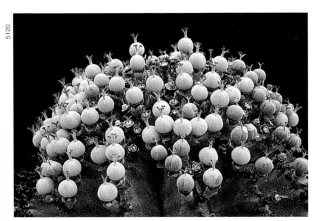

Euphorbia polygona Haw.
EUPHORBIACEAE
Fruits.
CITES App. II

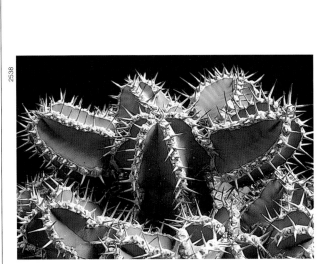

Euphorbia polyacantha Boiss.
EUPHORBIACEAE
Shrub 1-1.5 m high; branches 4-5-angled, 4 cm in diameter, spines 6 mm long; leaves grey, small, caducous; inflorescence at stem apices.
Ethiopia
CITES App. II

Euphorbia primulifolia Baker
EUPHORBIACEAE
Subterranean caudex 15 cm long, 7 cm thick, covered with a corky layer; one or more stems with 4-12 leaves arranged in rosettes; inflorescences with white to pink cyathia.
Madagascar
CITES App. II

Euphorbia pseudocactus A.Berger
EUPHORBIACEAE
Shrub to 1 m high; branches 3-5-angled constricted into segments, green with grey-green or yellow-green V-shaped markings; flowers yellow.
South Africa (Natal)   CITES App. II

Euphorbia ramiglans N.E.Br.
EUPHORBIACEAE
Caudex to 20 cm long and 15 cm in diameter; branches spineless, 2-4 cm long, tuberculate; leaves to 1 cm long at stem apices, deciduous; inflorescence on short peduncles at stem apices. Photograph by Charles H. Everson.
South Africa (Cape Province)
CITES App. II

Euphorbia ramiglans N.E.Br.
EUPHORBIACEAE
Cristate specimen. Photograph by Charles H. Everson.
                    CITES App. II

Euphorbia rivae Pax
EUPHORBIACEAE
Tuberous rootstock 12 cm long and 4 cm thick from which woody underground stems arise; branches prostrate to 15 cm long; leaves to 1.7 cm long, green with lower surface often tinged red; inflorescence on short peduncles, cyathia red.
Kenya
CITES App. II

Euphorbia rivae Pax
EUPHORBIACEAE
Inflorescence.
                    CITES App. II

Euphorbia robivelonae Rauh
EUPHORBIACEAE
Shrub much branched, to 1 m tall; branches covered with leaf scars; leaves to 8 cm long, dark green above, pale green below; inflorescence whitish.
Madagascar
CITES App. II

Euphorbia rossii Rauh & Buchloh
EUPHORBIACEAE
Shrub to 1 m high; stems thorny, branching from base, to 3 cm thick; leaves narrow, 4-5 cm long; inflorescence yellowish-green to red.
Madagascar
CITES App. II

Euphorbia rossii Rauh & Buchloh
EUPHORBIACEAE
Inflorescence.
CITES App. II

Euphorbia rudis N.E.Br.
EUPHORBIACEAE
Caudex mostly buried in the soil; branches to 15 cm long, cylindrical, whitish-green, crowded to form clumps to 20 cm in diameter; leaves at apex of branches, to 1 cm long; inflorescence on peduncles 2 cm long.
Namibia
CITES App. II

Euphorbia sakarahaensis Rauh
EUPHORBIACEAE
Shrub to 50 cm high, spiny; root tuberous; branches grey-brown with yellow-brown bark; leaves 2.5 cm long and 2-4 cm wide, dark green above, grey-green below; inflorescence near branch apices, cyathia light green to pinkish.
Madagascar
CITES App. II

Euphorbia sapini De Wild.
EUPHORBIACEAE
Stems suckering from base, roundish; leaves light green, sometimes with reddish edges, to 10 cm long, arising from the apex of stems; inflorescence long stalked, with yellow cyathia.
Angola
CITES App. II

Euphorbia schimperi J.Presl
EUPHORBIACEAE
Succulent shrub to 2 m high; green to glaucous-green cylindrical branches; leaves 5-10 mm long, triangular; inflorescence with yellow cyathia.
Arabia
CITES App. II

Euphorbia schimperi J.Presl
EUPHORBIACEAE
Flowering stem.

CITES App. II

Euphorbia schoenlandii Pax
EUPHORBIACEAE
Solitary plant; stem rarely branched, to 1.3 m high and 20 cm thick, cylindrical, tuberculate; tubercles spirally arranged, prominent; persistent peduncles to 5 cm long, pale brown or pale grey to whitish; leaves rudimentary, caducous, at apex of stem; inflorescence on peduncles 1-2.5 cm long. Plant photographed in habitat.
South Africa (Cape Province)
CITES App. II

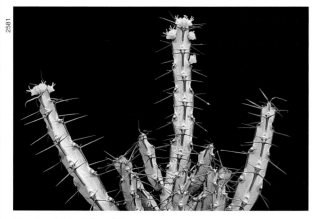

Euphorbia schinzii Pax
EUPHORBIACEAE
Small caudex with numerous branches from base; branches brown to olive green 15 cm long, conspicuously 4-angled; spines in pairs to 7 mm long; inflorescence with vivid yellow-green cyathia, at the end of the stems.
Botswana, South Africa, Zimbabwe

CITES App. II

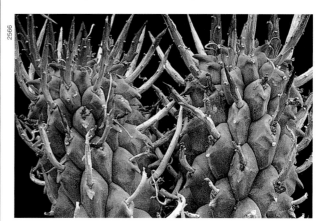

Euphorbia schoenlandii Pax
EUPHORBIACEAE
Cultivated specimen.

CITES App. II

Euphorbia schinzii Pax
EUPHORBIACEAE
Inflorescence.

CITES App. II

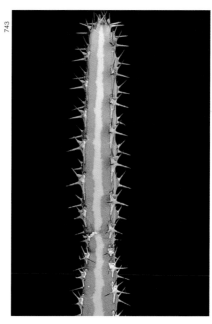

Euphorbia scitula
L.C.Leach
EUPHORBIACEAE
Woody tuberous root with one to several bright green stems with pale greenish-cream or white stripes, up to 50 cm long, 4-angled, spiny; leaves caducous, rudimentary; cyathia pale green.
Angola
CITES App. II

Euphorbia sekukuniensis R.A.Dyer
EUPHORBIACEAE
Tree to 5 m high; trunk cylindrical with crown of ascending branches to 1 m long; spines in pairs, to 1 cm long; inflorescence on very short peduncles. Young specimen.
South Africa (Transvaal)   CITES App. II

Euphorbia serendipita L.E.Newton
EUPHORBIACEAE
Shrub to 2 m high and 2 m in diameter; stem 4-angled, green with yellow streak in centre of each side; spines in pairs, red becoming grey when ageing; leaves rudimentary, caducous; inflorescence dark red.
Kenya
CITES App. II

Euphorbia silenifolia (Haw.) Sweet
EUPHORBIACEAE
Tuberous root 2-5 cm thick, brown, producing deciduous annual leaves; leaves to 10 cm long and 0.2-1.2 cm wide, linear, dark green to bluish-green; inflorescence on peduncles to 13 cm long.
Euphorbia elliptica Thunb.
South Africa (Cape Province)   CITES App. II

Euphorbia silenifolia (Haw.) Sweet
EUPHORBIACEAE
Flowering specimen.
                                             CITES App. II

Euphorbia sipolisii N.E.Br.
EUPHORBIACEAE
Shrub; branches leafless, 4-angled, segmented, grey-green to reddish, convex at angles, almost leafless; inflorescence with red cyathia.
Brazil   CITES App. II

Euphorbia sp.
EUPHORBIACEAE
Unrecognized species. Root tuberous; branches thick, round, 20-25 cm long; central spine recurved; flowers yellow.
Ethiopia (Awasha)
CITES App. II

Euphorbia sp.
EUPHORBIACEAE
Unrecognized species from Madagascar. Shrub with cylindrical spiny stem; leaves narrow, long, green; flowers red.
Madagascar
CITES App. II

Euphorbia sp. G.Marx 224
EUPHORBIACEAE
Undescribed species, collected by G. Marx, with thick, tuberculate branches.
South Africa
CITES App. II

Euphorbia sp.
EUPHORBIACEAE
Unrecognized plant found in cultivation. Stem 8-10-angled, green-pruinose; spines long, green when young, later brownish. Could be a hybrid of *E. heptagona* L. Photograph by Gaetano Palisano.
CITES App. II

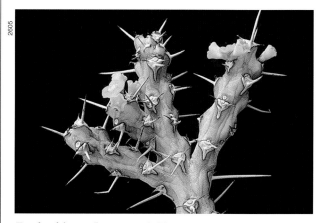

Euphorbia sp. Lavranos & Newton 1376
EUPHORBIACEAE
There are two forms of this plant; one has longer branches, grey spines 2-3 cm long; the other (illustrated here) is more compact and densely branched, with spines to 3 cm long and yellowish inflorescence.
Southern Africa
CITES App. II

Euphorbia sp. Delange 163
EUPHORBIACEAE
Undescribed species; dwarf plant; branches numerous, spineless, tuberculate.
South Africa
CITES App. II

Euphorbia sp. Leach 14143
EUPHORBIACEAE
A new species discovered by Leach in Tanzania. Stem thick, square, grey-green, freely branched; spines short and thin; flowers greenish-yellow.
Tanzania
CITES App. II

Euphorbia spinea N.E.Br.
EUPHORBIACEAE
Shrub to 25 cm high; branches sharp-pointed, rebranching and forming hemispherical mass to 1 m in diameter; leaves inconspicuous, caducous; inflorescence small, purple cyathia.
Namibia   CITES App. II

Euphorbia stellata Willd.
EUPHORBIACEAE
Dwarf species; tap root 15 cm long; stems prostrate to 15 cm long, green or purplish-brown with whitish variegation on upper surface; spines at apex of tubercles; flowers yellowish-green.
South Africa (Cape Province)   CITES App. II

Euphorbia suzannae Marloth
EUPHORBIACEAE
Stem to 10 cm high; tap root; several ribs each bearing prominent tubercles and deciduous leaves; inflorescence at apex of stem and branches, cyathia yellow. Plant photographed in habitat.
South Africa (Cape Province)   CITES App. II

Euphorbia suzannae Marloth
EUPHORBIACEAE
Cristate specimen. Photograph by Gaetano Palisano.
                                                   CITES App. II

Euphorbia tetragona Haw.
EUPHORBIACEAE
Tree to 15 m high; main trunk to 20 cm thick, with 1 to 5 stem-like branches ascending from base and crown branches at apex; branches ascending-spreading, deciduous; spines in pairs, to 1.5 cm long, light brown to grey; leaves scale-like; inflorescence on short peduncles, cyathia yellow.
South Africa (Cape Province)   CITES App. II

Euphorbia tirucalli L.
EUPHORBIACEAE
Shrub to 4 m tall or tree over 12 m tall; branches light green; leaves to 1.2 cm long, persisting only at tips of growing branches; inflorescence clustered at branch apices.
Euphorbia rhipsaloides Welw., *E. viminalis* Mill.
Tropical East Africa, southern Africa
CITES App. II

135

Euphorbia affinis triaculeata Forssk.
EUPHORBIACEAE
Plant forming small shrubs; branches erect; central spine 2-4 cm long, lateral spines shorter.
Probably Arabia

CITES App. II

Euphorbia trichadenia Pax
EUPHORBIACEAE
Tuberous caudex to 20 cm long and 15 cm thick; stems herbaceous to 10 cm long, spineless; leaves 5-8 cm long; inflorescence on short peduncles at fork of stems.
Angola, South Africa (Cape Province, Natal, Transvaal)   CITES App. II

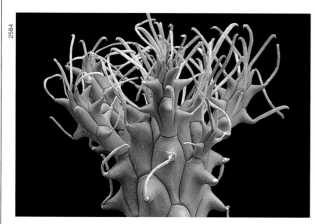

Euphorbia tuberculata Jacq.
EUPHORBIACEAE
Main stem partly buried in the soil continuing into the tap root, producing several branches and forming clumps to 75 cm in diameter; branches dull green to whitish when old, tuberculate, with persistent peduncles; leaves to 4 cm long, at branch apex, deciduous; inflorescence near the apex of stem, on peduncles 2 cm long. The photograph shows a young specimen.
Namibia, South Africa (Cape Province)   CITES App. II

Euphorbia tuberosa L.
EUPHORBIACEAE
Caudex 2.5 cm thick, buried in the soil; stem nearly absent; leaves to 8 cm long, crispy; inflorescence on peduncles 5 cm long.
South Africa (Cape Province)   CITES App. II

Euphorbia tubligans Marloth
EUPHORBIACEAE
Caudex with tap root 8-10 cm long and 4-5 cm thick; branches 5-angled, bluish-green, to 15 cm long; leaves rudimentary, caducous; inflorescence on short peduncles at apex of branches, cyathia yellow.
South Africa (Cape Province)
CITES App. II

Euphorbia valida N.E.Br.
EUPHORBIACEAE
Globose to elongate solitary stems, to 13 cm in diameter and 30 cm high, green with blue-green to reddish markings; peduncles persistent; inflorescence on erect peduncles, cyathia yellow.
South Africa (Cape Province)   CITES App. II

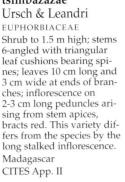

Euphorbia viguieri
M.Denis var.
tsimbazazae
Ursch & Leandri
EUPHORBIACEAE
Shrub to 1.5 m high; stems 6-angled with triangular leaf cushions bearing spines; leaves 10 cm long and 3 cm wide at ends of branches; inflorescence on 2-3 cm long peduncles arising from stem apices, bracts red. This variety differs from the species by the long stalked inflorescence.
Madagascar
CITES App. II

Faucaria tubercolosa (Rolfe) Schwantes
MESEMBRYANTHEMACEAE
Leaves dark green, to 2 cm long, with several teeth-like tubercles on upper surface; flowers yellow.
South Africa (Cape Province)

Euphorbia viguieri
M.Denis var.
tsimbazazae
Ursch & Leandri
EUPHORBIACEAE
Inflorescence.
CITES App. II

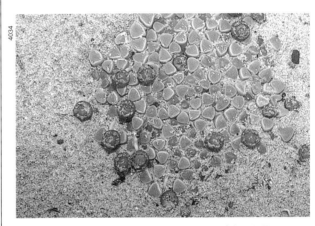

Fenestraria rhopalophylla (Schltr. & Diels) N.E.Br.
MESEMBRYANTHEMACEAE
Leaves light green, to 3 cm long, with transparent tips, forming cushions of 10 cm diameter and up; flowers white.
Namibia

Euphorbia woodii N.E.Br.
EUPHORBIACEAE
Caudex obconical, mostly subterranean; branches to 20 cm long, tuberculate, bright green; leaves rudimentary, at the centre of tubercles, deciduous; inflorescence on short peduncles, yellow cyathia.
South Africa (Natal)   CITES App. II

Fockea edulis (Thunb.) K.Schum.
ASCLEPIADACEAE
Caudex to 30 cm diameter; stems climbing or trailing, at least 80 cm long; leaves oblong. It may attain huge dimensions in habitat. Flowering stem.
Southern Africa

137

Fouquieria columnaris
(Kellogg) Kellogg
FOUQUIERIACEAE
Large, elongated caudex with numerous spiny stems to 15 m high; smaller branches arranged in spirals; leaves 2-4 cm long, greenish; flowers yellow.
Idria columnaris Kellogg
Mexico, USA (southwest California)
CITES App. II

Frithia pulchra N.E.Br.
MESEMBRYANTHEMACEAE
Cultivar «Minima», with smaller leaves.

Frithia pulchra N.E.Br.
MESEMBRYANTHEMACEAE
Stemless plant; leaves erect, 2 cm long, green to grey-green; leaf apex truncate, with transparent window; flower carmine or white.
South Africa (Transvaal)

Furcraea selloa K.Koch. var. marginata Trel.
AGAVACEAE
Single stemmed rosette up to 1.5 m high; leaves numerous, sword-shaped, green with yellow edges; inflorescence up to 6 m tall, flowers greenish-white.
Fureraea lindenii Jacobi
Guatemala, Mexico

Frithia pulchra N.E.Br.
MESEMBRYANTHEMACEAE
Large specimen.

× Gasterhaworthia bayfieldii (Salm-Dyck) G.D.Rowley
LILIACEAE
Rosette; leaves numerous, 10-15 cm long and 3 cm wide at base, triangular apex, horny margins, light green, reddish near the base and covered with prominent points; inflorescence 60-70 cm tall, flowers pale red. Hybrid between unknown species.
Aloe bayfieldii Salm-Dyck
Garden origin

Gasteria acinacifolia (Jacq.) Haw.
LILIACEAE

Stemless plant to 75 cm high and 65 cm wide, forming small groups; leaves erect to 60 cm long and 10 cm wide at base, lanceolate, erectly spreading, dark green with white spots; margins cartilaginous; inflorescence to 1 m tall; flowers pink. The photograph shows the flowers. Photograph by Ernst van Jaarsveld.

South Africa (Cape Province)

Gasteria bicolor Haw.
LILIACEAE

Plant with short stems to 50 cm tall, offsetting from base to form small groups; leaves distichous or spirally arranged, to 40 cm long and 6 cm wide at base, dark green with dense white spots; margin cartilaginous; inflorescence to 1.5 m tall; flowers light pink or white. Photograph by Ernst van Jaarsveld.
Gasteria maculata (Thunb.) Haw.
South Africa (Cape Province)

Gasteria batesiana G.D.Rowley
LILIACEAE

Stemless plant to 10 cm high and 30 cm in diameter forming small to large groups; leaves to 18 cm long and 4 cm wide at base, triangular, dark green with dense white spots and white or green tubercles; inflorescence to 45 cm long; flowers light pink. Photograph by Ernst van Jaarsveld.
South Africa (Natal, Transvaal)

Gasteria bicolor Haw. var. liliputana (Poelln.) vanJaarsv.
LILIACEAE

Leaves distichous or spirally arranged, to 10 cm long and 1.4 cm wide at base, dark green with dense white spots; margins cartilaginous; inflorescence to 40 cm long; flowers pink. Photograph by Ernst van Jaarsveld.
South Africa (Cape Province)

Gasteria baylissiana Rauh
LILIACEAE

Stemless plant forming small groups to 8 cm in diameter; leaves to 5.5 cm long and 2-3 cm wide at base, green with white cartilaginous tubercles; inflorescence to 35 cm long; flowers reddish-pink. Photograph by Ernst van Jaarsveld.
South Africa (Cape Province)

Gasteria brachyphylla (Salm Dyck) vanJaarsv.
LILIACEAE

Stemless plant to 25 cm tall and 25 cm in diameter; forming small groups; leaves distichous to 23 cm long and 8 cm wide at base, dark green with dense white spots; margins wavy; inflorescence to 90 cm tall; flowers pink. Photograph by Ernst van Jaarsveld.
Gasteria angustianum Poelln.; *G. nigricans* (Haw.) Duval
South Africa (Cape Province)

Gasteria brachyphylla (Salm Dyck) vanJaarsv.
LILIACEAE
Plant photographed in habitat.

Gasteria brachyphylla (Salm Dyck) vanJaarsv.
LILIACEAE
Plant photographed in habitat.

Gasteria carinata
(Mill.) Duval
LILIACEAE
Stemless plant offsetting
from base and forming
small groups to 80 cm in
diameter; leaves 5-18 cm
long and 1-5 cm wide at
base, triangular, green with
white spots; inflorescence
to 80 cm tall; flowers pink.
South Africa (Cape
Province)

Gasteria carinata (Mill.) Duval var. **retusa** vanJaarsv.
LILIACEAE
Variety with retuse or truncate leaves, smaller than the type species (to 9 cm long and 3.5 cm wide at base) and shorter inflorescence (to 45 cm tall). Photograph by Ernst van Jaarsveld.
South Africa (Cape Province)

Gasteria carinata (Mill.) Duval var. **verrucosa**
(Mill.) vanJaarsv.
LILIACEAE
Variety with linear-lanceolate leaves, tuberculate, distichous. This variety is very variable in size and leaf shape. Photograph by Ernst van Jaarsveld.
Gasteria verrucosa (Mill.) Duval
South Africa (Cape Province)

Gasteria carinata (Mill.) Duval var. **verrucosa**
(Mill.) vanJaarsv.
LILIACEAE
Another specimen in habitat. Photograph by Ernst van Jaarsveld.

Gasteria disticha (L.) Haw.
LILIACEAE
Stemless plant offsetting from base and forming small groups; leaves distichous to 1.5 cm long and 4.5 cm wide at base, green with dense white spots; margins undulate; inflorescence 20-90 cm tall with up to 180 pink to reddish flowers. Photograph by Ernst van Jaarsveld.
South Africa (Cape Province)

Gasteria excelsa Baker
LILIACEAE
Stemless rosette to 60 cm tall and 75 cm in diameter; leaves to 40 cm long and 18 cm wide at base, triangular, erect, dark green with white spots; margins white, semi-translucent, cartilaginous; inflorescence 55-75 cm tall; flowers light pink or white. Photograph by Ernst van Jaarsveld.
South Africa (Cape Province)

Gasteria glomerata vanJaarsv.
LILIACEAE
Stemless plant, offsetting from the base and forming small clusters to 20 cm in diameter; leaves distichous, 15-30 cm long and 15-20 cm wide at base, glaucous-green, unspotted; inflorescence 12-20 cm long; flowers pinkish-red. Photograph by Ernst van Jaarsveld.
South Africa (Cape Province)

Gasteria nitida (Salm-Dyck) Haw.
LILIACEAE
Stemless plant 6-20 cm tall, proliferating from base to form small groups; leaves distichous when young, then spirally arranged, to 20 cm long and 2.5-8 cm wide at base, dark green with white spots (juvenile leaves unspotted); inflorescence to 1.2 m long; flowers bright red. Photograph by Ernst van Jaarsveld.
Gasteria decipiens Haw.
South Africa (Cape Province)

Gasteria pillansii Kensit
LILIACEAE
Stemless plant offsetting from base and forming groups to 1 m in diameter with 10-150 plants; leaves to 20 cm long and to 5 cm wide at base, green spotted with tubercles; inflorescence to 1.6 m long; flowers pink. Photograph by Ernst van Jaarsveld.
South Africa (Cape Province)

Gasteria pillansii Kensit var. **ernsti-ruschii** (Dinter & Poelln.) vanJaarsv.
LILIACEAE
Smaller variety, with leaves to 7 cm long and inflorescence to 30 cm long.
Gasteria ernsti-ruschii Dinter & Poelln.
South Africa (Cape Province)

Gasteria pillansii Kensit var. **ernsti-ruschii** (Dinter & Poelln.) van Jaarsv.
LILIACEAE
Plant photographed in habitat by Ernst van Jaarsveld.

Gasteria pulchra (Aiton) Haw.
LILIACEAE
Stemless plant solitary or forming small groups; leaves 25-35 cm long and 2.5-4 cm wide at base, dark green with dense white spots; margins cartilaginous; inflorescence 30-150 cm tall; flowers reddish-pink. Photograph by Ernst van Jaarsveld.
Gasteria poellnitziana Jacobsen
South Africa (Cape Province)

Gasteria pulchra (Aiton) Haw.
LILIACEAE
Flowers. Photograph by Ernst van Jaarsveld.

Gasteria rawlinsonii Oberm.
LILIACEAE
Plant with pendulous stems to 1 m long; leaves distichous or spirally arranged, 3-8 cm long and 1-2.5 cm wide at base, green, unspotted or with faint white spots; margins denticulate; inflorescence 10-50 cm long; flowers reddish-pink. Photograph by Ernst van Jaarsveld.
South Africa (Cape Province)

Gasteria sp.
LILIACEAE
Variegated form of unidentified species of garden origin.

Gasteria vlokii vanJaarsv.
LILIACEAE
Stemless plant offsetting from base to form small groups; leaves distichous when young, then spirally arranged, 5-9 cm long and 2-3 cm wide at base, green with dense white spots; inflorescence 30-80 cm long; flowers reddish-pink. Photograph by Ernst van Jaarsveld.
South Africa (Cape Province)

Gasteria vlokii vanJaarsv.
LILIACEAE
Cultivated specimen.

Gibbaeum fissoides (Haw.) Nel
MESEMBRYANTHEMACEAE
Clump-forming plant; leaves of unequal size, to 3 cm long and 0.6-0.8 cm wide, grey to grey-green, sometimes tinged red; flowers red.
Antegibbaeum fissoides (Haw.) Schwantes.
South Africa (Cape Province)

Gethyllis namaquensis (Shönl.) Oberm.
AMARYLLIDACEAE
Bulbs 10-20 cm in diameter; leaves deciduous, appearing after flowering and fruiting; flowers white.
Klinja namaquensis Schönland
Namibia

Gibbaeum heatii (N.E.Br.) L.Bolus
MESEMBRYANTHEMACEAE
Caespitose plant; bodies subglobose, 2-3 cm high and 1-2.5 cm thick; leaves of equal size, green to whitish-green; flowers white to cream-white.
South Africa (Cape Province)

Gibbaeum esterhuyseniae L.Bolus
MESEMBRYANTHEMACEAE
Plant forming groups to 10 cm in diameter; leaves 2-5 cm long, green, glabrous; flowers pink. Plant photographed in habitat.
South Africa (Cape Province)

Gibbaeum pilosulum (N.E.Br.) N.E.Br.
MESEMBRYANTHEMACEAE
Caespitose plant; leaves united into obovate bodies to 2.5 cm high and 2 cm wide, light green, whitish, pubescent; flower red-violet.
South Africa (Cape Province)

Gibbaeum pubescens (Haw.) N.E.Br.
MESEMBRYANTHEMACEAE
Stems short, woody, with remains of dry leaves; leaves of unequal size, from 1 to 3 cm, whitish-grey; flowers violet-red.
South Africa (Cape Province)

Gibbaeum pubescens (Haw.) N.E.Br.
MESEMBRYANTHEMACEAE
Plant photographed in habitat.

Gibbaeum velutinum
(L.Bolus) Schwantes
MESEMBRYANTHEMACEAE
Plant caespitose, branched; leaves united at base, divaricate, of unequal size, from 4 cm to 5-6 cm; flowers pink.
South Africa (Cape Province)

Glottiphyllum cruciatum N.E.Br.
MESEMBRYANTHEMACEAE
Plant forming small groups; leaves light green to red when grown in full sun, 8-10 cm long, semi-cylindrical, curved outside; flowers light yellow. Plant photographed in habitat.
South Africa (Cape Province)

Glottiphyllum cruciatum N.E.Br.
MESEMBRYANTHEMACEAE
Plant photographed in habitat.

Glottiphyllum depressum (Haw.) N.E.Br.
MESEMBRYANTHEMACEAE
Small clumps; leaves erect, curving towards apex, to 10 cm long, green; flowers yellow. Plant photographed in habitat.
South Africa (Cape Province)

Glottiphyllum latifolium N.E.Br.
MESEMBRYANTHEMACEAE
Leaves of unequal size up to 8 cm long, soft, fleshy, with transparent dots; flowers yellow. Plant photographed in habitat.
South Africa (Cape Province)

Glottiphyllum regium N.E.Br.
MESEMBRYANTHEMACEAE
Erect shoots, each with 2 pairs; leaves of unequal size, from 2 to 10 cm, light green; flowers yellow. Plant photographed in habitat.
South Africa (Cape Province)

Glottiphyllum longum (Haw.) N.E.Br.
MESEMBRYANTHEMACEAE
Leaves erect, to 10 cm long and 2 cm wide, narrowed towards the apices, dark green; flowers yellow. Plant photographed in habitat.
South Africa (Cape Province)

Graptopetalum bellum (Moran & Meyran) D.R.Hunt
CRASSULACEAE
Compact rosettes to 5 cm in diameter, almost flat to the ground; leaves grey-green, 1-2 cm long; flowers over 2.5 cm diameter, magenta-pink. The photograph shows a cristate specimen.
Tacitus bellus Moran & Meyran
Mexico

Glottiphyllum oligocarpum L.Bolus
MESEMBRYANTHEMACEAE
Branches creeping; leaves of unequal size arranged in rows, 4 to 5 cm long, white-olive green with prominent dots, velvety; flowers yellow.
South Africa (Cape Province)

Graptopetalum bellum (Moran & Meyran) D.R.Hunt
CRASSULACEAE
Flowers.

Graptopetalum paraguayenese
(N.E.Br.) Walther
CRASSULACEAE
Stem to 30 cm long, decumbent; leaves 3-5 cm long and 1-2 cm wide, grey-green; inflorescence branched; flowers white spotted with red. Variegated form.
Mexico

Graptopetalum saxifragoides Kimnach
CRASSULACEAE
Rosettes stemless, small, compact; leaves grey-green; flowers white spotted with brownish tinge towards the tips of petals.

Graptopetalum pentandrum Moran ssp. superbum Kimnach
CRASSULACEAE
Stems short, freely branched; leaves blue-grey arranged in rosettes at the apex of branches.
Mexico

Graptopetalum saxifragoides Kimnach
CRASSULACEAE
Close-up of flowers.
Mexico

Graptopetalum rusbyi (Greene) Rose
CRASSULACEAE
Small plant; leaves in rosettes 1.5-2 cm long; flowers coral-red.
USA (Arizona)

Graptopetalum suaveolens R.T.Clausen
CRASSULACEAE
Rosettes with bluish-green leaves.
Mexico

Graptoveria cv. «Albert Baynesii»
CRASSULACEAE
Hybrid between *Graptopetalum* × *Echeveria*; leaves arranged in rosettes, bluish tinged with pink.
Garden origin

Graptoveria «Spirit of 76»
CRASSULACEAE
An intergeneric hybrid (*Graptopetalum* × *Echeveria*) with short stem and leaves in rosettes, bluish tinged with violet-pink.
Garden origin

Graptoveria cv. «Hahinii»
CRASSULACEAE
Hybrid between *Graptopetalum* × *Echeveria* with short stem and leaves arranged in rosettes.
Garden origin

Greenovia aurea (H.Christ) Webb & Berth.
CRASSULACEAE
Low shrub forming clumps of rosettes; leaves blue-green to pale green, pruinose; flowers yellow. During the dry season rosettes close-up to protect the apical meristem. Plant photographed in habitat.
Canary Islands (Tenerife, Gran Canaria, Hierro, Gomera)

Graptoveria opalina ISI 1853
CRASSULACEAE
Intergeneric hybrid (*Graptopetalum* × *Echeveria*); leaves arranged in rosettes, pale blue.
Garden origin

Haemanthus albiflos Jacq.
AMARYLLIDACEAE
Leaves elliptic, erect, to 40 cm long and 12 cm wide, sometimes with white spots; flowers white.
South Africa

Haemanthus coccineus L.
AMARYLLIDACEAE

Leaves 45 cm long and 15 cm wide, recurved or prostrate, fleshy, with white or maroon bands; flowers coral to scarlet with white markings. Photograph by Charles H. Everson.
South Africa (Cape Province)

Haemanthus humilis Jacq. ssp. hirsutus (Baker) Snijman .
AMARYLLIDACEAE

Leaves elliptic or lanceolate, erect, 30 cm long and 15 cm wide, pubescent; flowers white to pink.
Haemanthus nelsonii Bak.
South Africa

Haworthia angustifolia Haw.
LILIACEAE

Rosette stemless, 2-6 cm in diameter; leaves ascending, to 10 cm long and 1.5 cm wide, dull green or red when grown in full sun; margins with scattered teeth; inflorescence to 20 cm tall; flowers pinkish-white with brownish-pink veins.
South Africa (Cape Province)

Haworthia arachnoidea (L.) Duval
LILIACEAE

Rosette stemless, to 4-10 cm in diameter, clustering; leaves 2-7 cm long, incurved, green, semi-translucent; margins with white to pale brown teeth; inflorescence to 30 cm tall; flowers white with green veins. Photograph by Roberto Mangani.
South Africa (Cape Province)

Haworthia arachnoidea (L.) Duval
LILIACEAE

Specimens densely white-spined (from Ladysmith, Cape Province).

Haworthia arachnoidea (L.) Duval
LILIACEAE

Plant photographed in habitat by Charles H. Everson.

Haworthia aranea (Berger) M.B.Bayer
LILIACEAE
Rosette stemless, to 4-10 cm in diameter, clustering; leaves 5-10 cm long, incurved, green, semi-translucent, especially towards the tips; margins with white bristles; inflorescence to 30 cm tall; flowers white with green veins. This species may be a variant of *H. bolusi* Baker or *H. arachnoidea* (L.) Duval.
South Africa (Cape Province)

Haworthia asperula Haw.
LILIACEAE
Rosette stemless, 2-8 cm in diameter, offsetting from the base; leaves erect to recurved, to 3.5 cm long, with a triangular pellucid area at tips; inflorescence 55 cm tall; flowers whitish with greenish-brown veins. Bayer rejects this species and considers it «a dreadful source of confusion».
South Africa (Cape Province)

Haworthia bayeri J.D.Venter & S.A.Hammer
LILIACEAE
Rosettes stemless, to 9 cm in diameter; leaves to 4 cm long, 1.7 cm wide at the tip, green at base, reddish-brown toward the end with branched whitish «imbedded» markings; tip translucid; inflorescence to 30 cm tall; flowers white with brown veins.
South Africa (Cape Province)

Haworthia blackburniae W.F.Barker
LILIACEAE
Plant short stemmed, to 15 cm tall; leaves 10 cm long, glaucous-green, grooved; inflorescence to 25 cm tall; flowers white with brown veins.
South Africa (Cape Province)

Haworthia blackburniae W.F.Barker var. graminifolia M.B.Bayer
LILIACEAE
Plant with short stems to 4.5 cm tall; leaves erect to spreading, to 30 cm long, 3 mm wide and 1.5 mm thick, dull green; inflorescence to 60 cm tall; flowers white with green veins. Plant photographed in habitat.
Haworthia graminifolia G.G.Sm.
South Africa (Cape Province)

Haworthia bruynsii M.B.Bayer
LILIACEAE
Stemless plant to 6 cm in diameter; leaves erect, to 4 cm long and 1.4 cm wide at tip, yellow-green to reddish when grown in full sun; inflorescence 25 cm tall; flowers white with brown veins.
South Africa (Cape Province)

Haworthia cassytha Baker
LILIACEAE

Although in cultivation under this name, this species is quite uncertain. Baker, when describing the taxon, was not sure of the correct genus and stated: «it may be an *Aprica*». Other authors consider this taxon to be a complex of garden hybrids.

Haworthia cooperi Baker
LILIACEAE

Rosettes stemless, 5-8 cm in diameter; leaves to 4.5 cm long, pale green, translucent; inflorescence to 40 cm tall; flowers pinkish-white with greenish-brown veins. Photograph by Roberto Mangani.
South Africa (Cape Province)

Haworthia chloracantha Haw. var. subglauca Poelln.
LILIACEAE

Rosettes stemless, 3-5 cm in diameter; leaves to 3 cm long, brownish-green or light green; margins with translucent teeth; inflorescence to 20 cm tall; flowers white with green keels. This variety has nearly glaucous leaves.
South Africa (Cape Province)

Haworthia cooperi Baker
LILIACEAE

A compact form cultivated as forma «obtusa».
South Africa (Cape Province)

Haworthia comptoniana G.G.Sm.
LILIACEAE

Rosettes stemless, to 9 cm in diameter; leaves reddish-brown to green, with reticulated lines, to 4.5 cm long and 2 cm wide at base; inflorescence to 25 cm tall; flowers white with greenish-brown keels. The illustrated specimen is cultivated as forma «major».
Haworthia emelyae var. *comptoniana* J.D.Venter & S.A.Hammer
South Africa (Cape Province)

Haworthia cuspidata Haw.
LILIACEAE

Rosettes to 8 cm in diameter; leaves pale green with darker spots. This species is probably a hybrid of *H. retusa* (L.) Duval and *H. cymbiformis* (Haw.) Duval, widely cultivated.
Garden origin

Haworthia cymbiformis (Haw.) Duval
LILIACEAE
Stemless rosettes 10 cm in diameter; leaves 3-5 cm long, numerous, pale green, translucent with dark stripes; inflorescence 20 cm tall; flowers white with brownish-green veins. A variable species. The specimen illustrated here is a form with elongated stems.
Haworthia concava Haw.; *H. lepida* G.G. Sm.; *H. planifolia* Haw.
South Africa (Cape Province)

Haworthia cymbiformis (Haw.) Duval
LILIACEAE
The flowers.

Haworthia cymbiformis (Haw.) **Duval**
LILIACEAE
A variegated form.

Haworthia cymbiformis (Haw.) Duval
LILIACEAE
Another variegated form.

Haworthia decipiens Poelln.
LILIACEAE
Rosettes stemless 4-6 cm in diameter; leaves to 4.5 cm long, green to reddish; margins acute with pellucid teeth; inflorescence 35-40 cm tall; flowers greyish-white with greenish-brown veins.
South Africa (Cape Province)

Haworthia decipiens Poelln.
LILIACEAE
A specimen from Gerstkraal area (Cape Province).

151

Haworthia decipiens Poelln.
LILIACEAE
A smaller form from Prince Albert area (Cape Province).

Haworthia emelyae Poelln. var. **multifolia** M.B.Bayer
LILIACEAE
Variety with up to 60 leaves, suberect.
South Africa (Cape Province)

Haworthia emelyae Poelln.
LILIACEAE
Rosette stemless; leaves recurved, brownish-green, tip convex, translucent, with pinkish spots; inflorescence 30 cm tall; flowers white with brown veins.
Haworthia correcta Poelln.
South Africa (Cape Province)

Haworthia fasciata (Willd.) Haw. forma **browniana** (Poelln.) M.B.Bayer
LILIACEAE
Rosettes stemless, 7 cm in diameter and to 14 cm tall; leaves 4 cm long, green with white tubercles; inflorescence 40 cm tall; flowers reddish-white with brown veins. Variety with leaves longer and wider than the type, brownish in colour.
South Africa (Cape Province)

Haworthia emelyae Poelln.
LILIACEAE
Plant photographed in habitat.

Haworthia glauca Baker
LILIACEAE
Stem to 8 cm tall; leaves crowded, 2-3 cm long, the younger pale green, the old brownish to bluish-green; inflorescence to 30 cm tall; flowers greyish-white with brown veins.
South Africa (Cape Province)

Haworthia glauca W.F.Baker var. **herrei** Poelln.
LILIACEAE
A variety with longer stems.
Haworthia eilyae Poelln.; *H. herrei* Poelln.
South Africa (Cape Province)

Haworthia limifolia Marloth
LILIACEAE
Rosettes stemless to 12 cm in diameter; leaves recurved, spreading, 3-10 cm long and 2-4 cm wide, green with raised shining tubercles; inflorescence to 35 cm tall; flowers white with grey or green veins.
Mozambique, South Africa (Natal, Transvaal), Swaziland

Haworthia kingiana Poelln.
LILIACEAE
Rosettes stemless to 15 cm in diameter; leaves erect when young, later tapering, bright green with reddish tip; tubercles white; inflorescence to 40 cm tall; flowers white with green veins.
South Africa (Cape Province)

Haworthia lockwoodii Archibald
LILIACEAE
Rosettes stemless, to 10 cm in diameter; leaves erect, recurved, 6 cm long, yellow-green, with a papery-like tip; inflorescence 20 cm tall; flowers white with green and brown veins. Photograph by Roberto Mangani.
South Africa (Cape Province)

Haworthia koelmaniorum Oberm. & Hardy
LILIACEAE
Rosettes stemless, solitary, 7 cm in diameter; leaves to 4 cm long, recurved, dark purplish-brown; numerous rounded tubercles; inflorescence 35 cm tall, flowers white with grey-green veins.
Haworthia mcmurtryi C.L.Schott
South Africa (Transvaal)

Haworthia marginata (Lam.) Stearn
LILIACEAE
Rosettes stemless, 15 cm in diameter; leaves whitish-green, smooth, to 8 cm long; inflorescence to 50 cm tall; flowers pinkish-white with green veins.
South Africa (Cape Province)

Haworthia marginata (Lam.) Stearn
LILIACEAE
Cultivated specimen. Photograph by Roberto Mangani.

Haworthia minima (Aiton) Haw.
LILIACEAE
Rosettes stemless to 8 cm in diameter; leaves 7 cm long, triangular, with sharp pointed tip, tuberculate; inflorescence 50 cm tall; flowers white with green veins.
South Africa (Cape Province)

Haworthia marumiana Uitewaal
LILIACEAE
Rosettes stemless to 30 cm in diameter, forming small clumps; leaves to 2 cm long, brownish-green, with tubercles and teeth; inflorescence 25 cm tall; flowers white with green veins.
South Africa (Cape Province)

Haworthia mirabilis (Haw.) Haw.
LILIACEAE
Rosettes stemless 2.5-7 cm in diameter, forming clusters; leaves 3-4 cm long, yellow or yellow-green, armed with minute teeth; inflorescence 45 cm tall; flowers white with greenish-brown veins.
Haworthia willowmorensis Poelln.
South Africa (Cape Province)

Haworthia maughanii Poelln.
LILIACEAE
Stemless plant, to 5 cm in diameter; leaves arranged in spirals, semi-cylindrical, truncate tip with a translucid window, erect, to 2.5 cm long and 1.5 cm wide; inflorescence 20 cm tall; flowers white with brown veins. Bayer, in his recent monograph, considers this species as a variety of *H. truncata* var. *maughanii* (Poelln.) B.Fearn. Plant photographed in habitat.
South Africa (Cape Province)

Haworthia mucronata Haw. var. **helmiae** (Poelln.) M.B.Bayer
LILIACEAE
Rosettes stemless to 7 cm in diameter and forming clusters; leaves 3-4 cm long, erect (incurved when grown in dry conditions), smooth with green longitudinal lines, armed with teeth; inflorescence 40 cm tall; flowers white with brown and green veins.
Haworthia helmiae Poelln.; *H. unicolor* Haw. var. *helmiae* (Poelln.) M.B.Bayer
South Africa (Cape Province)

154

Haworthia mucronata
Haw. var. **inconfluens**
(Poelln.) M.B.Bayer
LILIACEAE
Rosettes stemless, 5-8 cm in diameter; leaves 2.5 cm long, light green or reddish, margins with teeth; inflorescence 25 cm tall; flowers white with green veins. This variety is more opaque in colour and is usually spineless. Photograph by Roberto Mangani.
Haworthia inconfluens (Poelln.) M.B. Bayer; *Haworthia habdomadis* Poelln. var. *inconfluens* (Poelln.) M.B.Bayer
South Africa (Cape Province)

Haworthia mutica Haw.
LILIACEAE
Rosettes stemless to 6 cm in diameter; leaves brownish to green, 4 cm long, with tips rounded and flattened; inflorescence 15 cm tall; flowers white with green veins.
Haworthia otzenii G.G.Sm.
South Africa (Cape Province)

Haworthia mucronata Haw. var. **rycroftiana** M.B.Bayer
LILIACEAE
Rosette stemless to 10 cm in diameter; leaves to 5 cm long, green with darker tips, turning to reddish-brown when in full sun, inflorescence 50 cm tall; flowers white with green veins.
Haworthia rycroftiana M.B.Bayer
South Africa (Cape Province)

Haworthia nigra (Haw.) Baker
LILIACEAE
Plant short stemmed, to 15 cm tall and 7 cm in diameter; leaves black-green, 1-4 cm long and to 2 cm wide at base, acuminate towards the tip; inflorescence 30 cm tall; flowers white with brown and green veins.
Haworthia schmidtiana Poelln.
South Africa (Cape Province)

Haworthia multilineata (G.G.Sm.) C.L.Scott
LILIACEAE
Rosettes stemless to 8 cm in diameter; leaves recurved, 4-5 cm long, green with white lines and spots; inflorescence 30 cm tall; flowers white with brown and green veins. Bayer considers this species to be a synonym of *H. retusa*. (L.) Duval. Photograph by Roberto Mangani.
South Africa (Cape Province)

Haworthia nortieri G.G.Sm.
LILIACEAE
Rosette stemless to 8 cm in diameter; leaves 2-4 cm long, mauvish-brown, translucid in the upper half; inflorescence 35 cm tall; flowers white with greenish-brown veins.
South Africa (Cape Province)

Haworthia picta Poelln.
LILIACEAE

Rosettes stemless to 6 cm in diameter; leaves grey-green, 3.5 cm long, truncate at the tip; tip translucent; inflorescence 25-30 cm long; flowers white with green veins. Bayer includes this species in *H. emelyae* Poelln.
South Africa (Cape Province)

Haworthia pumila (L.) Duval
LILIACEAE

Rosettes stemless to 20 cm in diameter; leaves reddish or dark green, 10 cm long, 3 cm wide at base, triangular with a pungent reddish-brown tip, white tubercles; inflorescence 40 cm tall; flowers whitish with brownish-white veins.
Haworthia margaritifera (L.) Mill.; *H. maxima* (Haw.) Duval
South Africa (Cape Province)

Haworthia pygmaea Poelln.
LILIACEAE

Rosette stemless to 10 cm in diameter; leaves to 5 cm long, brownish, papillate, translucid in the upper half; inflorescence 35 cm tall; flowers white with greenish-brown veins. Photograph by Roberto Mangani.
South Africa (Cape Province)

Haworthia reinwardtii
(Salm-Dyck) Haw.
LILIACEAE

Rosettes elongate to 15 cm tall and 5 cm in diameter; leaves green, 1-2 cm long, green with whitish tubercles; inflorescence 40 cm tall; flowers pinkish-white with greyish-brown veins. Variable species. Photograph by Roberto Mangani.
South Africa (Cape Province)

Haworthia reinwardtii (Salm-Dyck) Haw.
LILIACEAE

Stems of another specimen.

Haworthia reticulata Haw.
LILIACEAE

Rosette stemless to 8 cm in diameter; leaves to 6 cm long, greenish-white, translucid in the upper third, with green longitudinal lines; inflorescence 30 cm tall; flowers pinkish-white with pinkish veins.
Haworthia guttata Uitewaal
South Africa (Cape Province)

Haworthia retusa (L.) Duval
LILIACEAE
Rosette stemless to 14 cm in diameter, forming clumps; leaves to 6 cm long, green, shiny, turning to reddish-brown when in full sun, inflorescence 70 cm tall; flowers white with green veins. Plant photographed in habitat.
Haworthia caespitosa Poelln.; *H. turgida* Haw.
South Africa (Cape Province)

Haworthia retusa (L.) Duv.
LILIACEAE
A clump photographed in habitat.

Haworthia scabra Haw.
LILIACEAE
Rosette stemless to 6 cm in diameter; leaves to 7 cm long, erect, laterally curved, with pungent yellow tip; inflorescence 60 cm tall; flowers pinkish-white with grey-green veins.
South Africa (Cape Province)

Haworthia semiviva (Poelln.) M.B.Bayer
LILIACEAE
Rosettes stemless to 6 cm in diameter and forming small clusters; leaves to 6 cm long, incurved, pellucid with green longitudinal lines, armed with translucid lanceolate bristles; inflorescence 35 cm tall; flowers brownish-white with brown veins. Photograph by Roberto Mangani.
South Africa (Cape Province)

Haworthia springbokvlakensis C.L.Scott
LILIACEAE
Rosettes stemless; leaves 3.5-4 cm long, dark green to reddish-brown; tip to 1.8 wide, translucent with tubercles and reticulated lines; inflorescence 30 cm long; flowers white with dark brown veins.
South Africa (Cape Province)

Haworthia truncata Schönl.
LILIACEAE
Stemless plant; leaves distichous in opposite rows, 2-3.5 cm long and 1.5-3 cm wide, to 7 mm thick, brownish-green to reddish; upper surface truncate, convex, translucent, rough with minute tubercles; inflorescence 20 cm tall; flowers white with green veins. Plant photographed in habitat.
South Africa (Cape Province)

Haworthia truncata Schönl.
LILIACEAE
Small clump photographed in habitat.

Haworthia turgida Haw.
LILIACEAE
Rosette stemless 3-8 cm in diameter, very proliferous; leaves 2-5 cm long, green, shiny, turning to reddish-brown when in full sun, inflorescence 50 cm tall; flowers white with green veins. Plant photographed in habitat.
Haworthia caespitosa Poelln.
South Africa (Cape Province)

Haworthia venosa (Lam.) Haw. var. **woolleyi** M.B.Bayer
LILIACEAE
Rosettes stemless, 7-10 cm in diameter; leaves 7 cm long, light green with dark green lines, tuberculate; inflorescence 30 cm tall; flowers white with brownish-green veins.
Haworthia woolleyi Poelln.
South Africa (Cape Province)

Haworthia viscosa (L.) Haw.
LILIACEAE
Stems erect, leafy, proliferous from base, forming clumps; leaves 4 cm long, 1-2 cm wide at base, reddish-brown, olive or dark green; inflorescence 30 cm tall; flowers white with brown or green veins. Plant photographed in habitat.
Haworthia concinna Haw.
South Africa (Cape Province)

Haworthia wittebergensis Baker
LILIACEAE
Stemless plant, about 7 cm tall and 3 cm in diameter; leaves 7 cm long, purplish-green in the wild, becoming greener in cultivation; inflorescence 35 cm tall; flowers white with green veins.
South Africa (Cape Province)

Haworthia zantneriana Poelln.
LILIACEAE
Rosettes stemless to 9 cm in diameter, forming clusters; leaves 4-7 cm long, 6-8 mm wide narrowing towards tip, light grey-green or brownish-green; inflorescence to 25 cm tall; flowers white with pale green veins.
South Africa (Cape Province)

Haworthia zantneriana Poelln.
LILIACEAE
Cultivated specimen.

Hoodia macrantha
Dinter
ASCLEPIADACEAE
Stems erect to 80 cm high, 8 cm in diameter; ribs tuberculate, armed with spines; flowers 15-20 cm in diameter, purplish, yellow along the nerves, covered with purple hairs. Plant photographed in habitat by Charles H. Everson.
Namibia

Hoodia alstonii (N.E.Br.) D.C.H.Plowes
ASCLEPIADACEAE
Plant forming clumps; stems to 15 cm tall, 3-5 cm in diameter, green tinged with blue; ribs spiny-tuberculate. Plant photographed in habitat by Charles H. Everson.
Trichocaulon alstonii N.E.Br.
South Africa (Cape Province)

Hoodia sp.
ASCLEPIADACEAE
Unrecognized species from Cape Province, similar to *H. bainii* Dyer. Stems erect, 65-70 cm high, 4-4.5 cm in diameter, 13-15-angled; tubercles tipped with long spines, yellowish at first, later white; flowers 6-7 cm in diameter, yellow-cream tinged with pink, without hairs or papillae.
South Africa (Cape Province)

Hoodia gordonii (Masson) Sweet
ASCLEPIADACEAE
Stems erect with 12-14 tubercled ribs; spines brown, woody, 1 cm long; flowers 7-10 cm in diameter, flesh coloured or brownish with longitudinal and traverse furrows.
South Africa (Cape Province)

Hoya affinis Hems.
ASCLEPIADACEAE
Climbing shrub, freely branched; leaves pubescent, dark green; flowers 2.5-3 cm in diameter, waxy, brownish-purple with a yellow crown and dark brown centre. Photograph by Charles H. Everson.
Solomon Islands

159

Hoya albiflora Zipp. ex Blume
ASCLEPIADACEAE
Trailing plant; leaves opposite, fleshy, green; flowers in umbels, white, waxy, star-like. Photograph by Charles H. Everson.
Java, New Guinea

Hoya archboldiana C.Norman
ASCLEPIADACEAE
Shrub trailing; leaves large, dark green; flowers in umbels, 5 cm in diameter, rose-red inside, light green outside. Photograph by Ann Wayman.
New Guinea

Hoya australis R.Br.
ASCLEPIADACEAE
A variable species with leaves of different size, shape and colour, from light green to dark green; flowers waxy, white with carmine-pink centre. Photograph by Lina Paul.
Australia

Hoya campanulata Blume
ASCLEPIADACEAE
Plant climbing; leaves opposite, fleshy; flowers white, in umbels, waxy. Photograph by Ann Wayman.
Malaysia, Sumatra, Thailand

Hoya carnosa (L.) R.Br. cv. «Krimson Princess»
ASCLEPIADACEAE
Trailing shrub, fleshy; leaves ovate-cordate to ovate-elongate, 5-8 cm long, 4-5 cm wide; flowers in large umbels, 1.5 cm in diameter, white or flesh-coloured with red centre. This is a cultivar named «Krimson Princess» with leaves dark green, pink, white and yellow. Photograph by Charles H. Everson.
Asclepias carnosa L.
Australia, China

Hoya carnosa (L.) R.Br. cv. «Krincle 8»
ASCLEPIADACEAE
Another cultivar with thick dark, glossy green leaves. Photograph by Charles H. Everson.

Hoya ciliata Elmer
ASCLEPIADACEAE
Rambling shrub; leaves green, fleshy; flowers in umbels, dark purple-blackish with yellow centre, waxy. Photograph by Ann Wayman.
Philippines

Hoya crassicaulis Elmer
ASCLEPIADACEAE
Climbing shrub; leaves dark green, fleshy; flowers cream coloured, in large umbels, small, waxy. Photograph by Ann Wayman.
Philippines

Hoya cinnamifolia Hook.
ASCLEPIADACEAE
Climbing shrub, branched; leaves olive green, veins silver; flowers 25-30 in umbels, yellow with brownish-red centre, waxy. Photograph by Ann Wayman.
Java

Hoya curtisii King & Gamble
ASCLEPIADACEAE
Plant freely branching; leaves green; flowers star-like cream-yellowish. Photograph by Charles H. Everson.
Malaysia, Sumatra, Thailand

Hoya compacta C.M.Burton cv. «Hindu Rope»
ASCLEPIADACEAE
Twining plant; leaves green, large, curled; flowers in large umbels, white or pink, waxy. Photograph by Charles H. Everson.
Unknown origin

Hoya cv. «Gold Star»
ASCLEPIADACEAE
A cultivar with climbing stem; flowers yellow, waxy. Photograph by Ann Wayman.
Garden origin

Hoya cv. «Pinkie»
ASCLEPIADACEAE
A cultivar with dark green leaves; flowers white flushed with pink, waxy, in umbels. Photograph by Charles H. Everson.
Garden origin

Hoya diptera W.Seem.
ASCLEPIADACEAE
Climbing plant; stems thick, covered with dark green leaves; flowers white with pink centre, waxy, star-like. Photograph by Charles H. Everson.
Fiji

Hoya darwinii Loher
ASCLEPIADACEAE
Climbing plant; leaves 8 cm long, dark bluish-green, inhabited by ants in the wild; flowers pink-mauve with white crown and dark rose-red centre. Photograph by Ann Wayman.
Philippines

Hoya eritryna Rintz
ASCLEPIADACEAE
Climbing stems; leaves lime green, upper surface with deep green venation, lower surface dull maroon to pink; flowers in pendent umbels, buttery-yellow. Photograph by Ann Wayman.
Malaysia, Sumatra, Thailand

Hoya dimorpha F.M.Bailey
ASCLEPIADACEAE
Stems thin, climbing; leaves dark blue-green; flowers in umbels of 35-40, golden yellow with white crown. Photograph by Charles H. Everson.
New Guinea

Hoya excavata Teijsm. & Binn.
ASCLEPIADACEAE
Trailing plant; leaves dark green, opposite; flowers pink with red centre, in umbels, waxy. Photograph by Ann Wayman.
Malaysia, Sumatra, Thailand

Hoya gracilis Schltr.
ASCLEPIADACEAE
Climbing stems; leaves dark green, lanceolate; flowers in umbels, pink with red crown. Photograph by Ann Wayman.
Philippines

Hoya kerrii Craib
ASCLEPIADACEAE
Climbing plant; leaves succulent, heart-shaped, 5-15 cm long and wide; flowers in umbels, white to dark pinkish-brown with age, brown-maroon crown. Photograph by Charles H. Everson.
Malaysia, Sumatra, Thailand

Hoya guppyi Oliv.
ASCLEPIADACEAE
Climbing stems; leaves covered with hairs; flowers 2.5 cm in diameter, purple to maroon with yellowish centre. Photograph by Charles H. Everson.
Solomon Islands

Hoya macgillivrayi F.M.Bailey
ASCLEPIADACEAE
Leaves 10 cm long, 5 cm wide, dark green, copper when young; flowers pendent, waxy, 7-7.5 cm in diameter, purple, on slender pedicels. Photograph by Ann Wayman.
Australia

Hoya imperialis Lindl.
ASCLEPIADACEAE
Climbing stems; leaves fleshy, green elongate; flowers in umbels with 6-8 large flowers, 5-7 cm in diameter, coppery-pink to brownish-red with pure white crown. Photograph by Charles H. Everson.
Borneo

Hoya madulidii Kloppenb.
ASCLEPIADACEAE
Climbing stems; leaves opposite, lanceolate; flowers star-like, waxy, brownish with yellow centre. Photograph by Ann Wayman.
Philippines

Hoya meliflua (Blanco) Merril

ASCLEPIADACEAE

Climbing plant; leaves thick, glossy-green; flowers in globose umbels with 30 star-like flowers, deep pink. Photograph by Ann Wayman.

Philippines

Hoya nicholsoniae F.Mull.

ASCLEPIADACEAE

Twining stems; leaves green, purplish in sunshine; flowers in globose umbels, cream to yellow flushed with pink. Photograph by Ann Wayman.

Australia

Hoya mindorensis Schltr.

ASCLEPIADACEAE

Stems trailing; leaves green, fleshy; flowers white with red centre, waxy, in pendent umbels. Photograph by Ann Wayman.

Philippines

Hoya nummularioides Costantin

ASCLEPIADACEAE

Stems thin, climbing; leaves dull olive green, covered with fine hairs; flowers in umbels, small, white with pink centre. Photograph by Lina Paul.

Laos, Cambodia, Thailand, Vietnam

Hoya multiflora (Decne) Blume

ASCLEPIADACEAE

Climbing plant; leaves green, linear-elongate; flowers in umbels, star-shaped, dark yellow with white crown and purple centre. Photograph by Charles H. Everson.

Hoya coriacea Blume

Malacca

Hoya obavata Decne.

ASCLEPIADACEAE

Leaves thick, fleshy, round, dark green flushed with pink and white; flowers white to light pink with deep carmine-red centre. Photograph by Charles H. Everson.

Celebes, Malacca

Hoya obscura Elmer ex C.M.Burton
ASCLEPIADACEAE
Plant epiphytic with compact bushy growth; leaves light green; flowers waxy cream to pink. Photograph by Charles H. Everson.
Philippines

Hoya pubicalyx Merril cv. «Red Buttons»
ASCLEPIADACEAE
Climbing stems; leaves light green; flowers in umbels, star-like, purple-red. This is a cultivar named «Red Buttons». Photograph by Charles H. Everson.
Philippines

Hoya pachyclada Kerr
ASCLEPIADACEAE
Shrub; leaves thick, olive green; flowers in umbels, white with white crown. Photograph by Charles H. Everson.
Cambodia, Laos, Thailand, Vietnam

Hoya serpens Hook.
ASCLEPIADACEAE
Climbing shrub, freely branching; leaves round and small, deep green; flowers in pendent umbels, white, waxy. Photograph by Charles H. Everson.
India

Hoya pauciflora Wight
ASCLEPIADACEAE
Bush; stems thick; leaves narrow, olive green; flowers bell-shaped, white with red centre.
India, Sri Lanka

Hoya sheperdii Short ex Hook.
ASCLEPIADACEAE
Stems climbing; leaves dark green, 5-12 cm long, 1.5 cm wide; flowers 1-1.5 cm in diameter, white or pale pink with white crown and pink centre. Photograph by Ann Wayman.
India

Hoya sp. WMZ
ASCLEPIADACEAE
An unrecognized species with trailing stems and large decorative foliage. Photograph by Charles H. Everson.
Origin unknown

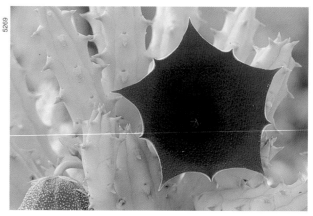

Huernia aspera N.E.Br.
ASCLEPIADACEAE
The flowers.

Hoya tsangii C.M.Burton
ASCLEPIADACEAE
Trailing stems; leaves fleshy, green; flowers red, in umbels. Photograph by Ann Wayman.
Philippines

Huernia brevirostris N.E.Br.
ASCLEPIADACEAE
Stems erect or ascending to 5 cm long, 1-2 cm thick, dull dark green or purplish, 4-5-angled, acutely toothed; flowers 2.5-4 cm in diameter, variable in colour: whitish to brown, dark crimson or blackish, tinged with maroon.
South Africa

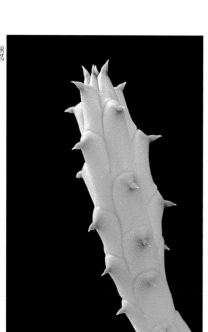

Huernia aspera
N.E.Br.
ASCLEPIADACEAE
Stems usually procumbent, 1-1.5 cm thick, to 20 cm long, tuberculate, 5-6-angled with small spreading teeth; leaves rudimentary at the apex of tubercles; flowers 2-2.5 cm in diameter, red-brown to blackish-purple.
Kenya, Malawi, Tanzania

Huernia campanulata
(Masson) R.Br.
ASCLEPIADACEAE
Stems erect or ascending 5-10 cm long, 1-2 cm thick, green spotted with red, 4-5-angled, angles dentate; flowers sulphur-yellow with large black-purple blotches.
South Africa (Cape Province)

Huernia confusa Phillips
ASCLEPIADACEAE

Stems erect, 6 cm high, 4-5-angled, greyish-green with small teeth along the angles; flowers 2.5-3.5 cm in diameter, cream to buff-coloured with irregular red markings. Considered a synonym of *H. insigniflora* Masson.
South Africa (Cape Province)

Huernia distincta N.E.Br.
ASCLEPIADACEAE

Stems 8-9-angled, strongly toothed; flowers 3-3.6 cm in diameter, dull yellow marked with red spots. Possible a natural hybrid of *H. clavigera* (Jacq.) Haw. × *H. pillansii* N.E.Br.
South Africa (Cape Province)

Huernia echidnopsioides (L.C.Leach) L.C.Leach
ASCLEPIADACEAE

Plant rhizomatose; stems 4-6 cm high, 1 cm thick, tuberculate, 7-9-angled, toothed; flowers 2-3 cm in diameter, yellowish to buff, densely papillate, covered with small red to brownish spots in labyrinthine pattern.
H. pillansi ssp. *echidnopsioides* L.C.Leach
South Africa (Cape Province)

Huernia guttata (Masson) N.E.Br.
ASCLEPIADACEAE

Stems decumbent or erect, 7 cm high, 1.5 cm thick, 4-5-angled, acutely toothed; flowers 2.5-7 cm in diameter, variably coloured and patterned, most commonly cream, blood red spots.
Huernia olentiginosa Haw., *H. cellata* (Jacq.) Schultes
South Africa (Cape Province)

Huernia hislopii Turrill
ASCLEPIADACEAE

Stems 5-angled, 5 cm high, 1 cm thick, bluish-green, strongly toothed; flowers 4-5 cm in diameter, whitish or cream, with red-brown spots.
Zimbabwe

Huernia hystrix (Hook f.) N.E.Br.
ASCLEPIADACEAE

Stems, erect or decumbent, 6-7 cm long, 5-angled, grey-green, strongly toothed; flowers 3-5 cm in diameter, densely papillose, yellow, marked with brown-red spots and lines.
H. appendiculata Berge
Mozambique, South Africa

167

Huernia insigniflora
Masson
ASCLEPIADACEAE
Stems erect, branching from base, 4-angled, grey-ish-green, toothed; flowers with greenish-white, ivory lobes and crimson to brown annulus.
South Africa (Transvaal)

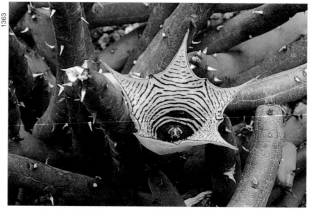

Huernia leachii Lavranos
ASCLEPIADACEAE
Stems prostrate to 1.5 m long, 0.5-0.8 cm thick, 4-angled, cylindric; flowers 2.5 cm in diameter, densely papillate, cream marked with purple lines.
Malawi, Mozambique

Huernia kennediana Lavranos
ASCLEPIADACEAE
Stems 6-10-angled, short stout, usually globose, grey-green to purplish; flowers 2-2.5 cm in diameter, papillose, cream to dull yellow, with transverse red-brown spots.
South Africa (Cape Province)

Huernia macrocarpa (A.Rich.) Sprenger
ASCLEPIADACEAE
Stems erect to 9 cm long, green, 5-angled, prominently toothed; flowers 2 cm in diameter, brownish-red to blackish-purple, papillate. Reputedly a synonym of *H. penzigii* N.E.Br.
Ethiopia, Somalia

Huernia kirkii N.E.Br.
ASCLEPIADACEAE
Stems 4-5-angled, 2.5-4.5 cm high, to 1.8 cm thick, strongly toothed, prostrate at the base; flowers 3-5 cm in diameter, cream marked with reddish-maroon spots, blackish in the tube.
H. bicampanulata Verd.
Zimbabwe, South Africa (Transvaal)

Huernia pendula E.A.Bruce
ASCLEPIADACEAE
Stems cylindric, grey-green tinged with purple, 0.5-0.8 cm thick, to 1.5 m long; flowers dark purple-brown, densely papillate.
South Africa (Cape Province)

Huernia procumbens (R.A.Dyer) L.C.Leach
ASCLEPIADACEAE
Stems trailing, tuberculate, 1-1.5 cm thick, 5-angled; flowers 4-5.5 cm in diameter, cream with a prominent annulus and narrow lobes.
Duvalia procumbens R.A.Dyer
South Africa

Huernia recondita M.G.Gilbert
ASCLEPIADACEAE
Stems cylindrical, procumbent, to 50 cm long, 1-1.2 cm wide, 4-angled; flowers yellow, marked with irregular red blotches, covered with papillae.
Ethiopia

Huernia sp. Collenette 7828
ASCLEPIADACEAE
An unrecognized species collected by Sheila Collenette. Plant caespitose, stems 4-angled, grey-green, strongly dentate.
Saudi Arabia

Huernia whitesloniana Nel
ASCLEPIADACEAE
Plant caespitose; stems to 5 cm high, 4-5-angled, strongly toothed, greenish-purple; flowers 1.2-2.2 cm in diameter, cream, with red purple spots, covered with minute papillae.
South Africa (Transvaal)

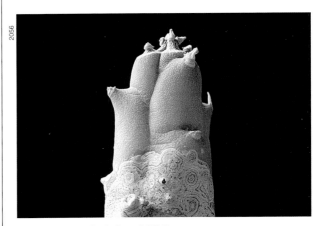

Huerniopsis decipiens N.E.Br.
ASCLEPIADACEAE
Stems decumbent, 3-7 cm long, caespitose, 4-5-angled, armed with acute spreading teeth; flowers 2.5 cm in diameter, dull purple somewhat yellowish spotted.
Botswana, Namibia, South Africa (Cape Province)

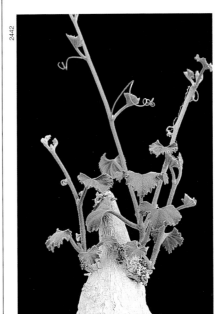

Ibervillea sonorae (S.Watson) Greene
CUCURBITACEAE
Large caudex more or less globose protruding above soil; stems over 3 m long, climbing, green turning whitish with age, with tendrils; leaves green, 4-7-lobed, hairy on both margins, deciduous; flowers green.
Mexico (Baja California)

Ibervillea tenuisecta Small
CUCURBITACEAE
Caudex from which many twining stems with tendrils arise; leaves trilobate; flowers yellow.
Mexico

Jacaratia hassleriana DC.
CONVOLVULACEAE
Caudex oblong; stems thin; leaves heart-shaped.
Tropical regions

Ipomoea holubii Baker
CONVOLVULACEAE
Caudex to 20 cm in diameter; stems numerous, thin; leaves green, filiform; flowers pink to purple. Photograph by Gaetano Palisano.
Botswana, Namibia

Jatropha macrantha Müll.Arg.
EUPHORBIACEAE
Plant to 1 m tall; stems green; leaves to 3.5 cm long, green on the upper surface, brownish on the lower; inflorescence with red flowers.
Mexico, USA (Texas).

Ipomoea sp.
CONVOLVULACEAE
Unidentified species from Karoo; caudex 10-12 cm in diameter, brown; stems annual, thin; leaves filiform, 3-5 cm long.
South Africa

Jatropha macrantha Müll.Arg.
EUPHORBIACEAE
Flowers.

Jatropha podagrica Hook.
EUPHORBIACEAE

Dichotomously branched shrub with caudex 50 cm tall, three-lobed; leaves approximately 18 cm long and wide, green-glaucous below, borne at branch apices; inflorescence dichotomously branched; flowers scarlet. Close-up of flowers.
Central America

Jordaaniella cupriata H.E.K.Hartmann
MESEMBRYANTHEMACEAE

Branches to 6 cm long, creeping and forming compact groups; leaves pale green, reddish in full sun, to 6.5 cm long; flowers to 8 cm in diameter, red. Plant photographed in habitat by Charles H. Everson.
Cephalophyllum cupreum L.Bolus
South Africa (Cape Province)

Kalanchoe beharensis Drake
CRASSULACEAE

Stem up to 3 m high; leaves up to 20 cm long and 10 cm wide, green with dense covering of fine hairs on both surfaces; inflorescence 60 cm tall; flowers greenish-yellow.
Madagascar

Kalanchoe blossfeldiana Poelln.
CRASSULACEAE

Dwarf shrub to 40 cm high, little branched; leaves 2-5 cm long, 4 cm wide, dark green. Many cultivars with flowers of different colours (yellow, red, pink, orange) have been produced in the last 20 years.
Kalanchoe globulifera var. *coccinea* Perr.
Madagascar

Kalanchoe blossfeldiana Poelln.
CRASSULACEAE

Flowers.

Kalanchoe citrina Schweinf.
CRASSULACEAE

Stem to 1 m tall; leaves obovate-lanceolate, 6 cm long, 1.2 cm wide, densely pubescent and with dentate margins; flowers yellow.
Arabia, Ethiopia, Kenya, Uganda

Kalanchoe daigremontiana Raym.-Hamet & Perr.
CRASSULACEAE
Brownish erect stem to 1 m high; leaves 15-20 cm long, 2-3 cm wide, brown-red spotted, producing adventitious plantlets; flowers red to red-violet.
Madagascar

Kalanchoe daigremontiana Raym.-Hamet & Perr.
CRASSULACEAE
Inflorescence.

Kalanchoe eriophylla Hilsenb. & Boyer
CRASSULACEAE
Slender stem, much branched at the base; leaves ovate-elongate, 1.5-2 cm long, covered with dense hairs, brown tips; flowers violet or blue-violet.
Cotyledon pannosa W.F.Baker
Madagascar

Kalanchoe farinacea Balf.
CRASSULACEAE
Stems to 40 cm tall; leaves obovate, 2-2.7 cm long, grey-green with darker spots; flowers red. Considered a synonym of *K. scapigera* Welw.
Angola, Yemen (Socotra)

Kalanchoe faustii Font Quer
CRASSULACEAE
Stem 30-70 cm high; leaves 6-8 cm long, 3-4 cm wide, ovate-acuminate, margins irregularly curled; flowers golden yellow.
Morocco

Kalanchoe flammea Stapf.
CRASSULACEAE
Stem to 40 cm high; leaves 6-7 cm long, 2.5-3 cm wide, narrowed at base, entire or crenate, pale grey-green; flowers bright orange-red. Considered a synonym of *K. glaucescens* Britten.
Somalia

Kalanchoe gastonis-bonnieri Raym.-Hamet & Perr.
CRASSULACEAE
Shrub to 60 cm high; leaves whitish-pruinose with brown-green spots, 16 cm long, 4 cm wide, adventitious plantlets at the apex; flowers pale green.
Madagascar

Kalanchoe gastonis-bonnieri Raym.-Hamet & Perr.
CRASSULACEAE
Young specimen. Photograph by Roberto Mangani.

Kalanchoe hildebrandtii Baill.
CRASSULACEAE
Shrubby or arborescent plant, 1.5 to 5 m high; leaves roundish 1.5-4 cm long, 1-3.5 cm wide, densely covered with white hairs; flowers white to cream.
Madagascar

Kalanchoe laciniata
(L.) DC.
CRASSULACEAE
Stem erect to 1 m high; leaves glabrous or hairy, pinnately or deeply lobed; flowers yellowish.
K. rohlfsii Engl.; *Kalanchoe schweinfurthii* Penz.
Eastern to southern Africa, south India

Kalanchoe lanceolata
(Forssk.) Pers.
CRASSULACEAE
Plant to 35 cm tall; leaves to 15 cm long and 6 cm wide, covered with fine hairs, margins entire or crenate; flowers yellow or orange.
Kalanchoe diversa N.E.Br.; *K. heterophylla* Wight
East Africa, India

Kalanchoe longiflora Schltr. ex J.M.Wood
CRASSULACEAE
Simple stem, 4-angled; leaves ovate-oblong, 5.6 cm long, grey-green to yellowish with dentate margins; flowers yellow to orange.
Natal

Kalanchoe luciae Raym.-Hamet
CRASSULACEAE
Leaves in rosettes, obovate, entire, 6-16 cm long, 3-9 cm wide, glabrous or hairy, grey-green to yellowish-green with red margins; flowers yellowish-green.
South Africa (Cape Province, Transvaal)

Kalanchoe peteri Werderm.
CRASSULACEAE
Plant 40-60 cm high; leaves 19 cm long and 10 cm wide, reddish-blue; margins crenate; flowers pale yellow.
Congo

Kalanchoe marmorata Baker
CRASSULACEAE
Stems branching from base; leaves obovate, 10 cm long, grey-green with brown spots and dentate margins; flowers white. Plant photographed in habitat.
Kalanchoe grandiflora A. Rich.
Eritrea

Kalanchoe pinnata (Lam) Persoon
CRASSULACEAE
Erect stem to 1 m high; leaves at first simple, later pinnate, 7-13 cm long, producing plantlets; flowers whitish-reddish.
Bryophyllum calycinum Salisb.
Africa, tropical Asia and America, Australia

Kalanchoe marneriana Jacobs
CRASSULACEAE
Small shrub 30 cm high, branched from base; leaves 1-2 cm long, 2-3 cm wide, grey-green; flowers yellow-orange to pink.
Madagascar

Kalanchoe prolifica (Bowie) Raym.-Hamet
CRASSULACEAE
Stem erect, 4-angled, off-setting at base, to 2 m tall; leaves simple or pinnate, 3-5 cm long, margins dentate; flowers greenish.
Madagascar

Kalanchoe serrata
G.Mann. & Boiteau
CRASSULACEAE
Small shrub to 60 cm high, branched from the base; leaves 4-6 cm long, 2.5-4 cm wide, bluish-pruinose with red spots and dentate margins; flowers red-orange.
Madagascar

Kedrostis crassirostrata Bremek.
CUCURBITACEAE
Caudex to 10 cm in diameter; stems erect, climbing; leaves green, dentate; flowers yellowish-green.
Central and southern Africa

Kalanchoe thyrsyfolia Harv.
CRASSULACEAE
Stem to 60 cm high; leaves 1-1.5 cm long, 5-7 cm wide, white-pruinose often with red margins; flowers yellow. Photograph by Charles H. Everson.
South Africa (Cape Province)

Lampranthus sp.
MESEMBRYANTHEMACEAE
An undescribed species photographed in habitat.

Kalanchoe tomentosa Baker
CRASSULACEAE
Shrub much branched, to 50 cm high; leaves 7 cm long, 2 cm wide, densely tomentose with dark blotches, margins entire or dentate; flowers yellow-brown. There are several cultivars in cultivation. This is a form with dark brown leaves.
Madagascar

Lenophyllum acutifolium Rose
CRASSULACEAE
Stems 10-40 cm tall; leaves in pairs, to 12 in number, elliptic-lanceolate, upper surface grooved; flowers pale yellow.
Mexico

Lenophyllum obtusum Moran
CRASSULACEAE
Stems 20-30 cm tall; leaves in pairs, ovate, 2-4 cm long and wide, glaucous when young, dull purplish-green or brownish later; flowers yellow.
Mexico

Lenophyllum sp.
CRASSULACEAE
Close-up of flowers.

Lenophyllum reflexum S.S.White
CRASSULACEAE
Stem to 4 cm high; leaves 2 cm long, 1.5 cm wide, green-reddish; flowers yellow.
Mexico

Lithops coleorum S.A.Hammer & R.Hijs
MESEMBRYANTHEMACEAE
Leaves grey-brown with darker spots arranged in bands.
South Africa (Transvaal)

Lenophyllum sp.
CRASSULACEAE
Unidentified species from Mexico with stems to 10 cm high and long, acute leaves.
Mexico

Lithops gracilidelineata Dinter
MESEMBRYANTHEMACEAE
Body 1.5-3 cm in diameter; fissure deep; leaves almost equal in size, pale grey with a pattern of dark lines; flowers yellow. Plant photographed in habitat by Charles H. Everson.
Namibia

Lithops herrei L.Bolus
MESEMBRYANTHEMACEAE
Body 2-3 cm in diameter; fissure deep; leaves divergent, grey to pale grey with dark lines; flowers yellow. Plant photographed in habitat by Charles H. Everson.
Lithops translucens L.Bolus
Namibia, South Africa (Cape Province)

Lithops karasmontana (Dinter & Schwantes) N.E.Br. ssp. bella (N.E.Br.) D.T.Cole
MESEMBRYANTHEMACEAE
Bodies 2-3 cm in diameter; leaves divergent, grey-green with olive green spots; flowers white. Plant photographed in habitat by Charles H. Everson.
Namibia

Lycium intricatum Boiss.
SOLANACEAE
Freely branched shrub; stems up to 1 m tall with horizontal branches up to 2 m long; leaves 1.5 cm long and 3-6 cm wide, glaucous-green; flowers violet-purple or white. Plant photographed in habitat.
Canary Islands, northern Africa

Lycium intricatum Boiss.
SOLANACEAE
The fruits. Plant photographed in habitat.
Canary Islands, northern Africa

Malephora lutea (Haw.) Schwantes
MESEMBRYANTHEMACEAE
Shrubs, forming mats over 30 cm wide; leaves fused at base, 2.5-4 cm long, semicylindrical, blue-pruinose to white-pruinose; flowers yellow. Plant photographed in habitat.
South Africa (Cape Province)

Malephora lutea (Haw.) Schwantes
MESEMBRYANTHEMACEAE
Flowering plant photographed in habitat.

177

Massonia depressa Houtt.
LILIACEAE
Bulbous plant; leaves 7-15 cm long, fleshy, usually 2 in number; inflorescence with 20-30 flowers green, yellowish-white or pink to red or brown. Plant photographed in habitat by Charles H. Everson.
South Africa (Cape Province)

Mesembryanthemum crystallinum Boiss.
MESEMBRYANTHEMACEAE
Plant photographed in South Africa by Charles H. Everson.

Mesembryanthemum crystallinum Boiss.
MESEMBRYANTHEMACEAE
Annual plant; stems succulent, creeping; leaves 10-15 cm long, undulate, succulent; stems and leaves covered with watery papillae; flowers white or pinkish. Plant photographed in habitat (Canary Islands).
Macronesia and Mediterranean region

Mesembryanthemum nodiflorum L.
MESEMBRYANTHEMACEAE
Annual plant; stems fleshy, to 20 cm long; leaves 1-2.5 cm long, grey-green with large papillae; flowers white.
South Africa (Cape Province); naturalized in southern Europe, Middle East and California.

Mesembryanthemum crystallinum Boiss.
MESEMBRYANTHEMACEAE
Flowering plant photographed in habitat (Canary Islands).

Mitrophyllum affine L.Bolus
MESEMBRYANTHEMACEAE
Branches, reddish-brown, to 15 cm long; leaves 3 cm long, fused for 1 cm at base; flowers yellow.
South Africa (Cape Province)

Mitrophyllum pillansii N.E.Br.

MESEMBRYANTHEMACEAE

Plant about 15 cm tall; leaves of two types: united in conical bodies 4-8 cm long and 2-3 mm thick, or free to 9 cm long and 2 cm wide at base ending in a short, papillose tip; flowers white.

South Africa (Cape Province)

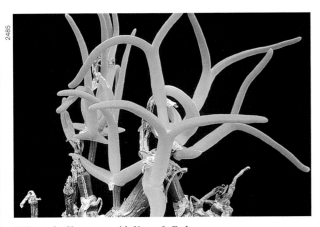

Mitrophyllum tenuifolium L.Bolus

MESEMBRYANTHEMACEAE

Plant to 6 cm tall; branches ascending, glabrous, brown or yellow-green; leaves of different sizes, from 0.5 cm to 2.5 cm long; flowers yellow.

South Africa (Cape Province)

Momordica repens Bremek.

CUCURBITACEAE

Roots tuberous; stems to 6 m long, with tendrils; leaves compound; flowers yellowish-orange.

South Africa (Transvaal)

Monadenium affinis orobanchoides P.R.O.Bally

EUPHORBIACEAE

Unidentified species close to *M. orobanchoides* P.R.O.Bally, with small caudex and ovate red on the lower surface.

Tanzania

Monadenium ritchiei P.R.O.Bally

EUPHORBIACEAE

Roots tuberous; stems cylindrical, trailing, sparsely branched, to 40 cm long, 1.5-2.5 cm thick; tubercles to 0.7 cm high, crowned by 3-5 spines; leaves fleshy, dark green with serrulate margins; inflorescence solitary, whitish-green with pale pink veins.

Kenya

Monadenium rubellum (P.R.O.Bally) S.Carter

EUPHORBIACEAE

Stems erect, fleshy, to 25 cm tall, striped green-purple; leaves 4.5 cm long, purple tinged; inflorescence forked; flowers pink. Close-up of flowers.

Kenya

Monadenium schubei
Pax
EUPHORBIACEAE
Stems erect or decumbent to 45 cm high, 4 cm thick, covered with prominent tubercles rectangular or hexagonal at base, to 1 cm tall, bearing 4-6 spines; leaves deciduous with undulate-crenate margins.
Mozambique, Zimbabwe

Monanthes laxiflora (DC.) Bolle
CRASSULACEAE
Small plant with woody reddish stems; leaves yellow-green to dark green sometimes with red dots; inflorescence with small flowers, yellow to red. Plant photographed in habitat.
Canary Islands (Tenerife, Gomera, Gran Canaria, Lanzarote, Fuerteventura)

Monadenium stapelioides Pax
EUPHORBIACEAE
Stems erect, decumbent, to 15 cm long; tubercles arranged in spirals; leaves green, 3-5 cm long, present on growing parts of stems; flowers pink.
Kenya, Tanzania

Monanthes minima (Bolle) H.Christ
CRASSULACEAE
Root tuberous with dense offset rosettes; leaves bluntly rounded, ciliate; flowers yellow, often with red stripes. Plant photographed in habitat.
Monanthes dasyphylla Svent.
Canary Islands (Tenerife)

Monanthes brachycaulon (Webb & Berthel) Lowe
CRASSULACEAE
Rosettes small; stems 5 mm in diameter forming small clumps; leaves greenish or reddish, to 1.5 cm long; inflorescence with small flowers 3-5 mm in diameter, pale yellow, with red stripes. Plant photographed in habitat.
Monanthes niphophila Svent.; *M. praegei* Bramwell
Canary Islands (Tenerife, Gran Canaria)

Monanthes pallens (Webb) H.Christ
CRASSULACEAE
Fibrous root with rosettes up to 5 cm in diameter; leaves acute or truncate at apex, soft, glaucous; flowers 3-4 mm in diameter, red-brownish sometimes with reddish-brown stripes. Plant photographed in habitat.
Monanthes silensis (Praeger) Svent.
Canary Islands (Tenerife, Hierro, Gomera)

Monilaria obconica Ihlenf. & S.Jörg.
MESEMBRYANTHEMACEAE
Leaves thin, 3-4 cm long, green, cylindrical; new growth covered in shining papillae; flowers white.
South Africa (Cape Province)

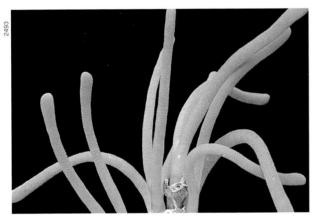

Monilaria salmonea L.Bolus
MESEMBRYANTHEMACEAE
Plant 10 cm tall; branches with 2-4 leaves; leaves green, 3-4 cm long; flowers salmon-red.
South Africa (Cape Province)

Moringa drouhardii Jum.
MORINGACEAE
Tree to 15 m tall; trunk swollen, to 2 m in diameter, covered with smooth white bark; branches numerous at top of trunk; leaves three-pinnate; flower in axillary panicles. Young plant.
Madagascar

Muiria hortense N.E.Br.
MESEMBRYANTHEMACEAE
Plant forming large clumps; leaves fused except for an apical slit, light green, covered with velvety hairs; flowers pink-white.
South Africa (Cape Province)

Myrmecodia lamii
G.Merr. & T.A.Perry
RUBIACEAE
Caudex to 1 m tall, 40 cm thick, spiny, with holes inhabited by ants; stems 10-40 cm long, spiny; leaves to 10 cm long; flowers white. Plant photographed in habitat by Agostino Tomasello.
New Guinea

Myrmecodia lamii
G.Merr. & T.A.Perry
RUBIACEAE
Specimen growing on a tree, photographed in habitat by Agostino Tomasello.

Nananthus transvaalensis (Rolfe) L.Bolus
MESEMBRYANTHEMACEAE
Stems thick; leaves 2-3 cm long, unequal in size, 2-3 cm long, dull green, with large tubercles toward leaf margins; flowers light yellow.
Aloinopsis tramsvaalensis (Rolfe) Schwantes.
South Africa (Transvaal)

Nolina longifolia
(Schult.) Hemsl.
AGAVACEAE
Stem to 2 m tall, base swollen; leaves to 1 m long, dark green with rough margins; flowers cream-white.
Mexico

Nolina microcarpa
S.Watson
AGAVACEAE
Leaves 60-100 cm long, grass-like, apex brush-like; flowers cream-white.
California, Mexico

Nolina recurvata
(Lem.) Hemsl.
AGAVACEAE
Caudex globose over 1 m in diameter; stems few, to 6 m tall; leaves dark green, to 1 m long and 1-2 cm wide; inflorescence branched; flowers white.
Beucarnea recurvata Lem.
Mexico

Nolina recurvata (Lem.) Hemsl.
AGAVACEAE
Flowering plant.

Oophytum nanum (Schltr.) L.Bolus
MESEMBRYANTHEMACEAE
Plant 2 cm tall; leaves fused into bodies 5-7 mm in diameter, green, covered with fine papillae; flowers white with red margins. Plant photographed in habitat by Charles H. Everson.
South Africa (Cape Province)

Orbeopsis lutea (N.E.Br.) L.C.Leach
ASCLEPIADACEAE
Stems branching from base, 5-10 cm high, dentate, 4-angled, green mottled purple; flowers in clusters, 5-7 cm in diameter, very variable in colour: yellow, reddish-brown, variegated red and yellow, ciliate with purple hairs.
Caralluma lutea N.E.Br.
Botswana, Mozambique, South Africa, Zimbabwe

Orbeopsis lutea (N.E.Br.) L.C.Leach ssp. **vaga** (N.E.Br.) L.C.Leach
ASCLEPIADACEAE
A variety with maroon flowers.
Caralluma vaga (N.E.Br.) A.C.White & B.Sloane
Angola, Namibia, South Africa

Orbeopsis melanantha (Schltr.) L.C.Leach
ASCLEPIADACEAE
Stems procumbent, 5-7 cm tall, 4-angled, with acute triangular teeth; flowers 5 cm in diameter, black-brown with concentric grooves and ciliate margins.
Caralluma melanantha (Schltr.) N.E.Br.; *Stapelia furcata* N.E.Br.
Mozambique, South Africa

Ornitogalum sp. Lavranos 26172
LILIACEAE
Undescribed species; bulb to 15 cm in diameter; leaves narrow, 30-40 cm long; flowers yellowish-green.
Southern Africa

Orostachys chanettii (Lév.) A.Berger
CRASSULACEAE
Rosettes small to 1.5 cm in diameter; leaves of two different lengths, linear, grey-green; flowers white with red outside.
China

Orostachys erubescens A.Berger
CRASSULACEAE
Rosettes small growing in clumps; leaves green or grey-green of two different lengths, soft tips; flowers white.
China, Japan, Korea

183

Orostachys spinosum (L.) A.Berger
CRASSULACEAE

Rosettes 8-10 cm in diameter, growing in clumps; leaves of two different lengths, grey-green with white soft spiny tips; flowers yellow.
East CIS, north and central Asia

Oscularia deltoides (L.) Schwantes
MESEMBRYANTHEMACEAE

Shrub 20-30 cm tall, freely branching; stems reddish, with numerous short shoots from axils; leaves blue-grey, 1 cm long, triangular, armed with reddish teeth and ending in a short tip; flowers pink.
South Africa (Cape Province)

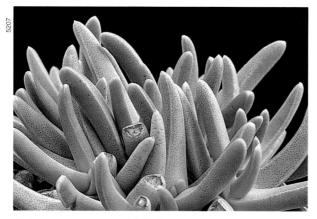

Orthopterum coegana L.Bolus
MESEMBRYANTHEMACEAE

Plant forming small clumps; leaves 3-4 cm long, crowded at stem apices, light green with darker green dots; flowers golden yellow.
South Africa (Cape Province)

Othonna armiana vanJaarsv.
COMPOSITAE

Caudex 3-7 cm in diameter with blackish-brown caudex; stems to 2 cm long, covering the upper surface of caudex; leaves green tinged with purple below; inflorescence to 10 cm tall; flowers yellow.
South Africa (Cape Province)

Orthopterum waltoniae L.Bolus
MESEMBRYANTHEMACEAE

Plant forming small clumps; leaves oblong-lanceolate, 2-3 cm long, light green covered with dark green dots; flowers golden yellow with reddish lower surface.
South Africa (Cape Province)

Othonna cacalioides L.f.
COMPOSITAE

Caudex to 10 cm in diameter, branches very short; leaves arising from woolly tufts of the caudex, to 2.5 cm long, grey-green; inflorescence to 8 cm tall; flowers yellow.
Namibia, South Africa (Cape Province)

Othonna cacalioides L.f.
COMPOSITAE
Flowers.

Othonna capensis Baill.
COMPOSITAE
Plant creeping and forming mats; branches prostrate, to 1 m long and 4 mm thick; leaves cylindrical, fleshy, green to deep red when grown in full sun; inflorescence to 15 cm tall; flowers yellow.
Othonna crassifolia Harv.; *O. filicaulis* Eckl.
South Africa (Cape Province)

Othonna euphorbioides Hutch.
COMPOSITAE
Shrubs to 30 cm in diameter; branches 2 cm thick, covered with peeling yellowish bark; remains of inflorescences persisting, to 4 cm long; leaves caducous, glaucous-green, to 4 cm long; inflorescence 3-5 cm long; flowers greenish-yellow.
South Africa (Cape Province)

Othonna hallii Nord.
COMPOSITAE
Caudex 4-8 cm in diameter with blackish-brown bark; branches very short; leaves deciduous; fleshy, to 8 cm long, glaucous blue-green; inflorescence to 25 cm tall; flowers yellow.
South Africa (Cape Province)

Othonna lepidocaulis Schltr.
COMPOSITAE
Taproot 2.5 cm in diameter, continuing into the stem; leaves caducous, to 9 cm long, glaucous grey-green; inflorescence to 20 cm long; flowers yellow.
South Africa (Cape Province)

Othonna quercifolia DC.
COMPOSITAE
Shrub with small spherical caudex; stems fleshy, slender, arising from caudex; leaves dark green, 6-7 cm long, 2.5 cm wide; inflorescence about 3 cm long; flowers yellow. Photograph by Alberto Marvelli.
Namibia, South Africa (Cape Province)

Othonna retrofracta Jacq.

COMPOSITAE

Caudex with peeling bark; stems to 40 cm tall, light brown; leaves caducous, 3-6 cm long, fleshy, dark or bluish-green; inflorescence to 5 cm long; flowers yellow.

Othonna lamulosa Schinz;
O. litoralis Dtr.;
O. pinnatilobata Sch.Bip.;
O. surculosa Muschl. ex Dtr.

Namibia, South Africa (Cape Province)

Pachyphytum bracteosum Link, Klotzsch & Otto

CRASSULACEAE

Stem to 30 cm tall; leaves whitish-grey, 6-10 cm long, 2-3 cm wide; inflorescence to 30 cm tall; flowers red.
Mexico

Othonna retrofracta Jacq.

COMPOSITAE

Flower.

Pachyphytum bracteosum Link, Klotzsch & Otto

CRASSULACEAE

Flowers.

Oxalis carnosa Molina

OXALIDACEAE

Stems fleshy, erect to sprawling, little branched, to 40 cm tall; leaves on petioles 8 cm long, succulent, shiny above; flowers bright yellow.
Bolivia, Chile, Galapagos Islands, Peru

Pachyphytum brevifolium Rose

CRASSULACEAE

Stem to 25 cm high, branched from base; leaves 2-4 cm long, blue often reddish; flowers carmine to dark red.
Mexico

Pachyphytum compactum Rose
CRASSULACEAE
Stem to 10 cm high; leaves cylindrical, 2-3 cm long, green to grey-white pruinose; flowers reddish. A cristate form.
Mexico

Pachyphytum oviferum J.A.Purpus
CRASSULACEAE
Short stem; leaves obovate 2-4 cm long; 2-2.5 cm wide, reddish or white pruinose; flowers red.
Mexico

Pachyphytum fittkaui Moran
CRASSULACEAE
Stem to 20 cm tall, 1.5 cm thick; leaves 3-5 cm long, flattened, green with grey-white minute spots; flowers red.
Mexico

Pachypodium baronii Const. & Bois var. **windsorii** Pichon
APOCYNACEAE
Stems globose, to 10 cm in diameter; branches thick, cylindrical; spines short; leaves at the ends of branches; flowers red.
Madagascar   CITES App. I

Pachyphytum longifolium Rose
CRASSULACEAE
Stem to 10 cm high; leaves 6 cm long, clavate or lanceolate, grey-green; flowers dark red.
Mexico

Pachypodium bispinosum (L.f.) DC.
APOCYNACEAE
Variant of *P. succulentum* with pink to dull purple flower. Photograph by Gaetano Palisano.
Madagascar   CITES App. II

Pachypodium lamerei Drake
APOCYNACEAE

Tree to 8 m tall, spiny; leaves dark green to 20 cm long, present at growing apices; flowers white. Photograph by Gaetano Palisano.
Madagascar
CITES App. II

Pachypodium namaquanum Welw.
APOCYNACEAE

Stems spiny, to 3 m tall, branching when old; spines brown, 5 cm long; leaves hairy, 8-12 cm long and 2-6 cm wide, clustered at stem apices; flowers brownish-red. Plant photographed in habitat by Charles H. Everson.
Namibia, South Africa (Cape Province)
CITES App. II

Pachypodium rosulatum Baker.
APOCYNACEAE

Caudex large; stems forked, to 3 m tall, spiny; spines to 1 cm long; leaves 3-8 cm long, elliptic; flowers on long peduncles, yellow. Plant photographed in habitat by Paolo Ormas.
Madagascar
CITES App. II

Pachypodium saundersei N.E.Br.
APOCYNACEAE

Stems clavate, with wide base and numerous erect branches; leaves 4-8 cm long, green, hairy; flowers white with red stripes.
South Africa (Natal), Zimbabwe
CITES App. II

Pachypodium succulentum DC.
APOCYNACEAE

Caudex to 15 cm in diameter growing underground in habitat; stems fleshy, branched, 20-60 cm long; leaves 5-8 cm long, 1 cm wide, present on new shoots; spines in pairs, 1-2 cm long; flowers pink.
South Africa (Cape Province)
CITES App. II

Pachypodium succulentum DC.
APOCYNACEAE

Plant photographed in habitat.
CITES App. II

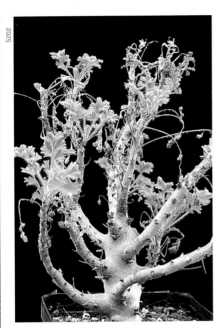

Pelargonium alternans H.Wendl.
GERANIACEAE
Plant to 40 cm tall and 40 cm in diameter; stems glaucous to dark grey-brown, succulent, branched, to 6 cm long; leaves stalked, green, hairy; flowers white to light pink.
South Africa (Cape Province)

Pelargonium histrix Harv.
GERANIACEAE
Plant to 10 cm tall; stems dark grey-black, covered with persistent stipules; leaves bipinnate, hairy; inflorescence to 10 cm tall with creamy white flowers.
South Africa (Cape Province)

Pelargonium echinatum Curtis
GERANIACEAE
Stems fleshy, to 60 cm tall, covered with recurved spines; leaves velvety; flowers white, pink or purple.
South Africa

Pelargonium xerophytum Schltr.
GERANIACEAE
Plant forming large cushions 30-60 cm tall; branches 1 cm thick, woody, green to dark green covered in grey skin and short spines; leaves 1 cm long at tips of branches; flowers white marked with red. Plant photographed in habitat by Charles H. Everson.
Namibia

Pelargonium fulgidum (L.) L'Hér.
GERANIACEAE
Stems succulent, woody, branched, to 60 cm tall; leaves to 10 cm long, silvery; inflorescence branched; flowers pink to scarlet. Plant photographed in habitat by Charles H. Everson.
South Africa

Peperomia asperula Hutchison & Rauh
PIPERACEAE
Stems erect, succulent; leaves to 2 cm long and 1 cm wide at base, folded along main vein, grey-green, translucent above.
Peru

Peperomia columella
Rauh & Hutchison
PIPERACEAE
Stems succulent, erect to sprawling, freely branching; leaves succulent, to 8 mm long and 6 cm wide, green to dark green with translucent shiny windows above.
Peru

Plectranthus ernestii Codd.
LABIATAE
Plant to 25 cm tall; stems thickened at base, to 2 cm in diameter; bark white-brown; leaves erect, 4 cm long, glandular; flowers pale bluish-mauve.
South Africa (Natal)

Peperomia columella
Rauh & Hutchison
PIPERACEAE
Inflorescence.

Plectranthus ernestii Codd.
LABIATAE
Flowers.

Peperomia longespicata DC.
PIPERACEAE
Stems succulent, sprawling, freely branching; leaves slightly succulent, ovate, to 4 cm long, green to dark green.
Central America

Pleiospilos nelii Schwantes
MESEMBRYANTHEMACEAE
Stemless plant, leaves in pairs, semi-cylindrical, grey-green with numerous dark dots; flowers yellow-pink to orange. Photograph by Charles H. Everson.
Pleiospilos pedunculatus L.Bolus
South Africa (Cape Province)

Plumeria hypoleuca Gasp.
APOCYNACEAE
Tree to 7 m tall; leaves green to dark green, to 20 cm long; flowers white.
Central America

Portulaca sp.
PORTULACACEAE
An unidentified species from Mexico, (Nuevo Leon, Sierra el Diablo), with small cylindrical fleshy leaves and terminal flowers.
Mexico

Portulaca cyanosperma Egler
PORTULACACEAE
Tap-root thick; stems cylindrical, green when young, later hairy; leaves cylindrical, greenish to reddish; flowers dark pink.

Portulacaria afra Jacq.
PORTULACACEAE
Shrub much branched; branches spreading, segmented, succulent; leaves obovate to 2 cm long, glossy green; flowers pale pink, in small clusters.
South Africa

Portulaca grandiflora Hook.
PORTULACACEAE
Stems to 30 cm long, ascending or prostrate; leaves cylindrical, to 2.5 cm long, succulent; flowers variable from red to yellow or white.
Argentina, Brazil, Uruguay

Pseudolithos caputviperae Lavranos
ASCLEPIADACEAE
Stems tuberculate, yellowish-grey or grey-green; flowers small, whitish spotted with red. Photograph by Gaetano Palisano.
Somalia

Pseudolithos caputviperae Lavranos
ASCLEPIADACEAE
Mature specimen. Photograph by Gaetano Palisano.

Pseudolithos migiurtinus (Chiov.) P.R.O.Bally
ASCLEPIADACEAE
Stems spherical to 12 cm high and 12 cm wide, pale green to grey-green; flowers 1-1.5 cm in diameter, purple-brown. Photograph by Gaetano Palisano.
Pseudolithos sphaericus (P.R.O.Bally) P.R.O.Bally; *Whitesloanea migiurtina* Chiov.
Somalia

Pseudolithos migiurtinus (Chiovenda) P.R.O.Bally
ASCLEPIADACEAE
Specimen with ripening follicles releasing seeds. Photograph by Gaetano Palisano.

Psilocaulon parviflorum Schwantes
MESEMBRYANTHEMACEAE
Shrubs to 30 cm tall; branches cylindrical; leaves small, opposite, cylindrical; flowers white. Plant photographed in habitat.
South Africa

Pterodiscus sp.
PEDALIACEAE
An unrecognized species with fleshy caudex and erect branches; leaves dark green, hairy below, glabrous above, undulate margins; flowers pale yellow with purple blotch in the tube and suffused mauve lobes.
Kenya

Pterodiscus speciosus Hook.
PEDALIACEAE
Caudex obconic or cylindrical, to 40 cm in diameter; branches few, to 15 cm long; leaves linear with margins dentate; flowers purple-red.
South Africa

Pterodiscus speciosus Hook.
PEDALIACEAE
Flower. Photograph by Gaetano Palisano.

Rosularia alpestris (Kar. & Kiroloff) A.Boriss.
CRASSULACEAE
Small rosettes 1.5-6 cm in diameter; leaves fresh green; flowers white with red stripes.
Sempervivella acuminata (Decne.) A.Berger
Himalayas, Pamir, Tibet

Rabiea albipuncta (Haw.) N.E.Br.
MESEMBRYANTHEMACEAE
Leaves 6-8 together, 2.5 to 4 cm long, green with numerous tuberculate dots; flowers 3 cm in diameter, straw yellow to flesh-coloured. Photograph by Alessandro Mosco.
Aloinopsis albipuncta (Haw.) Schwantes
South Africa (Orange Free State)

Rosularia sedoides (Decne.) H.Ohba
CRASSULACEAE
Small rosettes 2-3.5 cm in diameter; leaves light green, hairy; flowers white.
Sempervivella alba (Edgew.) Stapf.
Kashmir

Rhinephyllum macradenium (L.Bolus) L.Bolus
MESEMBRYANTHEMACEAE
Stems short, woody, covered at base with remains of old leaves; leaves unequal in size, 2-6 cm long, triangular, greenish; flowers yellowish. Plant photographed in habitat.
South Africa (Cape Province)

Rosularia sedoides (Decne.) H.Ohba
CRASSULACEAE
Leaves.

Rosularia sedoides (Decne.) H.Ohba
CRASSULACEAE
Flowers.

Rosularia serpentinica (Werderm.) Muirhead
CRASSULACEAE
Small rosettes; leaves bluish-green; flowers cream-white.
Turkey

Rosularia sempervivum (Marsh & M.Bieb.) A.Berger
CRASSULACEAE
Leaves in small rosettes, grey-green to dark green; flowers whitish to pink.
Iran, Turkey, Syria, Lebanon, Israel

Ruschia diutina
L.Bolus
MESEMBRYANTHEMACEAE
Small shrubs; leaves triangular, fused around stems; flowers white.
Polymita diutina (L. Bolus) L. Bolus
South Africa (Cape Province)

Rosularia sempervivum (Marsh & M.Bieb.) A.Berger
CRASSULACEAE
Flowers.

Ruschia maxima
(Haw.) L.Bolus
MESEMBRYANTHEMACEAE
Shrub 30 cm tall; leaves 4.5 cm long, 2 cm wide, grey to white-grey, 3-angled, compressed laterally with an arcuate keel; flowers pink.
South Africa (Cape Province)

194

Ruschia multiflora (Haw.) Schwantes
MESEMBRYANTHEMACEAE
Shrub to 1 m tall and 2 m in diameter; branches brown with grey skin, erect, forked; leaves fused at base, 1-2 cm long, grey-green with transparent dots; flowers white.
South Africa (Cape Province)

Ruschia perfoliata (Mill.) Schwantes
MESEMBRYANTHEMACEAE
Shrub to 50 cm tall; leaves light grey flushed with red, 1-2 cm long, fused at base, triangular, with a reddish spinescent tip; flowers rose-red.
South Africa (Cape Province)

Ruschia rubricaulis L.Bolus
MESEMBRYANTHEMACEAE
Small shrub with angled reddish branches; leaves 2-4 cm long and 4-6 mm wide, 3-angled, with slight cartilaginous margins, green; flowers pale purple.
South Africa (Cape Province)

Ruschia sarmentosa (Haw.) Schwantes
MESEMBRYANTHEMACEAE
Shrub to 60 cm wide; branches spreading, prostrate, rooting at nodes; leaves light green with transparent dots, triangular with rounded edges and reddish tip; flowers reddish.
South Africa (Cape Province)

Ruschia sp.
MESEMBRYANTHEMACEAE
Unidentified species photographed in habitat.
South Africa (Cape Province)

Sansevieria aethiopica Thunb.
AGAVACEAE
Leaves erect ending in a withered tip, to 50 cm tall and 1.5 cm wide, dark green with pale green bands; flowers white to green. Photograph by Roberto Mangani.
Southern and tropical Africa

Sansevieria conspicua
N.E.Br.

AGAVACEAE

Subterranean rhizome; leaves few, up to 60 cm long and 7 cm wide, dark green with red margins; inflorescence up to 75 cm tall; flowers whitish. Plant photographed in habitat.
Southern Africa

Sansevieria desertii
N.E.Br.

AGAVACEAE

Plant photographed in habitat.

Sansevieria cylindrica
Bojer

AGAVACEAE

Leaves to 75 cm tall, cylindrical, banded with pale green when young; flowers withish-green. Photograph by Roberto Mangani.
Angola

Sansevieria gracilis N.E.Br.

AGAVACEAE

Short stems, to 8 cm long; leaves 20-60 cm long and 9 cm in diameter, dark green. Photograph by Roberto Mangani.
Southern Africa

Sansevieria desertii
N.E.Br.

AGAVACEAE

Subterranean rhizome; leaves to 1 m long and 3 cm wide, deeply sulcate, dull green; flowers white, in clusters. Plant photographed in habitat.
Botswana, Transvaal, Zimbabwe

Sansevieria grandis
Hook.

AGAVACEAE

Few leaves , broadly lanceolate, to 60 cm long and 15 cm wide, dull green with paler marks. Photograph by Roberto Mangani.
Tropical Africa

Sansevieria hyacinthoides
(L.) Druce
AGAVACEAE

Rhizome elongated; leaves up to 45 cm long and 8 cm wide, leaves few, dark green with transverse pale green bands; flowers green-white. Plant photographed in habitat.
Southern Africa

Sansevieria hyacinthoides (L.) Druce
AGAVACEAE
A smaller form photographed in habitat beside an *Aloe* sp.

Sansevieria kirkii Baker
AGAVACEAE
Leaves to 1 m long, 7-8 cm wide, grey-green with paler marks, flat; margins undulate, red-brown. Photograph by Roberto Mangani.
Tropical East Africa

Sansevieria powellii
N.E.Br.
AGAVACEAE

Stems to 50 cm long; leaves arranged in spirals, 40-70 cm long and to 5 cm wide, slightly recurved, banded. Probably a natural hybrid between *S. arborescens* Hort ex Gentil and *S. ehrenbergii* Schweinf. ex Baker. Photograph by Roberto Mangani.

Southern Africa

Sansevieria raffillii
N.E.Br.
AGAVACEAE

Leaves 60-100 cm long and 7-12 cm wide, erect, green with pale spots and bars. Photograph by Roberto Mangani.
Tropical East Africa

Sansevieria rorida (Lanza) N.E.Br.
AGAVACEAE
Stems to 35 cm tall; leaves distichous, triangular, grey-green, ending in a strong spine; inflorescence to 1 m tall, branched; flowers whitish with reddish stripes.
Sanseverina rorida Lanza
Somaliland

Sansevieria singularis N.E.Br.
AGAVACEAE
Leaves to 45 cm long, banded, arising from soil. The photograph shows a young plant. Photograph by Roberto Mangani.
Tropical Africa

Sansevieria trifasciata Prain
AGAVACEAE
Leaves erect, to 75 cm tall, 7 cm wide, in cluster of 1-5 per shoot, glaucous, banded pale and dark green. Photograph by Roberto Mangani.
Nigeria

Sansevieria zeylanica (L.) Willd.
AGAVACEAE
Leaves with light and dark green bands, erect, 45-75 cm long, arranged in rosettes. Photograph by Roberto Mangani.
Sri Lanka

Sarcocaulon crassicaule Rehm
GERANIACEAE
Shrub to 50 cm tall; branches thick with spines 2-3 cm long; leaves caducous, 1.5 cm long, 1 cm wide; flowers white or light pink. Plant photographed in habitat by Charles H. Everson.
Namibia, South Africa (Cape Province)

Sarcocaulon crassicaule Rehm
GERANIACEAE
Flower. Plant photographed in habitat.

Sarcocaulon paniculatum Moffett
GERANIACEAE
Shrub to 10 cm tall, 20 cm in diameter; stems branching at ground level, grey-white; leaves ciliate, 5 cm long; flowers rose to pale pink. Plant photographed in habitat by Charles H. Everson.
Namibia

Sarcocaulon patersonii (DC.) G.Don
GERANIACEAE
Shrub to 50 cm tall, 2 cm long; leaves caducous, 1.2 cm long, 0.8 cm wide; flowers rose pink, light magenta or purple. Plant photographed in habitat by Charles H. Everson.
South Africa

Sarcocaulon rigidum Schinz
GERANIACEAE
Low plant; main stem 3-4 cm thick; branches growing horizontally, 1 cm in diameter, to 15 cm long, with spines to 3 cm long; leaves bilobed, green; flowers bright red. Plant photographed in habitat.
Namibia

Sarcocaulon vanderritiae L.Bolus
GERANIACEAE
Plant to 15 cm tall, 25 cm in diameter; stems 1 cm thick, with thin spines to 3.5 cm long; leaves thick, glabrous; flowers pale pink.
South Africa (Cape Province)

Sarcocaulon vanderritiae L.Bolus
GERANIACEAE
Flower.

Sarcostemma viminale R.Br.
ASCLEPIADACEAE
Stems erect, cylindrical, 5 mm thick, light green, dichotomously branching; leaves inconspicuous; flowers white-yellowish. Photograph by Charles H. Everson.
Namibia, South Africa (Cape Province)

Schlechteranthus hallii L.Bolus
MESEMBRYANTHEMACEAE
Dwarf shrubs with woody roots; leaves to 1 cm long, armed with 1-2 teeth, fused at base to half their length; flowers purple-rose.
Namibia, South Africa (Cape Province)

199

Scilla pauciflora Baker
LILIACEAE
Small bulbs, offsetting and forming large clumps; leaves pale green with dark green marks; flowers greenish.
South Africa

Sedum acre L.
CRASSULACEAE
Low herb, caespitose; stems erect, much branched; leaves imbricated, appressed to one another, 15 mm long, glabrous, light green; flowers bright yellow.
Europe, northern Africa

Sedeveria cv. «Harry Butterfield» Hort
CRASSULACEAE
Hybrid between *Sedum morganianum* Walther and *Echeveria derenbergii* J.A. Purpus. Stems pendent covered with fleshy yellowish-green leaves; flowers pale pink-yellow. Close-up of stem tips.

Sedum cepaea L.
CRASSULACEAE
Plant annual or biennial; leaves linear-ovate, mid-green, in flat rosette elongated to produce a terminal pyramid of flowers; flowers white with a purple keel.
Sedum galioides All.; *S. paniculatus* Lam.
Central and southern Europe

Sedeveria cv. «Harry Butterfield» Hort
CRASSULACEAE
Flowers.

Sedum clavatum Clausen
CRASSULACEAE
Creeping stems, marked with old leaf scars; leaves pale green-glaucous, often tinged red, crowded at the tips of stems; flowers white.
Mexico

Sedum compressum Rose
CRASSULACEAE

Subshrub to 20 cm high; leaves 2 cm long, 1 cm wide, oblanceolate, grey-green with cartilaginous margins, in loose rosettes at the stem tips; flowers golden yellow to orange.
Mexico

Sedum hispanicum L.
CRASSULACEAE

Annual plant, 5-15 cm high, branched from the base; leaves linear to elongate-lanceolate, 1-2.5 cm long, glaucous-green or grey becoming pink; flowers white with a pinkish tipped vein.
Sedum aristatum Ten.; *S. hungaricum* Poir.; *S. puberulum* DC.
Europe, Asia Minor

Sedum dasyphyllum L.
CRASSULACEAE

Low herb, 2-6 cm high; leaves opposite, crowded along the stems, ovate, 3-7 mm long, blue-green, glandular-papillose or pubescent; flowers white with a pink keel. Variable species.
Sedum burnatii Briq.; *S. glanduliferum* Guss.; *S. glaucum* Lam.
North Africa, Europe

Sedum lucidum Clausen
CRASSULACEAE

Stems prostrate to 35 cm long, branched; leaves alternate, elongate, 4 cm long, 6-1.9 mm wide, yellowish-green; flowers white.
Mexico

Sedum frutescens Rose
CRASSULACEAE

Stem stout, arborescent; leaves 2-6 cm long, light green, loosely crowded at the branch tips; flowers white.
Mexico

Sedum moranense Humb., Bonpl. & Kunth.
CRASSULACEAE

Small herbs, branched from the base; leaves 2-3 cm long, 2 mm wide, green with red tips; flowers white.
Mexico

Sedum nussbaumeranum Bitter

CRASSULACEAE

Subshrub to 15 cm high; leaves lanceolate, 4 cm long, yellow-greenish, crowded at the tips of the stems and scattered along lower parts; flowers pure white. Photograph by Roberto Mangani.

Mexico

Sedum rubrotictum cv. «Aurora» Hort

CRASSULACEAE

Stems leafy, erect or decumbent; leaves colour salmon with silvery tinge, red purple in full sun; flowers cream. Photograph by Roberto Mangani.

Sedum oxypetalum Humb., Bonpl. & Kunth.

CRASSULACEAE

Arborescent plant to 90 cm high; stems with several branches, bare at base, with peeling bark; leaves ovate-lanceolate, 2.5-3.8 cm long, bright green; flowers white, flushed purple. The photograph shows a young plant.

Mexico

Sedum spectabile Boreau

CRASSULACEAE

Stems 30-50 cm tall, arising from base annually; leaves 7.5 cm long, 5 cm wide, glabrous green-glaucous, edges faintly dentate; flowers pink.

Japan, central China

Sedum oxypetalum Humb., Bonpl. & Kunth.

CRASSULACEAE

Close-up of leaves.

Sedum treleasii Rose

CRASSULACEAE

Subshrub with woody branches; leaves crowded along the branches, oblong-ovate, 3 cm long, blue-green, grey, pruinose; flowers yellow.

Mexico

Sedum winkleri (Willk.) Wolley-Dod
CRASSULACEAE
Erect stems, few branched, leaves at growing apices, light green-yellowish; flowers white with a reddish-green dorsal vein. Considered a synonym of *S. hirsutum* All.
Iberian peninsula

Sempervivum balcanicum Stoj. & Stef.
CRASSULACEAE
Rosettes 3-4 cm in diameter; leaves green to orange-red, glabrous with dark tip.
Bulgaria

Sempervivum andreanum Wale
CRASSULACEAE
Rosette 1.5-4 cm in diameter; leaves glabrous, margins ciliate, tip reddish-brown: flowers pale pink to red. According to Smith, this is a form of *S. tectorum* L.
Spain

Sempervivum ballsii Wale
CRASSULACEAE
Stolons 1-1.5 cm in diameter, to 10 cm long; rosettes 3 cm in diameter; leaves erect near the centre, 1.8 cm long, yellow-green; flowers pink with red centre.
Greece, Caucasus

Sempervivum arachnoideum L. × **pittonii** Schott, Nyn. Kotschy
CRASSULACEAE
Rosettes 3-4 cm in diameter; leaves pale green with reddish translucent apex with a tuft of hair, margins ciliate; flowers pink or yellow. Natural hybrid.
Austria

Sempervivum charadzae M.Gurgen.
CRASSULACEAE
Rosettes 8-12 cm in diameter, stolons to 30 cm long; leaves pale green, short hairs on upper and lower surfaces; flowers pink-red.
Georgia

Sempervivum cv. «Aglow» Ed Skrochi, USA 1981
CRASSULACEAE
Rosettes 6 cm in diameter; leaves purplish-red, short hairs.

Sempervivum cv. «Bedivere» Ed Skrochi, USA 1973
CRASSULACEAE
Rosettes 2-3 cm in diameter, stoloniferous; leaves green with base and tip purple-red.

Sempervivum cv. «Apache» Martin Haberer, Germany 1980
CRASSULACEAE
Rosettes 4 cm in diameter; leaves elongated, pale green, hairy, ciliate, with a tuft of hair at the tip.

Sempervivum cv. «Belladonna» Sandy McPherson, USA 1970
CRASSULACEAE
Rosettes 5 cm in diameter; leaves purple-red, velvety.

Sempervivum cv. «Aross» Ben Zonneveld, Netherlands 1982
CRASSULACEAE
Rosettes 1-1.5 cm in diameter, stoloniferous; leaves dark red with a tuft of hair at the tip. Hybrid of *S. arachnoideum* L. × *S. ossetiense* Wale.

Sempervivum
cv. «Black Velvet»
David Ford, UK 1985
CRASSULACEAE
Rosettes 5-6 cm in diameter; leaves linear, dark red.

Sempervivum cv. «Bronco» Martin Haberer, Germany 1980
CRASSULACEAE
Rosettes 3-4 cm in diameter; leaves brownish-red, base paler.

Sempervivum cv. «Carmen» Helen Payne, USA
CRASSULACEAE
Rosettes 8 cm in diameter; leaves yellowish-green with brownish-red tip.

Sempervivum cv. «Cafe» David Ford, UK 1984
CRASSULACEAE
Rosettes 2-3 cm in diameter; leaves brownish-green with brown tips.

Sempervivum cv. «Corsair» David Ford, UK 1976
CRASSULACEAE
Rosette 5-7 cm in diameter, very stoloniferous; leaves crimson-red with white long cilia.

Sempervivum cv. «Candy Floss» David Ford, UK 1976
CRASSULACEAE
Rosettes 2-3 cm in diameter; leaves flushed red with long white hairs.

Sempervivum cv. «Dakota» Martin Haberer, Germany
CRASSULACEAE
Rosettes 7-8 cm in diameter; leaves glabrous, brownish-green with pink-purplish base and dark tip.

Sempervivum cv. «Dark Beauty» Tom Lewis, UK
CRASSULACEAE
Rosettes 5-6 cm in diameter; leaves dark, almost black in summer.

Sempervivum cv. «Edge of Night» Kevin Vaughn, USA 1977
CRASSULACEAE
Rosettes 4 cm in diameter; leaves green with brownish-red tip.

Sempervivum cv. «Deepfire» Ed Skrocki, USA 1986
CRASSULACEAE
Rosettes 3-4 cm in diameter, stoloniferous; leaves orange-red with long white cilia.

Sempervivum cv. «El Toro» David Ford, UK
CRASSULACEAE
Rosettes 5-6 cm in diameter; leaves dark red with green tip.

Sempervivum cv. «Director Jacobs» Gustaaf van der Steen, Belgium 1975
CRASSULACEAE
Rosettes 4-5 cm in diameter; leaves numerous, dark red with silvery cilia.

Sempervivum cv. «Excalibur» Ed Skrocki, USA 1972
CRASSULACEAE
Rosettes 3 cm in diameter, stoloniferous; leaves pinkish-green, hairy, base and tip red.

Sempervivum cv. «Festival» Otakar Cmiral, Czech Rep.
CRASSULACEAE
Rosettes 8 cm in diameter; leaves wide, pale green with red tips.

Sempervivum cv. «Georgette» David Ford, UK 1985
CRASSULACEAE
Rosettes 2-2.5 cm in diameter; leaves elongated, pale green to red, very hairy and ciliate.

Sempervivum cv. «Flaming Heart» Patty Brown, USA 1974
CRASSULACEAE
Rosettes 4 cm in diameter; leaves red with green base.

Sempervivum cv. «Gipsy» David Ford, UK 1979
CRASSULACEAE
Rosettes 8 cm in diameter; leaves glabrous, dark red with green base.

Sempervivum cv. «Frosty» David Ford, UK 1985
CRASSULACEAE
Rosettes 3-4 cm in diameter; leaves green, hairy, tip dark brown.

Sempervivum cv. «Greenwich Time» Kevin Vaughn, USA 1968
CRASSULACEAE
Rosettes 2.5-3 cm in diameter; leaves elongated, green tinged pink.

Sempervivum cv. «Greyola» Ed Skrocki, USA 1981
CRASSULACEAE
Rosettes 4 cm in diameter; leaves brownish-green, velvety.

Sempervivum cv. «Jack Frost» Anna Adams, UK
CRASSULACEAE
Rosettes 3.5-4 cm in diameter; leaves green, long cilia.

Sempervivum cv. «Happy» Ed Skrocki, USA 1981
CRASSULACEAE
Rosettes 5-7 cm in diameter; leaves wine-red with green tip.

Sempervivum cv. «Jewel Case» Ed Skrocki, USA 1976
CRASSULACEAE
Dense rosettes 2-3 cm in diameter; leaves glossy red.

Sempervivum cv. «Hot Peppermint» Anna Adams, UK
CRASSULACEAE
Rosettes 3-3.5 cm in diameter; leaves hairy, pale green flushed with red.

Sempervivum cv. «Jungle Fire» Shirley Rempel, USA
CRASSULACEAE
Rosettes 2-3 cm in diameter; leaves dark red flushed with brown.

Sempervivum cv. «King George» A. Hansen, UK
CRASSULACEAE
Rosettes 2 cm in diameter; leaves elongate, hairy.

Sempervivum cv. «Medallion» Ed Skrocki, USA 1976
CRASSULACEAE
Rosettes 5-6 cm in diameter, stoloniferous; leaves flat, brownish.

Sempervivum cv. «Lavander and Old Lace» Helen Payne, USA
CRASSULACEAE
Rosettes 4 cm in diameter; leaves narrow, pink-purple to green-glaucous, silvery cilia.

Sempervivum cv. «Mystic» David Ford, UK 1981
CRASSULACEAE
Rosettes 5-6 cm in diameter; leaves pale green tinged with pink.

Sempervivum cv. «Lilac Time» E. Milton, UK
CRASSULACEAE
Rosettes 5-6 cm in diameter; leaves pale lilac.

Sempervivum cv. «Noir» Nicholas Moore, UK 1950
CRASSULACEAE
Rosettes 6-8 cm in diameter; leaves numerous, reddish-brown.

Sempervivum cv. «Pippin» Betty Brown, USA
CRASSULACEAE
Rosettes 5-6 cm in diameter; leaves with brownish-red tip and long cilia.

Sempervivum cv. «Seminole» Martin Haberer, Germany 1984
CRASSULACEAE
Rosettes 3-3.5 cm in diameter; leaves velvety, grey-green tinged with pink.

Sempervivum cv. «Pixie» Bill Nixon, USA 1972
CRASSULACEAE
Rosettes 2-3 cm in diameter; leaves green to reddish with a tuft of white hair at the apex.

Sempervivum cv. «Superama» Ed Skrocki, USA 1972
CRASSULACEAE
Rosettes 5-6 cm in diameter; leaves green tinged with dark red, long cilia.

Sempervivum cv. «Risque» Kevin Vaughn, USA 1976
CRASSULACEAE
Rosettes 4 cm in diameter; leaves purple-pink.

Sempervivum cv. «Topaz» Goos & Koenemann, Germany 1937
CRASSULACEAE
Rosettes 3 cm in diameter; leaves golden-green with red tips.

Sempervivum cv. «Zaza» Nicholas Moore, UK
CRASSULACEAE
Rosettes 2-3 cm in diameter; leaves glaucous-green with brownish-red tips.

Sempervivum macedonicum Praeger
CRASSULACEAE
Rosette 2-3 cm in diameter, stoloniferous; leaves dark green, often tinged with red, hairy; flowers crimson-red.
Yugoslavia (former)

Sempervivum giuseppii Wale
CRASSULACEAE
Rosettes 2.5-3.5 cm, stoloniferous; leaves pale green, hairy and ciliate, tip red; flowers pink to red. It is probably a hybrid between *S. arachnoideum* L. and *S. cantabricum* J.A.Huber.
Spain

Sempervivum marmoreum Griseb.
CRASSULACEAE
This is a form from Monte Tirone (Italy) with pale green leaves and ciliate margins. It could be a form of *S. italicum* Ricci.
Italy (Alburni)

Sempervivum ingwersenii Wale
CRASSULACEAE
Rosettes 3-4 cm in diameter with numerous reddish stolons up to 15 cm long; leaves 1-1.5 cm long, with red-brownish tip; flowers red with white margins.
Caucasus

Sempervivum marmoreum Griseb. cv. «Brunneifolium»
CRASSULACEAE
Rosette 5 cm in diameter; leaves green, the outer tinged with red, tip brown, margins ciliate; flowers variable, crimson or pink with white margins. The plant illustrated is a cultivar with leaves red in winter and brown in summer.
Eastern Europe

Sempervivum octopodes Turrill var. **apetalum** Turrill
CRASSULACEAE
Rosette 2.5-3 cm in diameter; leaves numerous, green with brownish tinge at the apex; flowers without petals and stamens.
Yugoslavia (former) (Mt Peristeri)

Sempervivum sosnowskii Ter-Chatsch.
CRASSULACEAE
Rosette 6-8 cm in diameter; leaves glabrous, green, tip reddish-brown; flowers yellow.
Caucasus

Sempervivum ossetiense Wale
CRASSULACEAE
Rosette 3 cm in diameter; leaves hairy, pale green with brown tip; flowers crimson with white margins.
Caucasus

Sempervivum tectorum L.
CRASSULACEAE
Extremely variable species, rosettes 3-15 cm in diameter or more; leaves yellow-green to dark green or red-brown, with or without brown tips and purple base, glabrous or hairy; flowers pink. The photograph shows a natural form with leaves brownish-green in summer, and purple-red base.
Pyrenees, Alps, Appennines, northern Balkan regions

Sempervivum reginae-amaliae Heldr. & Guicc.
CRASSULACEAE
Rosettes 2-3 cm in diameter; leaves hairy, ciliate, variable in colour; flowers crimson with median band and white margins. Possibly a form of *S. marmoreum* Griseb.
Albania, Greece

Sempervivum tectorum L.
CRASSULACEAE
This form has red leaves with green tip.

Senecio abbreviatus
S.Moore
COMPOSITAE

Stems prostrate, rooting, 20 cm long and more; leaves very succulent, erect, ovoid, glaucous grey-green with longitudinal translucent stripes; inflorescence to 6 cm tall; flowers yellow. Plant photographed in habitat.

South Africa (Cape Province)

Senecio crassissimus
Humb.
COMPOSITAE

Shrub to 80 cm tall; branches numerous, leafy towards top, leaf-scarred below; leaves to 10 cm long, variable in colour, veined; inflorescence to 100 cm tall; flowers yellow.

Madagascar

Senecio acaulis (L.f.) Sch.Bip.
COMPOSITAE

Plant with tuberous root and short thick stems to 10 cm tall; leaves cylindrical, to 15 cm long, grass green with a longitudinal translucent window; inflorescence to 20 cm tall; flowers yellow.

South Africa (Cape Province)

Senecio crassulifolius (DC.) Sch.Bip.
COMPOSITAE

Plant to 15 cm tall; branches 8-10 cm long, covered with leaves; leaves elliptic to clavate, to 6 cm long, green with red tips when grown in full sun; inflorescence to 20 cm tall; flowers white. Plant photographed in habitat.

Kleinia crassulaefolia DC.
South Africa (Cape Province)

Senecio anteuphorbium (L.) Sch.Bip.
COMPOSITAE

Shrub 1-2.5 m tall; branches glaucous, succulent, ascending, divergent, pale green, striated and with white spots; leaves deciduous, grey-green; inflorescence to 10 cm tall; flowers greenish or yellowish-white.

Kleinia anteuphorbium (L.) Haw.; *K. pteroneura* DC.; *Senecio-pteroneuros* (DC.) Sch.Bip. & Hook.f.
Arabia, Oman, North & East Africa

Senecio crassulifolius (DC.) Sch.Bip.
COMPOSITAE

Plant photographed in habitat.

Senecio ficoides (L.) Sch.Bip.
COMPOSITAE

Shrub to 1 m tall; branches covered in leaf scars below; leaves 10-15 cm long, bluish-white, waxy, with longitudinal translucent stripes; inflorescence 30-60 cm tall; flowers white. Plant photographed in habitat.
Kleinia ficoides (L.) Haw.; *Senecio crassicaulis* Hutch.

Senecio kleinia (L.) Less.
COMPOSITAE

Dichotomously branched shrub up to 3 m tall; leaves 10-20 cm long and 1-2 cm wide, crowded at stem apices, grey-green; inflorescence 6 cm long; flowers white. Plant photographed in habitat.
Kleinia neriifolia Haw.; *Senecio neriifolius* (Haw.) Baill.
Canary Islands (Palma, Gomera, Hierro, Tenerife, Gran Canaria, Lanzarote, Fuerteventura).

Senecio nyikensis Baker
COMPOSITAE

Shrub to 2 m tall with swollen base and soft stems; branches fleshy, glaucous tinged with purple; leaves pale green or purplish; inflorescence 20-40 cm tall; flowers bright red to deep pink.
Central and East Africa

Senecio nyikensis Baker
COMPOSITAE
Flower.

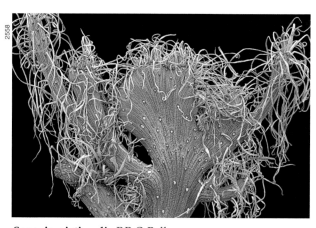

Senecio picticaulis P.R.O.Bally
COMPOSITAE

Plant with swollen base and succulent stems; branches erect, to 30 cm tall; leaves to 11 cm long, cylindrical, deciduous; inflorescence 20 cm tall; flowers bright red. The photograph shows a cristate specimen.
Senecio subulatus (Bally) Jacobs.; *S. subulatifolius* G.D.Rowley
East Africa

Senecio pyramidatus DC.
COMPOSITAE

Shrub to 1.5 m tall with few erect branches; leaves present at the top of branches, cylindrical, 8-12 cm long; inflorescence 15-30 cm tall; flowers yellow.
South Africa (Cape Province)

Senecio radicans (L.f.) Sch.Bip.

COMPOSITAE

Plant prostrate, creeping, forming mats; branches 1 m long or more, with adventitious roots; leaves erect, 2-3 cm long, green to purple in sunny conditions, with a longitudinal window and several translucent stripes; inflorescence to 15 cm long; flowers white. Plant photographed in habitat.

South Africa (Cape Province)

Senecio radicans (L.f.) Sch.Bip.

COMPOSITAE

Plant photographed in habitat.

Senecio scaposus DC.

COMPOSITAE

Plant stemless or with very short stem; few branches, succulent; leaves in rosettes, cylindrical, 3-10 cm long; inflorescence 20-40 cm tall; flowers yellow. Plant photographed in habitat.

South Africa (Cape Province)

Senecio sempervivus (Forssk.) Sch.Bip.

COMPOSITAE

Plant with swollen caudex and soft stems, to 40 cm tall; leaves crowded in terminal rosettes, 5-10 cm long, pale bluish-green sometimes flushed with purple; inflorescence 30-40 cm tall; flowers red to pinkish-purple.

East Africa, Yemen

Senecio serpens G.D.Rowley

COMPOSITAE

Stems prostrate; leaves sub-cylindrical, depressed or grooved on upper surface, light grey-bluish, pruinose; flowers white.

Kleina repens (L.) Haw.; *Senecio repens* (L.) Muschl.; *S. succulentus* Sch.Bip.

South Africa (Cape Province)

Sphalmanthus sp.

MESEMBRYANTHEMACEAE

Unidentified specimen photographed in habitat.

South Africa (Cape Province)

215

Sphalmanthus viridiflorus (Aiton) N.E.Br.
MESEMBRYANTHEMACEAE
Roots woody; stems fleshy, branching, to 40 cm long; leaves green, persisting as short spines after drying; flowers pale green.
Nycteranthus viridiflorus (Aiton) Schwantes

Stapelia gigantea N.E.Br.
ASCLEPIADACEAE
Specimen with yellowish flowers and central depression. Photograph by Gaetano Palisano.

Stapelia comparabilis A.C.White & B.Sloane
ASCLEPIADACEAE
Hybrid between *Stapelia* and *Tromotriche*, similar to *Stapelia incomparabilis* N.E.Br.
South Africa

Stapelia grandiflora Masson
ASCLEPIADACEAE
Stems to 25 cm high, hairy; flowers 13-16 cm in diameter, pale red to brown-purple with yellow transverse lines and covered with purple hairs. Very variable species.
Stapelia ambigua Masson; *S. desmetiana* N.E.Br.; *S. flavirostris* N.E.Br.; *S. spectabilis* Haw.
South Africa (Cape Province)

Stapelia gigantea N.E.Br.
ASCLEPIADACEAE
Stems to 25 cm high, pubescent, 4-angled; leaves caducous, acute, 0.2-0.3 cm long; flowers 12.5-40 cm in diameter, flat or with deep central depression, light yellow to buff, reddish or purplish, covered with pale purplish hairs. A variable species.
S. marlothii N.E.Br.; *S. nobilis* N.E.Br.
Botswana, Kenya, Malawi, Mozambique, Tanzania, Zambia, Zimbabwe

Stapelia grandiflora Masson
ASCLEPIADACEAE
Close-up of flower.
South Africa (Cape Province)

Stapelia hirsuta L.
ASCLEPIADACEAE
Stems erect to 20 cm high, dull green armed with minute teeth; flowers 10-12 cm in diameter, dull reddish-yellow covered with soft purple hairs.
Stapelia pulvinata Donn
South Africa (Cape Province)

Stapelia hirsuta
ASCLEPIADACEAE
Cristate specimen.

Stapelia hirsuta L.
ASCLEPIADACEAE
Close-up of flower of another specimen.

Stapelia incomparabilis N.E.Br.
ASCLEPIADACEAE
Stems 8-15 cm high with toothed angles; flowers 7.5-8.5 cm in diameter, rugose, purple-red sometimes with transverse yellowish lines.
Hybrid of *Stapelia* × *Tromotriche*
South Africa

Stapelia hirsuta L.
ASCLEPIADACEAE
Plant photographed in habitat.

Stapelia mutabilis Jacq.
ASCLEPIADACEAE
Stems to 15 cm high, greyish-green with spreading teeth; flowers 7 cm in diameter, greenish-yellow covered with transverse brownish lines and dots, tips brown. A hybrid of *Stapelia* sp. × *Tromotriche* sp.
Orbea mutabilis Sweet; *Stapelia passerini* Tod.
South Africa

217

Stapelia praeterissa
L.C.Leach
ASCLEPIADACEAE
Erect stems 12-15 cm high, 4-angled, toothed; flowers 3-5 cm in diameter, reddish-purple to dark maroon, covered with fine hairs.
South Africa (Cape Province)

Stapelia sp.
ASCLEPIADACEAE
Probably a hybrid of *Stapelia gettlifei* Pott.

Stapelia prognatha P.R.O.Bally
ASCLEPIADACEAE
Stems to 10 cm long, erect or procumbent, branching from base and forming clumps; ribs toothed; flowers to 3 cm in diameter, blue-purple.
Orbea prognatha (P.R.O.Bally) L.C.Leach
Somalia

Stapelia sp.
ASCLEPIADACEAE
Probably another hybrid of *Stapelia gettlifei* Pott.

Stapelia sp.
ASCLEPIADACEAE
An unrecognized plant found in cultivation. Probably a hybrid of *Stapelia gigantea* N.E.Br.

Stapelia variegata L. var. curtisii (Haw.) N.E.Br.
ASCLEPIADACEAE
Plant caespitose; stems 5-10 cm high with acute teeth along the angles, green or greyish-green mottled purple; flowers 5-8 cm in diameter, greenish-yellow with brown spots. Considered a synonym of *Orbea variegata* Haw.
Orbea curtisii Haw.; *Orbea inodora* Haw.
South Africa (Cape Province)

Stapelia variegata L. var. **pallida** N.E.Br.
ASCLEPIADACEAE
Flowers pale yellow with brownish spots. A plant with unusual six lobed flowers. Considered a synonym of *Orbea (Stapelia) variegata* Haw.
South Africa (Cape Province)

Stapelianthus decaryi Choux
ASCLEPIADACEAE
Stems erect, brownish, 10 cm tall, 7-8-angled, dentate; teeth armed with small spines; flowers cream with dark purple spots, fleshy papillae and minute hairs inside.
Madagascar

Stapelia variegata L. var. **picta** (Donn) N.E.Br.
ASCLEPIADACEAE
Flowers 5-5.5 cm in diameter, yellow or sulphur yellow marked with black-purple transverse stripes and confluent large spots. Considered a synonym of *Orbea (Stapelia) variegata* Haw.
Orbea picta Haw.; *Stapelia picta* Donn
South Africa (Cape Province)

Suadea fruticosa (L.) Forssk.
CHENOPODIACEAE
Shrubs 30-60 cm tall, spreading; leaves linear, thick, sub-cylindrical, to 1 cm long, pale green; flowers inconspicuous, red. Worldwide distributed in salty meadows along shore.

Stapelia variegata L. var. **rugosa** (Donn) N.E.Br.
ASCLEPIADACEAE
Flowers greenish-yellow with dark purple-brown spots and irregular transverse lines. Considered a synonym of *Orbea variegata* Haw.
Orbea rugosa Haw.; *Stapelia rugosa* Donn; *Tridentea rugosa* Schult.
South Africa (Cape Province)

Talinum paniculatum (Jacq.) Gaertn.
PORTULACACEAE
Roots tuberous; stems erect, to 1 m tall; leaves 10 cm long, elliptic; flowers red to yellow.
Southern USA to Central America

Talinum sp. Nuovo Leon
PORTULACACEAE
Leaves fleshy, linear, 6-7 cm long, grey-green; flowers white.
Mexico

Tinospora caffra
(Miers)Troupin
MENISPERMACEAE
Shrubs woody, small; leaves 2-5 cm long, 2-5 cm wide, dark green, pubescent.
Kenya, Sudan, Uganda

Talinum sp. Transvaal
PORTULACACEAE
Small caudex with erect stems; leaves dark green, margins undulate; flowers light yellow.
South Africa (Transvaal)

Titanopsis calcarea
(Marloth) Schwantes
MESEMBRYANTHEMACEAE
Rosettes 10 cm wide; leaves 2.5 cm long with truncate tips, densely covered with grey-white tubercles; flowers golden yellow to almost orange. Photograph by Alessandro Mosco.
South Africa (Cape Province)

Tanquana prismatica (Schwantes) H.E.K.Hartmann & Liede
MESEMBRYANTHEMACEAE
Leaves triangular, 3-4 cm long, green to grey with dark spots, convex lower surface; leaves in pairs, 1-2 pairs of leaves from each shoot, forming small clumps; flowers yellow.
Pleiospilos prismaticus (Marloth) Schwantes.
South Africa (Cape Province)

Trachyandra saltii (Baker) Oberm.
LILIACEAE
Bulbous plant with basal green leaves.
South Africa

Trachyandra tortilis
(Baker) Oberm.
LILIACEAE
Bulbous plant to 25 cm tall; leaves basal, folded transversely. Photograph by Charles H. Everson.
South Africa

Tradescantia zebrina Hort. ex Boiss
COMMELINACEAE
Stems creeping, rooting at nodes; leaves to 10 cm long, 1.5-3.5 cm wide, succulent, green or purple, hairy, often with silver stripes; flowers pink or violet-blue.
Tradescantia pendula (Schniz.) D.R.Hunt; *Zebrina pendula* Schniz.
Mexico

Tradescantia navicularis Ortgies
COMMELINACEAE
Stems creeping, rooting and forming mats; leaves 1-3 cm long, canaliculate, green above, purple beneath; flowers magenta or mauve. Plant photographed in habitat by Alessandro Mosco.
Callisia navicularis (Ortgies) D.R.Hunt
Mexico

Tradescantia zebrina Hort. ex Boiss
COMMELINACEAE
Flower.

Tradescantia navicularis Ortgies
COMMELINACEAE
Close-up of flowers.

Trichocaulon cactiforme N.E.Br.
ASCLEPIADACEAE
Stem sub-cylindrical, 10 cm tall, 5-6 cm thick, tuberculate, grey-green; flowers 1-1.5 cm in diameter, pale yellow spotted with red. Variable species. Photograph by Gaetano Palisano.
South Africa (Cape Province)

Trichocaulon cactiforme N.E.Br.
ASCLEPIADACEAE
Close-up of flowers. Photograph by Gaetano Palisano.

Trichocaulon dinterii A.Berger
ASCLEPIADACEAE
Stems globose, branched from base, 4-6 cm long, 3-5 cm wide, tuberculate, dull green; flowers 7-8 mm in diameter, light coloured at base with red-brown spots which are more dense and confluent on lobes. Plant photographed in habitat by Charles H. Everson.
Namibia

Trichocaulon affinis cactiforme N.E.Br.
ASCLEPIADACEAE
Stems sub-cylindrical, tuberculate, branched from base; flowers whitish spotted with red. Probably a form of *T. cactiforme* N.E.Br.
South Africa

Trichocaulon dinterii A.Berger
ASCLEPIADACEAE
Flowering specimen. Photograph by Alberto Marvelli.
Namibia

Trichocaulon affinis cactiforme N.E.Br.
ASCLEPIADACEAE
Close-up of flowers.

Trichocaulon simile N.E.Br.
ASCLEPIADACEAE
Stems erect, globose; 4-5 cm tall, 4 cm wide, grey-green, tuberculate; flowers yellowish spotted with red.
South Africa

3625

Trichocaulon sp.
ASCLEPIADACEAE
Unidentified species with erect cylindrical stems 15-20 cm tall, 5 cm in diameter, grey-green, tuberculate; flowers whitish marked with purple-brown. It could be a form of *T. perlatum* Dinter. Photograph by Gaetano Palisano.
South Africa

2065

Trichodiadema intonsum (Haw.) Schwantes
MESEMBRYANTHEMACEAE
Stems 15-25 cm tall; leaves 1.5 cm long, semi-cylindrical, covered with grey papillae and 8-10 brown bristles at tip; flowers white or pink.
South Africa (Cape Province)

2636

Tridentea gemmiflora (Masson) Haw.
ASCLEPIADACEAE
Stems 7-15 cm tall, greyish-green, glabrous; angles obtuse, toothed; flowers 8 cm in diameter, black-brown or violet-brown, lobes mottled with yellow spots at base.
Stapelia gemmiflora Masson; *Tridentea stygia* Haw.
South Africa (Cape Province)

4008

Tridentea longipes (C.A.Luckh.) L.C.Leach
ASCLEPIADACEAE
Stems glabrous, much branched, green; angles toothed; flowers light red-brown. Photograph by Charles H. Everson.
South Africa (Cape Province)

2478

Tylecodon buchholzianus (Schuldt & P.Stephan) Toelken
CRASSULACEAE
Shrub with swollen base; branches 30 cm long, leaves usually linear, 0.5-1.5 cm long, 0.2-0.3 cm wide, but very variable in shape and size, dull green with brown stripes; flowers pink to deep red.
Cotyledon buchholziana Schuldt & P.Stephan
Namibia, South Africa (Cape Province)

3357

Tylecodon ellephiae vanJaarsv.
CRASSULACEAE
Caudex subterranean, 1-3 cm in diameter, light brown with yellowish-grey peeling flakes; branches grey-green, to 2 cm long; leaves ovate, 2-4 cm long; flowers yellow-green.
South Africa (Cape Province)

Tylecodon paniculatus (L.f.) Toelken

CRASSULACEAE

Stem to 1.5 m high, much branched and with yellow peeling bark; leaves 6-12 cm long, 3-10 cm wide, obovate, green to yellowish-green; flowers yellow-orange to red. Plant photographed in habitat.

Cotyledon fascicularis Ait.; *C. mollis* Dinter; *C. paniculata* L.f.; *C. tardiflora* Bonpl.

Namibia, South Africa (Cape Province)

Tylecodon paniculatus (L.f.) Toelken

CRASSULACEAE

Specimen 25 years old. Photograph by Charles H. Everson.

Tylecodon paniculatus (L.f.) Toelken

CRASSULACEAE

Flowers.

Tylecodon pearsonii (Schönl.) Toelken

CRASSULACEAE

Stem with swollen base 15 cm high, few branches, with brown peeling bark; leaves linear-lanceolate, 1.5-4 cm long, 0.2-0.4 cm wide, grey-green to greyish-brown; flowers pale brown.

Cotyledon pearsonii Schönl.

Namibia, South Africa (Cape Province)

Tylecodon reticulatus (L.f.) Toelken

CRASSULACEAE

Stem fleshy, swollen towards base, covered with yellow-brown peeling bark; leaves cylindrical to 5 cm long, greyish-green to yellow-green; flowers yellowish-green.

Cotyledon reticulata L.f.

Namibia, South Africa (Cape Province)

Tylecodon reticulatus (L.f.) Toelken

CRASSULACEAE

Plant photographed in habitat.

Tylecodon schaeferianus (Dinter) Toelken
CRASSULACEAE
Underground tuber with one to several branches to 15 cm long with pale flaking bark; leaves elliptic to obovate 0.8-2 cm long, 0.3-1.5 cm wide, green to pale brown with red stripes; flowers pink-violet rarely white. Close-up of flowers.
Cotyledon schaeferiana Dinter; *C. sinis-alexandri* Poelln.
Namibia, South Africa (Cape Province)

Tylecodon scadens vanJaarsv.
CRASSULACEAE
Small plant with short «zig-zag» branches and small succulents leaves.
South Africa (Cape Province)

Tylecodon striatus (Hutchison+) Toelken
CRASSULACEAE
Tuberous base; few branches, erect, to 25 cm long with remains of old leaves attached; leaves linear, 3.5 cm long, 0.2-0.5 cm wide, greyish-green; flowers yellowish-green with red-brown veins. Young specimen.
Cotyledon striata Hutchison
South Africa (Cape Province)

Tylecodon wallichii (Harv.) Toelken
CRASSULACEAE
Stems erect, to 80 cm high, much branched, covered with elongate phyllopodia; leaves linear 6-12 cm long, grey-green to grey-brown; flowers yellow. Photograph by Charles H. Everson.
Cotyledon wallichii Harv.
South Africa (Cape Province)

Tylecodon wallichii (Harv.) Toelken
CRASSULACEAE
Plant photographed in habitat.

Umbilicus horizontalis (Guss.) DC.
CRASSULACEAE
Bulbous plant with annual succulent stems up to 30 cm tall; leaves 3-10 cm in diameter, circular with undulate margins, brownish-green; inflorescence horizontal; flowers reddish-greenish. Plant photographed in habitat.
Mediterranean regions

Umbilicus rupestris (Salisb.) Dandy
CRASSULACEAE
Tuber to 5 cm in diameter; leaves on long petioles, green sometimes lined with reddish, or brown-red in sunny conditions; flowers greenish.
Umbilicus pendulinus DC.
Mediterranean regions

Uncarina grandidieri (Baill.) Stapf.
PEDALIACEAE
Tree to 2.5 m tall; leaves 5-7-lobed, pubescent; flowers yellow.
Harpagophytum grandidieri Baill.
Madagascar

Uncarina roeoesliana Rauh
PEDALIACEAE
Tree to 2 m tall; caudex thick; leaves to 12 cm long, to 2 cm wide, variable in shape, margins undulate; flowers yellow.
Madagascar

Veltheimia capensis (L.) DC.
LILIACEAE
Bulbs to 13 cm long, ovoid, flattened at base; leaves 30 cm long, 4 cm wide, glaucous-green; flowers white-pink or with red spots. Photograph by Charles H. Everson.
South Africa (Cape Province)

Welwitschia mirabilis Hook.f.
WELWITSCHIACEAE
Plant with shallow tap-root and many lateral roots just below the soil surface. Each plant has a short, nearly circular trunk, dark grey, fissured. Only two opposite leaves are produced from marginal grooves on the crown, each splitting into many parallel sections, twisting. The leaves continue to grow throughout the life of the plant, and in habitat may reach a length of 4 m and over. Male cones. *Welwitschia bainesii* (Hook.f.) Carr
Angola, Namibia

Welwitschia mirabilis Hook.f.
WELWITSCHIACEAE
Female cones.

CITES App. II

Xerosicyos pubescens Keraudren
CUCURBITACEAE
Caudex hemispherical to 2 m in diameter, covered with silver grey bark; stems thin, pubescent; leaves triangular, green, woolly; flowers inconspicuous.
Madagascar

Yucca brevifolia Engelm.
AGAVACEAE
Arborescent plant, to 9 m tall, branching, fissured bark; leaves 40 cm long and 4 cm wide at the base, green to brownish green, yellow-green denticulate margins; inflorescence 50 cm tall; flowers yellow to cream, tinged with green, malodorous. Plant photographed in habitat.
USA (California to SW Utah).

Yucca aloifolia L. cv. «Tricolor»
AGAVACEAE
Stems to 8 m tall; leaves 40 cm long, 6 cm wide at base, ending in a pungent tip, green striped yellow or with central white stripe; flowers white.

Yucca elephantipes A.Regel
AGAVACEAE
Arborescent plant, to 10 m tall, densely branching; leaves stiff, 50-100 cm long; inflorescence to 1 m tall; flowers white.
Yucca guatemalensis Baker
Guatemala, Mexico

Yucca aloifolia L. var. **draconis** (L.) Engelm.
AGAVACEAE
This variety differs from the type in having larger and more flexible leaves.
Yucca draconis L.
Mexico

Yucca filifera Chabaud
AGAVACEAE
Arborescent plant, to 10 m tall; leaves 55 cm long, 5 cm wide at base, glaucous; inflorescence to 1.5 m tall, cylindric; flowers cream-white.
Mexico

Yucca gloriosa L.
AGAVACEAE

Stems to 2.5 m tall, rarely branched; leaves to 60 cm long, 7 cm wide at base, glaucous; inflorescence to 1.5 m tall; flowers creamy-white, sometimes tinged with red or green.
Mexico

Yucca vomerensis Spreng.
AGAVACEAE

Hybrid between *Y. aloifolia* L. and *Y. gloriosa* L. with thick leaves; inflorescence to 2 m tall and flowers white tinged with green.
Garden origin

Yucca treculeana Carr
AGAVACEAE

Stems to 5 m tall; leaves blue-green, to 110 cm long, 7 cm wide at base; flowers white sometimes tinged with purple.
Mexico, USA (Texas)

Zygophyllum fontanesii Webb & Berthel.
ZYGOPHYLLACEAE

Small shrub, succulent, with woody base, branching; stems 10-60 cm tall, greyish-yellowish to light brown; leaves up to 2.5 cm long, glaucous-green to yellow, sub-cylindrical; flowers white-pinkish. Plant photographed in habitat.
Macaronesia

Yucca treculeana Carr
AGAVACEAE

Flowers.

Zygophyllum fontanesii Webb & Berthel.
ZYGOPHYLLACEAE

Flowers.
Macaronesia

CHECKLIST OF ALTERNATIVE NAMES

The following list contains some of the synonyms in common use.
This is a partial listing, and several obsolete names that are seldom used have been omitted.

Genus	Species	... See
Adromischus	cuneatus	Adromischus cooperi
	estivus	Adromischus cooperi
	halesowensis	Adromischus cooperi
Adromischus	juttae	Adromischus schuldtianus ssp. juttae
Aeonium	bertoletianum	Aeonium tabulaeforme
	caespiitosum	Aeonium simsii
	macrolepum	Aeonium tabulaeforme
Agave	colymus	Agave potatorum
	engelmannii	Agave polyacantha
	filamentosa	Agave filifera
	mitis	Agave celsii var. albicans
	rigida var. elongata	Agave fourcroydes
	saundersii	Agave potatorum
	verschaffeltii	Agave potatorum
Aloe	albo-cincta	Aloe striata
	bainesii	Aloe barberae
	bayfieldii	Gasterhaworthia bayfieldii X
	davyana	Aloe greatheadii var. davyana
	gariusana	Aloe gariepensis
	hanburyana	Aloe striata
	hodocincta	Aloe striata
	paniculata	Aloe striata
	punctata	Aloe variegata
Aloinopsis	albipuncta	Rabiea albipuncta
	tramsvaalensis	Nananthus transvaalensis
Anacampseros	alstonii	Avonia quinaria ssp. alstonii
	dinteri	Avonia dinteri
	meyeri	Avonia papyracea ssp. namaensis
	papyracea	Avonia papyracea
	recurvata	Avonia recurvata
	rhodesica	Avonia rhodesica
Antegibbaeum	fissoides	Gibbaeum fissoides

Genus	Species	... See
Asclepias	carnosa	Hoya carnosa
Beucarnea	recurvata	Nolina recurvata
Bryophyllum	calycinum	Kalanchoe pinnata
Callisia	navicularis	Tradescantia navicularis
Caralluma	lutea	Orbeopsis lutea
	melanantha	Orbeopsis melanantha
	vaga	Orbeopsis lutea ssp. vaga
Cephalophyllum	cupreum	Jordaaniella cupriata
Conophytum	calitzdorpense	Conophytum truncatum var. wiggettiae
	helenae	Conophytum tantillum ssp. helenae
	wiggettiae	Conophytum truncatum var. wiggettiae
Cotyledon	ausana	Cotyledon orbiculata
	buchholziana	Tylecodon buchholzianus
	elata	Cotyledon orbiculata
	fascicularis	Tylecodon paniculatus
	mollis	Tylecodon paniculatus
	paniculata	Tylecodon paniculatus
	pannosa	Kalanchoe eriophylla
	pearsonii	Tylecodon pearsonii
	ramosa	Cotyledon orbiculata
	reticulata	Tylecodon reticulatus
	spuria	Cotyledon orbiculata var. spuria
	striata	Tylecodon striatus
	tardiflora	Tylecodon paniculatus
	teretifolia	Cotyledon campanulata
	wallichii	Tylecodon wallichii
	schaeferiana	Tylecodon schaeferianus
	sinis-alexandri	Tylecodon schaeferianus
Crassula	alooides	Crassula hemisphaerica
	anthurus	Crassula perforata

Genus	Species	... See
Crassula	bakeri	Crassula grisea
	bolusii	Crassula cooperi
	conjuncta	Crassula perforata
	decipiens	Crassula tecta
	hystrix	Crassula hirtipes
	lucens	Crassula portulacea
	monticola	Crassula rupestris
	nitida	Crassula portulacea
	obvallata	Crassula albiflora
	perfilata	Crassula perforata
	punctulata	Crassula biplanata
	rhomboidea	Crassula deltoidea
Duvalia	compacta	Huernia compacta
	procumbens	Huernia procumbens
Echeveria	akontiophylla	Echeveria subalpina
	elegans	Echeveria harmsii
	palmeri	Echeveria subrigida
	peacockii	Echeveria subsessilis
	pusilla	Echeveria amoena
	sanguinea	Echeveria atropurpurea
	sangusta	Echeveria subrigida
	schaffneri	Echeveria paniculata
	scopulorum	Echeveria obtusifolia
Echinothamnus	pechuelii	Adenia pechuelii
Euphorbia	antankara	Euphorbia pachypodioides
	boyeri	Euphorbia milii
	breviarticulata	Euphorbia grandicornis
	decariana	Euphorbia hedyotoides
	elliptica	Euphorbia silenifolia
	enneagona	Euphorbia aggregata
	glomerata	Euphorbia globosa
	milii	
	var. bosseri	Euphorbia neobosseri
	regis-jubae	Euphorbia obtusifolia
	rhipsaloides	Euphorbia tirucalli
	rubella	Euphorbia brunellii
	rubella	
	var. brunellii	Euphorbia brunellii
	splendens	
	var. vulcanii	Euphorbia milii var. vulcani
	viminalis	Euphorbia tirucalli
Fureraea	lindenii	Furcraea selloa var. marginata
Gasteria	nigricans	Gasteria brachyphylla
	angustianum	Gasteria brachyphylla
	decipiens	Gasteria nitida
	ernsti-ruschii	Gasteria pillansii var. ernsti-ruschii
	maculata	Gasteria bicolor

Genus	Species	... See
Gasteria	poellnitziana	Gasteria pulchra
	verrucosa	Gasteria carinata var. verrucosa
Guillauminia	albiflora	Aloe albiflora
Haemanthus	nelsonii	Haemanthus humilis ssp. hirsutus
Haworthia	caespitosa	Haworthia retusa
	concava	Haworthia cymbiformis
	concinna	Haworthia viscosa
	correcta	Haworthia emelyae
	eilyae	Haworthia glauca var. herrei
	emelyae	
	var. comptoniana	Haworthia comptoniana
	graminifolia	Haworthia blackburniae var. graminifolia
	reticulata	Haworthia guttata
	habdomadis	
	var. inconfluens	Haworthia mucronata var. inconfluens
	helmiae	Haworthia mucronata var. helmiae
	herrei	Haworthia glauca var. herrei
	inconfluens	Haworthia mucronata var. inconfluens
	lepida	Haworthia cymbiformis
	planifolia	Haworthia cymbiformis
	margaritifera	Haworthia pumila
	maxima	Haworthia pumila
	mcmurtryi	Haworthia koelmaniorum
	otzenii	Haworthia mutica
	rycroftiana	Haworthia mucronata var. rycroftiana
	schmidtiana	Haworthia nigra
	turgida	Haworthia retusa
	unicolor	
	var. helmiae	Haworthia mucronata var. helmiae
	willowmorensis	Haworthia mirabilis
	woolleyi	Haworthia venosa woolleyi
Hoya	coriacea	Hoya multiflora
Huernia	appendiculata	Huernia hystrix
	bicampanulata	Huernia kirkii
	cellata	Huernia guttata
	echidnopsioides	Huernia echidnopsioides
	guttata sensu	Huernia plowesi
	olentiginosa	Huernia guttata
	pillansi ssp.	Huernia echidnopsioides
Idria	columnaris	Fouquieria columnaris

Genus	Species	... See
Kalanchoe	diversa	Kalanchoe lanceolata
	globulifera	
	var. coccinea	Kalanchoe blossfeldiana
	grandiflora	Kalanchoe marmorata
	heterophylla	Kalanchoe lanceolata
	ohlfsii	Kalanchoe laciniata
	schweinfurthii	Kalanchoe laciniata
Kleina	repens	Senecio serpens
	anteuphorbium	Senecio anteuphorbium
	crassulaefolia	Senecio crassulifolius
	ficoides	Senecio ficoides
	neriifolia	Senecio kleinia
	pteroneura	Senecio anteuphorbium
Klinja	namaquensis	Gethyllis namaquensis
Lithops	translucens	Lithops herrei
Monanthes	dasyphylla	Monanthes minima
	niphophila	Monanthes brachycaulos
	praegei	Monanthes brachycaulos
	silensis	Monanthes pallens
Nananthus	malherbei	Aloinopsis malherbei
	orpenii	Aloinopsis orpenii
Nycteranthus	viridiflorus	Sphalmanthus viridiflorus
Orbea	curtisii	Stapelia variegata var. curtisii
	inodora	Stapelia variegata var. curtisii
	mutabilis	Stapelia mutabilis
	picta	Stapelia variegata var. picta
	prognatha	Stapelia prognatha
	rugosa	Stapelia variegata var. rugosa
Othonna	crassifolia	Othonna capensis
	filicaulis	Othonna capensis
	lamulosa	Othonna retrofracta
	litoralis	Othonna retrofracta
	pinnatilobata	Othonna retrofracta
	surculosa	Othonna retrofracta
Pleiospilos	pedunculatus	Pleiospilos nelii
	prismaticus	Tanquana prismatica
Pseudolithos	sphaericus	Pseudolithos migiurtinus
Rochea	albiflora	Crassula albiflora
	coccinea	Crassula coccinea
Sedum	aristatum	Sedum hispanicum
	burnatii	Sedum dasyphyllum

Genus	Species	... See
Sedum	galioides	Sedum cepaea
	glanduliferum	Sedum dasyphyllum
	glaucum	Sedum dasyphyllum
	hungaricum	Sedum hispanicum
	paniculatus	Sedum cepaea
	puberulum	Sedum hispanicum
Sempervivella	acuminata	Rosularia alpestris
	alba	Rosularia sedoides
Senecio	crassicaulis	Senecio ficoides
	neriifolius	Senecio kleinia
	pteroneuros	Senecio anteuphorbium
	repens	Senecio serpens
	subulatifolius	Senecio picticaulis
	subulatus	Senecio picticaulis
	succulentus	Senecio serpens
Stapelia	ambigua	Stapelia grandiflora
	ciliata	Diplocyatha ciliata
	desmetiana	Stapelia grandiflora
	flavirostris	Stapelia grandiflora
	furcata	Orbeopsis melanantha
	gemmiflora	Tridentea gemmiflora
	marlothii	Stapelia gigantea
	nobilis	Stapelia gigantea
	passerini	Stapelia mutabilis
	picta	Stapelia variegata var. picta
	pulvinata	Stapelia hirsuta
	rugosa	Stapelia variegata var. rugosa
	spectabilis	Stapelia grandiflora
	reclinata	Duvalia reclinata
Tacitus	bellus	Graptopetalum bellum
Testudinaria	elephantipes	Dioscorea elephantipes
Trichocaulon	alstonii	Hoodia alstonii
Tridentea	rugosa	Stapelia variegata var. rugosa
	stygia	Tridentea gemmiflora
Tromotriche	ciliata	Diplocyatha ciliata
Welwitschia	bainesii	Welwitschia mirabilis
Whitesloanea	migiurtina	Pseudolithos migurtinus
Yucca	draconis	Yucca aloifolia var. draconis
	guatemalensis	Yucca elephantipes
Zebrina	pendula	Tradescantia pendula

231

FURTHER READING

GENERAL

Arnold T.H., de Wet B.C. (eds.), 1993: Plants of southern Africa: names and distribution. *Memoirs of the Botanical Survey of South Africa*, No. 62.

Bramwell D., Bramwell Z., 1990: *Flores Silvestres de las Islas Canarias*. Editorial Rueda S.L., Madrid, Spain.

Brummitt R.K., Powell C.E., 1992: *Authors of plant names*. Royal Botanic Gardens, Kew, UK.

Court D., 1981: *Succulent flora of southern Africa*. A.A. Balkema, Rotterdam, The Netherlands.

Eggli U., 1994: *Sukkulenten*. Ulmer, Stuttgart, Germany.

Griffiths M., 1994: *The New Royal Horticultural Society Index of Garden Plants*. Macmillan Press Ltd, London, UK.

Huxley A., Griffiths M., 1992: *The New Royal Horticultural Society Dictionary of Gardening*. Macmillan Press Ltd, London, UK.

Index Kewensis on compact disc, 1997. Oxford University Press, Oxford, UK.

Jacobsen H., 1960: *A Handbook of Succulent Plants* (3 vols.). Blandford Press, Poole, UK (reprint 1978).

Palgrave K.C., 1977: *Trees of Southern Africa*. C. Struik, Cape Town, South Africa.

Smith G.F., van Jaarsveld E., Arnold T.H., Steffens F.E., Dixon R.D., Retief J.A., 1997: *List of Southern African Succulent Plants*. Umdaus Press, Pretoria, South Africa.

Rauh W., 1984: *The Wonderful World of Succulents*. Smithsonian Press, Washington D.C., USA.

Rauh W., 1995: *Succulent and Xerophytic Plants of Madagascar* - Volume I. Strawberry Press, Mill Valley, California, USA.

Rauh W., 1998: *Succulent and Xerophytic Plants of Madagascar* - Volume II. Strawberry Press, Mill Valley, California, USA.

Rowley G.D., 1986: *Piante Grasse*. Zanichelli, Bologna, Italy.

Rowley G.D., 1987: *Caudiciform & Pachycaul Succulents*. Strawberry Press, Mill Valley, California, USA.

Sajeva M., Costanzo M., 1994: *Succulents: The Illustrated Dictionary*. Cassell plc, London, UK.

Willert D.J., Eller B.M., Werger M.J.A., Brinckmann E., Ihlenfeldt H.D., 1992: *Life Strategies of Succulents in Deserts*. Cambridge University Press, Cambridge, UK.

CITES

Carter S., Eggli U., 1997: *The CITES Checklist of Succulent Euphorbia Taxa (Euphorbiaceae)*. German Federal Agency for Nature Conservation, Bonn, Germany.

Davis A.P., 1999: *CITES Bulb Checklist*. Royal Botanic Gardens, Kew, UK.

Eggli, U. *et al.* (in prep.): *CITES Aloe and Pachypodium Checklist*. Royal Botanic Gardens, Kew, UK and Städtische Sukkulenten-Sammlung, Zürich, Switzerland.

Hunt. D., 1992: *CITES Cactaceae Checklist*. Royal Botanic Gardens, Kew, UK.

Hunt D., 1999: *CITES Cactaceae Checklist* (Second Edition). Royal Botanic Gardens, Kew, UK.

Mereu U., 1995: *Commercio e tutela di animali e piante. Guida alla regolamentazione del commercio e della detenzione di esemplari e prodotti derivati da specie animali e vegetali tutelate dalla Convenzione di Washington - CITES*. EdAs - Editori Associati per la Comunicazione, Frascati, Italy.

Roberts J.A., Beale C.R., Benseler J.C., McGough H.N., Zappi D.C., 1995: *CITES Orchid Checklist Volume 1*. Royal Botanic Gardens, Kew, UK.

Roberts J.A., Allman L.R., Beale C.R., Butter R.W., Crook K.R., McGough H.N., 1997: *CITES Orchid Checklist Volume 2*. Royal Botanic Gardens, Kew, UK.

Sajeva M., Cattabriga A., Orlando A.M., Oddo E., 1992: Manuale per l'identificazione delle Cactaceae e di altre piante succulente incluse nell'Appendice I della CITES. *Piante Grasse*, **12**(suppl.): 1-31.

Sajeva M., Orlando A.M., 1990: Manuale per l'identificazione delle Cactaceae incluse nell'Appendice I della Convenzione Internazionale sul Commercio di Specie di Flora e Fauna minacciate da estinzione (CITES). *Piante Grasse,* **9**(suppl.): 1-32.

Sandison M.S., Clemente Muñoz M., de Konig J., Sajeva M., 1999: *CITES and Plants - A Users Guide*. Royal Botanic Gardens, Kew, UK.

Wijnstekers W., 1992: *The Evolution of CITES*. Secretariat of the Convention on International Trade in Endangered Species of Wild Flora and Fauna (3rd Edition). Lausanne, Switzerland.

AGAVACEAE

Chahinian B.J.,1986: *The Sansevieria trifasciata Varieties*. Trans Terra Publ., Reseda, California, USA.

Gentry H.S., 1982: *Agaves of Continental Northern America*. University of Arizona Press, Tucson, Arizona, USA.

Matuda E., Pina Lujan I., 1980: *Las Plantas Mexicanas del Genero Yucca.* Coleccion Miscelanea Estado de Mexico, Toluca, Mexico.

Ulrich B., 1992: On the discovery of Agave schidigera Lemaire and status of certain taxa of the section Xysmagave Berger. *British Cactus & Succulent Journal,* **10**: 61-70.

ASCLEPIADACEAE

Bruyns P.V., 1985: Notes on Ceropegias of the Cape Province. *Bradleya*, **3**: 1-47.

Bruyns P.V., 1988: A revision of the genus Echidnopsis Hook.f. (Asclepiadaceae). *Bradleya*, **6**: 1-48.

Dyer R.A., 1983: *Ceropegia, Brachystelma and Riocreuxia in Southern Africa.* A.A. Balkema, Rotterdam, The Netherlands.

Gilbert M.G., 1990: A review of Caralluma R.Br. and its segregates. *Bradleya*, **8**: 1-32.

Kloppenburg D., Wayman A., 1992: *The Hoya Handbook - a guide for grower & collector.* Orca Publishing Co., Medford, USA.

Masson F., 1796: *Stapeliae Novae: or, a collection of several new species of that genus; discovered in the interior parts of Africa. By Francis Masson.* Reprint by Le Lettere, Firenze, Italy (1998).

White A., Sloane B.L., 1937: *The Stapeliae.* Abbey San Encino Press, Pasadena, California, USA.

BROMELIACEAE

Rauh W., 1979: *Bromeliads for Home, Garden and Greenhouse.* Blandford Press, Poole, UK.

COMPOSITAE

Halliday P., 1988: Noteworthy Species of Kleinia. *Hooker's Icones Plantarum,* vol. 39, part IV.

Rowley G.D., 1994: *Succulent Compositae.* Strawberry Press, Mill Valley, California, USA.

CRASSULACEAE

Evans R.L., 1983: *Handbook of Cultivated Sedum.* Science Reviews Ltd., Northwood, Middlesex, UK.

Liu Ho-Yih, 1989: *Systematic of Aeonium (Crassulaceae).* Special Publication number 3, National Museum of Natural Science.

Pilbeam J., Rodgerson C., Tribble D., 1998: *Adromischus.* Cirio Publishing Services Ltd, Southampton, UK.

Toelken H.R., 1985: Crassulaceae. In *Flora of Southern Africa* vol. 14 (Ed. O.A. Leistner). Botanic Research Institute, Pretoria, South Africa.

Walther E., 1972: *Echeveria.* California Academy of Sciences, San Francisco, California, USA.

DIDIEREACEAE

Choux P., 1934: Les Didiereacees, Xerophytes de Madagascar. *Memoires de l'Academie Malgache,* vol. 17.

Rowley G.D., 1992: *Didiereaceae, Cacti of the Old World.* British Cactus & Succulent Society, UK.

EUPHORBIACEAE

Bally P.R.O., 1961: *The Genus Monadenium.* Benteli Publ., Berne, Switzerland.

Carter S., 1982: New Succulent Spiny Euphorbias from Eastern Africa. *Hooker's Icones Plantarum,* vol. 39, part III.

Carter S., Eggli U., 1997: *The CITES checklist of succulent Euphorbia taxa (Euphorbiaceae).* German Federal Agency for Nature Conservation, Bonn, Germany.

Carter S., Smith A.R., 1989: Euphorbiaceae (part 2) in: *Flora of Tropical East Africa* (ed. R.M.Polhill). A.A. Balkema, Rotterdam, The Netherlands.

Euphorbia Journal, 1983-1996, vols. 1-10. Strawberry Press, Mill Valley, California, USA.

White A., Dyer R.A., Sloane B.L., 1941: *The Succulent Euphorbiae (Southern Africa).* Abbey Garden Press, Pasadena, California, USA.

FOUQUIERIACEAE

Humphrey R.R.,1974: *The Boojum and Its Home.* University of Arizona Press, Tucson, Arizona, USA.

GERANIACEAE

Van der Walt J.J.A., 1977: *Pelargoniums of Southern Africa.* Purnell, Cape Town, South Africa.

Van der Walt J.J.A., 1981: *Pelargoniums of Southern Africa* (vol. 2). Juta & Co. Ltd, Kenwyn, South Africa.

Van der Walt J.J.A., Vorster P.J., 1988: *Pelargoniums of Southern Africa* (vol. 3). National Botanic Gardens, Kirstenbosch, South Africa.

LILIACEAE

Bayer M.B., 1982: *The New Haworthia Handbook.* National Botanic Gardens, Kirstenbosch, South Africa.

Bayer M.B., 1999: *Haworthia revisited, A revision of the genus.* Umdaus Press, Hatfield, South Africa.

Jeppe B., 1969: *South African Aloes.* Purnell, Cape Town, South Africa.

Pilbeam J., 1983: *Haworthia and Astroloba a Collector's Guide.* Batsford, London, UK.

Reynolds G.W., 1966: *The Aloes of Tropical Africa and Madagascar.* The Aloes Book Fund, Mbabane, Swaziland.

Reynolds G.W., 1982: *The Aloes of South Africa.* A.A. Balkema, Rotterdam, The Netherlands.

Scott C.L., 1985: *The Genus Haworthia, a taxonomic revision.* Aloe Books, Johannesburg, South Africa.

van Jaarsveld E., 1992: The genus Gasteria: a synoptic review. *Aloe,* **29**(special issue): 1-32.

van Jaarsveld E., 1994: *Gasterias of South Africa, a new revision of a major succulent group.* Fernwood Press, Vloeberg, South Africa.

van Wyk B., Smith G., 1996: *Guide to the Aloes of South Africa.* Briza Publications, Pretoria, South Africa.

MESEMBRYANTHEMACEAE

Cole D., 1988: *Lithops: Flowering Stones.* Acorn Press, Randburg, South Africa.

Hammer S.,1988-91: Conophytum, an annotated checklist. *Bradleya* (A-C **6**: 101-120; D-K **7**: 41-62; L-R **8**: 53-84; S-Z **9**: 105-128).

Hammer S., 1995: Note su alcune succulente sudafricane.

Piante Grasse, **15**(suppl.): 1-96.

Herre H.,1973: *The Genera of the Mesembryanthemaceae.* A.A. Balkema, Rotterdam, The Netherlands.

Smith G.F., Chesselet P., van Jaarsveld E., Hartmann H., Hammer S., van Wyk B., Burgoyne P., Klak C., Kurzweil H., 1998: *Mesembs of the World.* Briza Publications, Pretoria, South Africa.

PORTULACACEAE

Mathew B., 1989: *The Genus Lewisia.* Timber Press, Portland, Oregon, USA.

Rowley G.D., 1995: *Anacampseros, Avonia, Grahamia. A grower's handbook.* British Cactus and Succulent Society, UK.

WELWITSCHIACEAE

Bornman C.H., 1978: *Welwitschia.* C. Struik, Cape Town, South Africa.

Wetschnig W., Debisch B., 1999: Pollination biology of Welwitschia mirabilis Hook.f. *Phyton* (Austria) **39**: 167-183.